I WANT YOU AROUND

I WANT YOU AROUND

THE RAMONES AND THE MAKING OF
ROCK 'N' ROLL HIGH SCHOOL

STEPHEN B. ARMSTRONG

Backbeat
Books

Essex, Connecticut

Backbeat
Books

An imprint of Globe Pequot, the trade division of
The Rowman & Littlefield Publishing Group, Inc.
4501 Forbes Blvd., Ste. 200
Lanham, MD 20706
www.rowman.com

Distributed by NATIONAL BOOK NETWORK

British Library Cataloguing in Publication Information available

Library of Congress Cataloging-in-Publication Data

Names: Armstrong, Stephen B., author.
Title: I want you around : The Ramones and the making of Rock 'n' roll high
    school / Stephen B. Armstrong.
Description: Essex, Connecticut : Backbeat Books, [2023] | Includes
    bibliographical references and index.
Identifiers: LCCN 2023003384 (print) | LCCN 2023003385 (ebook) | ISBN
    9781493064496 (paperback) | ISBN 9781493064502 (epub)
Subjects: LCSH: Rock 'n' roll high school (Motion picture) | Ramones
    (Musical group) | Rock films—United States—History—20th century.
Classification: LCC PN1997.R5753325 A76 2023 (print) | LCC PN1997.R5753325
    (ebook) | DDC 791.43/72—dc23/eng/20230217
LC record available at https://lccn.loc.gov/2023003384
LC ebook record available at https://lccn.loc.gov/2023003385

♾™ The paper used in this publication meets the minimum requirements of American
National Standard for Information Sciences—Permanence of Paper for Printed
Library Materials, ANSI/NISO Z39.48-1992.

For Lona, whom we always wanted around.

CONTENTS

Take a teaspoon of *Grease*, a dash of *Animal House*, add to that some *Beach Blanket Bingo* and a bit of *Rock Around the Clock* and you've got the Ramones in their debut movie—*Rock 'n' Roll High School*.

—Lisa Robinson

Where does middle-class morality end and punk liberation begin? Or are they always . . . inextricably linked?

—Richard Riegel

FOREWORD

n early 1977, I got my first break in Hollywood, working on John Cassavetes's *Opening Night*. One night when I was dropping off negative from the film at the MGM film laboratory, I overheard a woman saying that she was dropping off negative for Roger Corman's New World Pictures. I struck up a conversation, and she invited me to visit their editing rooms in Hollywood. There I learned that a new movie called *Rock 'n' Roll High School* was starting up, and since I was finishing up with Cassavetes, my interest was piqued. I got the address of the production office and showed up unknown and unannounced. I got to meet director Allan Arkush and producer Mike Finnell, and from that day on I haunted them—turning up repeatedly to make sure that my intention to work on their movie was crystal clear. One day I got a call from Mike saying that he wanted to hire me. He asked how many movies I had assisted on. "Two," I lied. Being a cagey and skilled producer (this was his first film in that capacity), he lowered his initial offer to $150 a week, which I gladly took.

I had been attending punk shows in small clubs in LA and had done interviews for *Slash* and *Search & Destroy* magazines. I frequented the rock 'n' roll hangout the Tropicana Motel (where the Ramones stayed during filming), mainly for breakfast at Duke's Coffee Shop, sitting among the scenesters.

So when the choice of bands for the movie came down to Cheap Trick or the Ramones, I was firmly for the boys from Queens. I was overjoyed when they chose the Ramones.

Filming started in late November 1978, and we all hit the ground running. It was a crazily tight schedule. The atmosphere in the cutting room was electric. There were so many enthusiastic people experiencing their first break in pursuing their dream of working in the movies. No one was making any money, but lifelong friendships were being forged. In addition to Allan and Mike there were Larry Bock, Joe Dante, Paul Bartel, and so many others. Mark Helfrich was the set PA, and we became fast friends. We were both at the beginning of our careers, and we both loved punk / new wave music. I wasn't able to get to the set very much, but the night they blew up the high school is engraved in my memory. And, of course, the day of the concert at the Roxy was wild.

After filming wrapped, Mark managed to get himself hired as the second assistant editor. We had a ball tearing into that footage, and the "anything goes" atmosphere in the cutting rooms really encouraged experimentation. Larry Bock, Gail Werbin, and Allan were very generous in allowing Mark and me the chance to experiment and to kibitz. All ideas were welcomed. Mark and I asked for and got the job of cutting the trailer, which we did in the best New World tradition.

A week after shooting, the Ramones did a show at the Whisky a Go Go on the Sunset Strip, and much of the cast and crew from the movie were there. I interviewed the band at length for an article published in Washington, DC's *Unicorn Times* (a title left over from the not-so-distant hippie days). We were all disappointed when New World basically dumped the film (it opened in Texas, not New York or Los Angeles). We were all very proud of the movie and had no inkling that it would go on to become a cult classic.

I hope you enjoy Stephen's deep dive into one of the most incredible experiences of my life.

Kent Beyda
Los Angeles, CA
November 2, 2022

Kent Beyda's credits as a film editor include *This is Spinal Tap*, *Get Crazy*, *Fright Night*, *Gremlins 2: The New Batch*, and *Scooby-Doo*.

INTRODUCTION

This Is *Rock 'n' Roll High School*

In the summer of 1978, a thirty-year-old movie director named Allan Arkush flew from Los Angeles to New York City to catch the Ramones play a gig in Midtown Manhattan at a nightclub called Hurrah. He was so astounded by what he heard and saw that night that he returned to California certain that the four rock 'n' rollers—Marky, Joey, Dee Dee, and Johnny—would be perfect as the featured band for a musical comedy he was planning to make called *Rock 'n' Roll High School*.

The Ramones had been approached about appearing in movies before, but they'd always passed, concerned about a tendency in Hollywood to make rockers look like morons. But they'd warmed to Arkush quickly. He liked the same music they did—bands like The Who and the Stones—and his boss, Roger Corman, had directed and produced several horror and science fiction movies, with titles like *Creature from the Haunted Sea*, *Not of This World*, and *Attack of the Crab Monsters*, they admired. They hoped that a movie would help introduce them and their music to new audiences as *A Hard Day's Night* had for the Beatles. Shooting took place in the late fall of 1978, and good feelings between

Allan and the band flourished as the cameras rolled. But when *Rock 'n' Roll High School* opened in movie theaters and drive-ins in the spring of 1979, it failed to find audiences—a distressing development for all involved. Yet bolstered by midnight movie screenings, strong home-video sales, and frequent broadcasts on television, the picture found an audience, not exactly huge, perhaps, but quite devoted all the same. It's a cult movie, in other words.

For any respectable Ramones fan, an encounter with *Rock 'n' Roll High School* is inevitable. To illustrate: When I was growing up in Maryland in the '80s, the pack I ran with all liked the Ramones. The first kid in our group to get turned on to the band's songs was Adam Brown, who loaned me his copies of *Leave Home* and the *Rock 'n' Roll High School* soundtrack album. While *Leave Home* was good, the soundtrack album was better. On its first side alone there was a fabulous five-song Ramones mini-concert, along with two studio recordings that bore repeated listening (and still do): the movie's catchy eponymous theme song and a poignant power-pop singalong called "I Want You Around." A collaboration between the Ramones and the Paley Brothers ("Come On Let's Go") made the record a complete killer. And the non-Ramones songs in the collection were all pretty good too, especially scorchers like Chuck Berry's "School Days" and Eddie and the Hot Rods' scorching "Teenage Depression."

Adam was also the first in our group to see *Rock 'n' Roll High School*—this was in 1984 when MTV scheduled an expurgated version of the PG movie periodically on Sunday nights. "You gotta watch it," he counseled me.

By that point, I was reading a lot of music criticism, and I'd found somewhere that *Rock 'n' Roll High School* depicted the Ramones in an unflattering manner, making them look like dummies. "I don't wanna not like them anymore," I said.

"Nah," Adam said. "It's a good movie. Don't worry."

So the next time MTV broadcast *Rock 'n' Roll High School*, I snuck down into the basement where my family had a hulking RCA connected to a cable box, and with the volume set low, as my sister and my parents slept upstairs, I watched Riff Randell and the Ramones wage war against the principal at Vince Lombardi High School, the fascist Miss Togar, along with her Hitler-youth hall-monitor flunkies, and win. Even with commercials wedged into it and significant holes wrought by the channel's censors, I was in love. "Goddamn, what a movie!" I remember saying afterward.

Rock 'n' Roll High School has always had this ability to win over doubters. "Even when punked-out fans of the band reluctantly watch it, they are captivated," Marky Ramone points out in his memoir, *Punk Rock Blitzkrieg*. At that point in my life, I wasn't myself "punked-out," but soon after seeing the movie I sewed a Clash patch onto my letterman's jacket and grew my bangs out like the Misfits' Glenn Danzig. I started buying records like *Talking Heads: 77*, the Ramones' *Pleasant Dreams*, and Black Flag's *My War* at Tower Records in DC, which was next door to an ice cream parlor, where, it was rumored, Henry Rollins had once worked.

The *sound* of *Rock 'n' Roll High School* was reason enough for me to love the film. And even though I probably listened more to Blondie and Lou Reed back then, the Ramones were up there on my list of favorite bands. They played the kind of music I always wanted to hear—hard, fast, with elements of sweetness tossed in like the slices of apple in a Waldorf salad. In the decades since that night in the basement, however, I've come to value another aspect of the film more: its implicit support for the students at Vince Lombardi High School as they take their stand against bullies. On its face, *Rock 'n' Roll High School* may be a musical comedy, and a parody of '50s rock 'n' roll movies like *Hot Rod Gang* and *Rock, Rock, Rock*, and an exploitation flick for hot-blooded (and hot-headed) teens, but it's also in its own weird way a political film, a chronicle of the dispossessed defying anti-democratic, anti-human authority, just like the French Resistance fighters in Melville's *Army of Shadows*, perhaps, or the guerrillas in Pontecorvo's *The Battle of Algiers*. But who cares about history?

As I write this in the fall of 2022, the Ramones' fiftieth anniversary approaches—the band formed in Forest Hills, Queens, in 1974. New (and renewed) interest in *Rock 'n' Roll High School* is certain: The movie and the band are inseparable. And this book has been written with the hope of satisfying or, as Roger Corman might say, *exploiting* this Ramones-mania. It contains numerous insights provided to me by people who worked on the picture and draws heavily on materials that the movie's producer, Michael Finnell, prepared, including the shooting schedule and call sheets. I worked constantly with the film's shooting script too. Any errors in this rendering of long ago events are unintentional, and the author cries "Mea culpa!" in advance. Out of convention, if not correctness, I refer to the movie throughout as *Rock 'n' Roll High School*. Confusion over the title has existed since at least the production of the film's promotional materials—Bill Stout's beautiful lobby poster, for example, features two spellings, *Rock 'N' Roll High School* and *Rock 'n' Roll High School*. And while the former spelling appears in the film's opening credits, in the trailer the spelling changes to *Rock N' Roll High School*.

In the back section of this book, a detailed plot summary appears along with information about cast and crew and the songs director Allan Arkush and Mike Finnell secured for the soundtrack with help from an attorney named Paul Almond. Were it not for the kindness of many, many people, writing this book would have been far less pleasant, and so a huge thanks and Gabba Gabba Hey to P. J. Soles, Jon Davison, Joe Dante, Mike Finnell, Joseph McBride, Russ Dvonch, Richard Whitley, Frances Doel, Jerry Zucker, Gale Anne Hurd, Loren Lester, Clint Howard, Dey Young, Vince Van Patten, Alan Toomayan, Barbara Boyle, Paul Almond, Cynthia Brown, Spencer Drate, Deborah Brock, Ed Stasium, Monte A. Melnick, Jake Fogelnest, Deborah Nadoolman Landis, John Landis, Jane Ruhm, Danny Fields, Brendan Toller, Henry Rollins, Harley Flanagan, Jack Rabid, Nick Marden, Bill Stout, Merrill Alighieri, Denise Mercedes, Vera Ramone, Andy Paley, Jonathan Paley, Bun E. Carlos, Kristian Hoffman, Gary Lachman, Ginger Coyote, Cherry Vanilla, Mandy Stein, Peter Crowley, Trudie Arguelles-Barrett, Stephen Lee, UT College of Humanities & Social Sciences, UT Research Office, Michael Lacourse, Richard B. Williams, Mike Peterson, AmiJo Comeford, Matt Smith-Lahrman, Cindy King, Randy Jasmine, Rico Del Sesto,

Leslie Twitchell, Diane Aldrich, Adam Brown, Bernie Bennett, Dan Lopez, Hope Lopez, April Chambers, Brittany and Ryan McMichael, Zane W. Levitt, Adam Walderman, Mike White and the Production Booth, and John Holmstrom. My boundless gratitude to Allan Arkush and warmest thoughts to Lee Sobel and Lee Sobel Literary Agency, Janet and Mike Oliveri, Jane and Jay Hudiburg, Dean and Mimi Armstrong, and my reasons for being, Katie and Charlotte.

CHAPTER ONE

WILL YOUR SCHOOL BE NEXT?

Through the summer of 1973 and into the early fall, as the syrupy humidity in New York waned and the nights grew longer, Allan Arkush drove a cab around Manhattan trying to earn enough in fares and tips to pay for a plane ticket to Los Angeles. Not that he hated the city. Never. He'd grown up in Fort Lee, on the New Jersey side of the Hudson, just a couple of blocks from the George Washington Bridge. He'd gone to film school at NYU, where Martin Scorsese was his professor. He'd worked at the Fillmore East in the Village, lighting shows for The Who, Neil Young, John Lennon and Yoko Ono, the Beach Boys, and the Grateful Dead. New York had given him a lot. But he was twenty-five years old, living in the West Village, frustrated and poor. He wanted more. He wanted to direct movies. That was it. And the best way to bring this about, he knew, was to leave home, to go west, to get himself to Hollywood.

Allan's fascination with films began early, in 1953, when his mother, Rochelle, took him into Manhattan to see *Peter Pan*, the music-packed Disney cartoon about the never-aging boy who protects his pals from the cruel and bullying Captain Hook. Allan was five. He and his mom watched the picture at the Roxy Cinema on West 50th Street. The experience imbued in him an early distaste for authoritarian adults, as well as an appreciation for the places where entertainers put on shows. "The Roxy was so big—easily the size of Radio City," he told me. "They ran 'Bear Country,' the Disney nature short, and they had a stage production with an ice-skating bear."

Allan and his family liked going to the movies closer to home, too, at the Lee Theater, a single-screen fifteen-hundred-seat hippodrome located on Main Street in downtown Fort Lee. The Lee had a slabby concrete facade and a low-slung rectilinear marquee, which protruded from the building at a right angle like the head of a putter. Next door, there was a Warncke's ice cream parlor, and before screenings, customers would congregate on the stretch of sidewalk that linked the two businesses, enjoying their cones and malts and egg creams as the skyscrapers of Uptown Manhattan loomed toward them from across the Hudson, half a mile away. "I grew up on the Disney animated things, Disney movies and Jerry Lewis. I loved Jerry Lewis. I remember going to see *The Horse Soldiers*. I liked westerns. And *Rio Bravo*. *Rio Bravo* left a big impression. Then *Lawrence of Arabia*."

Television also nurtured Allan's cinephilia. He would often watch *Million Dollar Movie*, a syndicated program that ran old Hollywood pictures, like *King Kong*, *Friendly Persuasion*, *She Wore a Yellow Ribbon*, and the W. C. Fields comedies *You Can't Cheat an Honest Man* and *The Bank Dick*. Allan's father, Jacob, an embroidery-company executive, "would tell me which movies to watch if he saw they were on TV, and that's how I saw *Lost Horizon*, because he loved that movie, and *I Was a Fugitive from a Chain Gang*. In high school, I remember my dad saying, 'You should stay up and watch this movie called *Citizen Kane*.'"

As a teenager in the second half of the '60s, when British-Invasion bands like the Kinks, the Animals, the Rolling Stones, and the Beatles ruled the American charts, Allan loved rock 'n' roll with the same passionate intensity he had for movies. Manhattan, especially around Bleecker Street in the Lower East Side, was a good source for getting vinyl, and he started collecting records. He cultivated an appreciation for music criticism, too, buying copies of *Crawdaddy!* to read Richard Meltzer, Jon Landau, and Sandy Perlman, writers who took rock 'n' roll as seriously as he did. Another guide was Murray the K, the first disc jockey in the New York–New Jersey region to evangelize for the Beatles.

Many of the films Allan enjoyed growing up were American studio productions made by directors like George Cukor, Billy Wilder, Preston Sturges, Vincente Minnelli, John Ford, Frank Capra, Howard Hawks, and Orson Welles. He was responsive to movies brought in from other countries too. On one family trip into Manhattan, Allan remembered, "My parents took me—I think I was about thirteen or fourteen—to see my first foreign movie, *The World of Apu*," Indian director Satyajit Ray's existential study of a young man experiencing a personality crisis. "That left an enormous impression. It really did. Once I responded to that, they would point out foreign movies that I might like, and I would go to the city. I saw *Great Expectations* that way."

Movies and rock 'n' roll offered a revitalizing contrast for Allan to the drudgery of public school education. He attended Fort Lee High School, which, with its red-brick exterior walls and colonnaded front entrance, was stately and awful, like a colonial-era plantation manor. The days at Fort Lee High were very long, very dull. "No jeans, no sandals, no rock 'n' roll music, no long hair and absolutely no dissent were tolerated." Teachers and administrators did what they could to stymie free thought. "High school was the wrong system for me. High school had no critical thinking. High school was repetition and spitting stuff back," back," Allan told me. In French class, he would often look out the window, he told *Variety*, "and make scenarios in my head, daydreaming of crazy things I'd like to happen at school." He explained to *Fresh Air*'s Terry Gross, "One vision was having my favorite band come play a concert. As a teenager of the '60s, I envisioned the Rolling Stones or the Yardbirds. I knew then it would make a great movie." He "daydreamed that we'd blow up the high school. And then we had motorcycle racing around the hallways. These are all things that I kept with me for years."

The film that meant the most to Allan as a teenager was *A Hard Day's Night*, the first Beatles movie, which Richard Lester, an American, had directed. Allan caught the picture on its opening night, August 11, 1964, at the Lee Theater. *A Hard Day's Night* gave smart-guy rock 'n' roll nuts like him their own cinematic jewel, inundating the eyes as much as the ears with Paul, George, John, and Ringo when the Mop Tops were still the most charming band in the world. In a brief essay Arkush wrote for the Criterion Collection's website, he recalled: "When my parents asked me about the movie afterward, I said, 'I think it was really well-directed.' I was aware that someone had controlled what was on-screen in a very specific way, and that was something that I knew a little bit about but had never experienced in such a personal way. . . . I hadn't actually thought about directors and what they were thinking when they made their films. But here, someone had taken the Beatles and made them look joyous, [while] expressing an anti-establishment point of view."

Rochelle and Jacob Arkush may have first pointed their son toward the movies, but they had little desire to see him pursue a career in show business, preferring instead for Allan eventually to practice law or medicine, hoping he would head off to Harvard or Yale after Fort Lee High. But though his grades were fine, Allan didn't get into any of the Ivy League schools he applied to. He wound up at Franklin & Marshall, instead, a liberal arts college in sleepy Lancaster, Pennsylvania, three hours by car from Fort Lee, where he started in the fall term of 1966, with psychology as his declared major.

The intellectual climate at the tiny college stimulated Allan, but he sensed quickly that he'd probably made a mistake moving to Lancaster. Since seeing *A Hard Day's Night*, all he could imagine himself doing professionally was directing movies, and Franklin & Marshall didn't have any kind of film program. There were no women to date at the all-male school either. And Lancaster was a bore: Its biggest attraction was Dutch Wonderland, a theme park with an elevated monorail ride that looked out over pumpkin patches, cornfields, and horse-drawn buggies tended by Amish farmers. The city had just two movie theaters, and good bookstores and record shops were scarce.

But Franklin & Marshall wasn't a total bust. Allan managed to have fun spinning discs for the college's radio station during his year there. The selections he featured when he had the air were heavy on the new, hard sound of West Coast rock, acts like Jefferson Airplane, Jimi Hendrix, and the Grateful Dead. "When I went to Franklin & Marshall and I was a deejay on the radio, there was pushback from the college kids— that I was not playing the hits. I had a four-hour radio show every Friday. In response to anybody making a suggestion of what I should play, I put on one of my rock records. I would put on something that I knew would put them off, like the Mothers of Invention. What worried people about rock 'n' roll in Lancaster was not so much how the music sounded but what it signified. All the music was tied into a new world. The San Francisco scene and the hippie scene were all tied into a change, societal change. Different songs became emblematic of the anti-war movement and civil rights."

Before the end of his first semester, the urge to learn how to make movies was such that Allan knew he had to transfer to a college and a city that were more amenable to his tastes and sensibilities. He needed an institution that could equip him with an understanding of cinematic technique that would lead to long-term employment in the American film industry. Working somewhere from nine-to-five, wearing a necktie, a starched shirt, a jacket, and polished loafers appealed to him about as much as enlisting in the Army. Undergraduate film programs were scarce in the United States, but New York University had one. So Allan applied, and before the end of his second semester at Franklin & Marshall, in the spring of 1967, the good news came that he'd been admitted to study in NYU's department of film.

Allan moved to New York City that summer and started his studies in August. The film program at NYU occupied the eighth floor of a worn-out and cramped midrise on Greene Street, which it shared with a small library dedicated to Serbo-Croatian publications. Haig P. Manoogian oversaw the department. In the fall of 1968, during Allan's junior year, Manoogian had to fire a member of the faculty, Harry Hurwitz, for using film-student labor to make a skin flick called *These Raging Loins*.

For Hurwitz's replacement, Manoogian hired the first graduate of the NYU film department's master's degree program, Martin Scorsese.

Scorsese started teaching in January 1969. The future director of *Taxi Driver* and *Raging Bull* revered American movies, the commercially oriented ones made by the big studios, the sort *Million Dollar Movie* broadcast. He sensed that his students didn't appreciate commercial pictures enough, though, and that they'd fallen too heavily under the spell of the French New Wave, opting for Jean-Luc Godard and Claude Chabrol over Alfred Hitchcock and John Ford. "Marty would come in at the start of every class with *TV Guide* and *Cue* magazine. *TV Guide* he'd read off what was on, which channel, and at what hour the movies we should see. That was our syllabus," Arkush said. On Tuesday afternoons, Scorsese would screen 16-millimeter prints of films in the Greene Street building he thought were ideal for illustrating and underscoring technical ideas he thought his students should know, pictures like *The Searchers*, *Force of Evil*, *Shock Corridor*, *Rear Window*, *The Band Wagon*, *The Big Heat*, *Johnny Guitar*, and *The Nutty Professor*.

One of Allan's friends in the program at NYU, Jonathan Kaplan, would go on to direct several excellent movies, ranging from low-budget action flicks like *Truck Turner* and *The Slams* to *The Accused*, an anti-rape drama starring Jodie Foster in an Academy Award–winning performance. Kaplan recalled for Chris Nashawaty that the first picture Scorsese showed his students on the eighth floor "was *The Searchers*. We were all appalled that he was showing us a film with John Wayne, who was for the war. We were like 'What the hell? Who is this little Italian guy showing us this right-wing crap?!' He'd show the film once, and then you'd take a break, and then he'd show it again and stop and start, and he would talk about it. It was fantastic."

Professor Scorsese, "Marty," as he liked to be called, also had his students read *The American Cinema*, Andrew Sarris's 1968 book-length study of Hollywood movie directors that helped popularize the auteur theory in the United States—the auteur theory elevates the film director to the position of most importance and greatest influence in a motion picture's creation.

While the faculty in the film program at NYU were great, the equipment the students had access to was exasperatingly limited. "Haig Manoogian coped as best he could, but all he could offer was enthusiasm and Bell & Howard Filmos. Filmos were virtually indestructible cast-iron cameras that had to be wound up with a doorknob because all the keys had disappeared years ago," Arkush recalled in an article he wrote for *Film Comment.* "We had four Moviolas that ate student films at an alarming rate and only one camera capable of sound."

The inadequacy of the equipment and the tightness of space at Greene Street prompted Allan and some classmates, among them Oliver Stone and Billy Crystal, with Scorsese's encouragement, to demand access to better resources from the school's administration. The students held a "watch-in" to express their discontent. "When the film school went on strike," Allan said, "we stayed up all night, occupying the building so we would get our own courses in film history and get more space. . . . We marched on the dean's office singing 'Shall We Gather at the River,'" an old Protestant hymn John Ford inserted into several films, most famously *My Darling Clementine*, which the protestors watched that night. The fellow traveler who supplied the movies to the strikers was Jon Davison, the future producer of blockbusters like *Airplane!*, *RoboCop*, and *The 6th Day* (and the underrated antiwar satire *Starship Troopers*). "It was a really great all night movie session," said Allan, "with a lot of cheap pot."

During his junior and senior years at NYU, Allan worked at the Fillmore East, a former Yiddish theater that music promoter Bill Graham had converted into a rock 'n' roll concert hall and opened to the public in March 1968. The Fillmore East was on Second Avenue, a short walk from the NYU film department's building on Greene Street (the buildings shared a wall). Graham booked hard-rock acts when doing so was novel. The first time Allan headed over to the Fillmore East, he was a paying customer: Jimi Hendrix was the featured act. Two months later, Allan joined Graham's staff, starting first as an usher, taking tickets and seating guests before shows. Then he worked on the stage crew. Then he was hired by the company the Fillmore East used for lighting concerts, The Joshua

Light Show, which specialized in projecting color-soaked LSD-friendly swirls of light against the stage. The impact this experience had upon Allan's development as a filmmaker was significant. "[A]t the Fillmore East, I must have seen over four hundred rock concerts. If you are very interested in filmmaking and very interested in rock 'n' roll, you cannot see four hundred concerts and not come away with very strong feelings about how they should be filmed." Several of Allan's best friends from NYU—who'd all play a role in his eventual relocation from New York to Los Angeles—Jon Davison, Jonathan Kaplan, Danny Opatoshu—worked at the Fillmore East too.

The student strike in Haig P. Manoogian's fragile but splendid film department led to a favorable outcome for Allan and his peers. The university's administration moved the Serbo-Croatian library off the Greene Street building's eighth floor and expanded the number of classrooms for the film program from three to five. In these improved conditions, Allan, under the supervision of his faculty advisor (Scorsese), made a thirty-five-minute student film called "Septuagenarian Ball," which drew upon his experiences at the Fillmore East. "Bill Graham . . . did the nicest thing anyone could ever do for me," Arkush told filmmaker Daniel Griffith, the director of an excellent documentary about *Rock 'n' Roll High School*'s production history titled *Class of '79: 40 Years of Rock 'n' Roll High School*. "He let me have the theater to make my student film in, which was a musical about the rise and fall of a rock star in five days." "Septuagenarian Ball" went on to take a third prize award in the Fifth National Student Film Festival in 1970.

Allan graduated from NYU in June 1970. A year later, the Fillmore East closed, a result, Kembrew McLeod relates in *The Downtown Pop Underground*, of the "changing economics of the concert industry and an inhospitable atmosphere in the surrounding neighborhood." The Lower East Side at the start of the '70s, as Lou Reed put it, was "something like a circus or a sewer," thick with open-air drug dealing, prostitutes, and flophouses. The Joshua Light Show hung on, though, and Allan stayed with the company as it changed its name to Joe's Lights, lighting shows up and down the Eastern Seaboard. Joe's Lights later secured a commission to light concerts in the United Kingdom, and Allan, by then the company's artistic director, followed. The lighting team worked a series of Who shows at the Rainbow Theatre in London, as well as several gigs for the Grateful Dead. Working with the Grateful Dead fostered a friendship between Allan and the Dead's lead guitarist and vocalist, Jerry Garcia, which would last until the musician died in 1995. The two liked watching movies together. Garcia would contribute music to two of Allan's films, as a matter of fact, the bloody motorcycle movie *Deathsport* and an Andy Kaufman robot comedy titled *Heartbeeps*.

EL CENTRO

During the two years Allan worked for Joe's Lights, several of his NYU chums landed filmmaking jobs in Los Angeles at New World Pictures, an independent production company owned by Roger Corman. Before creating New World in 1970, Corman had directed and produced dozens of profitable low-budget features, including several films starring Vincent Price that had been adapted from the short stories of Edgar Allan Poe, like *The Pit and the Pendulum*, *The Tomb of Ligeia*, and *The House of Usher*. A series of frustrating professional experiences with American-International Pictures (AIP), which distributed Corman's movies throughout the '60s, had prompted him to create his own company and leave film directing behind. During its first couple of years of operation, New World pumped out low-budget exploitation movies loaded with sex and violence, with suggestive, sometimes garish, titles like *The Student Nurses*, *Private Duty Nurses*, *Cover Page Models*, *Summer School Teachers*, *The Big Doll House*, *The Big Bird Cage*, and *Angels Hard as They Come*. New World produced movies *and* distributed them, placing its films primarily in hard-top movie theaters and drive-ins throughout North America.

"Clean and imperially slim," as E. A. Robinson might have found him, Corman ran New World Pictures out of a shabby, but neat, penthouse office in West Hollywood on the Sunset Strip. Despite paying employees minimal salaries, "At New World, we have a tendency to hire young, talented people. Young people are aware of this and find their way here," Corman told film writer Ed Naha in 1979. "There's a constant flow." Several well-regarded directors, producers, writers, editors, directors of photography, composers, production designers, costumers, and makeup people at early, pivotal points in their careers worked under Corman at New World, among them future Academy Award–winning directors Jonathan Demme, James Cameron, and Ron Howard.

Corman liked to hire talent based on the recommendations of people whose opinions he valued. One of these contacts was Haig Manoogian at NYU. In 1971, Corman needed to fulfill a contractual obligation with AIP, a hangover from the once-good years he'd had with the company. The picture Corman owed was *Boxcar Bertha*, a low-budget Depression-era pot-boiler in which Barbara Hershey and David Carradine were to star. He didn't have time to direct the picture himself, nor the inclination. He liked producing movies better. Manoogian recommended Corman hire Martin Scorsese for *Boxcar Bertha*, and by doing so cost himself a faculty member, as Scorsese soon quit NYU and left for LA for the directing job.

Scorsese's great intellect and skill were quickly evident to Corman. And when the older filmmaker said he needed a director for another picture he was developing, this one for New World, called *Night Call Nurses*, he asked Marty's recommendation of someone who had good nerves and real talent and who could direct a picture fast and cheap. Scorsese offered several names, one of them Jonathan Kaplan, his pupil at NYU. "I came home from the Fillmore one night, and I was pretty tired, it had been a long weekend," Kaplan told me. "The phone rang, and it was Roger Corman saying, 'I've talked to Martin Scorsese, and he's recommended you. The director of the third in our Nurses cycle,

Night Call Nurses, has had a disagreement. Creative differences. And my wife is producing it. Are you available to come out tomorrow and direct *Night Call Nurses?*'" Once Kaplan realized the call wasn't a prank, he said, "Yes."

Corman's wife, Julie Corman, in her role as *Night Call Nurses'* producer, decided that the movie needed a new script, and she permitted Kaplan to hire two of his friends from NYU—Danny Opatoshu and Jon Davison—for the rewrite. The two were to work up *Night Call Nurses* as a "three-girl picture," so it was explained to them, which meant building a plot around three female characters' personal lives and professional pursuits, with action and sex scenes squeezed in every ten pages to keep audiences titillated. Many of the pictures New World made exploited this plotting method, not just pictures about nurses, but also teachers and flight attendants. "It was a genre Roger believed in," Larry Woolner, a longtime Corman associate, explained. "He could have three different plots [with] three different sorts of ethnic types: a brunette, a blonde and a black woman, or a brunette, blonde, and a Hispanic woman. Each plot could be something totally different." Roger and Julie Corman both identified as feminists and insisted on featuring strong female characters in New World productions—women who could kick ass, riding motorcycles, practicing kung fu, hurling knives, swinging swords—but they also expected softcore elements to proliferate through their films, especially "breast nudity," as New World story editor Frances Doel referred to it. "One is fruitful only at the cost of being rich in contradictions," observed Nietzsche.

Working for Corman was always a low-pay affair. The independent mogul financed his movies with house money; and to ensure as high a return as he could, he spent as little as he could get away with on production costs, which entailed paying workers crumbs. Corman, the vigorous capitalist with left-wing sympathies, and perhaps the most successful independent film producer in Los Angeles at the time, attracted a certain ambitious-filmmaker type: obsessive cineastes who traded the harsh exploitation of their labor and their talents for the opportunity to use and to develop these talents through their labor. No one at New World who wanted to be there was there for money. The editors, writers, producers, and directors who worked for Roger had to be intellectually quick, college-educated, appreciative of what the master could teach them. They were an impoverished elite for whom making movies was akin to a religious calling, and Roger was their patron saint.

Kaplan had handled *Night Call Nurses* well, delivering it in on time and within budget, and he was retained to helm another three-girl picture, *The Student Teachers*. Corman also gave Jon Davison, who'd aspired since childhood to be a movie producer, a full-time position at New World as its marketing chief, which entailed overseeing the company's post-production department. "As luck would have it, Roger's director of advertising had just committed suicide—so I got offered the job. That put me in charge of advertising and publicity. As there was no other person in the department: "I was it," Jon told me. He designed press kits and coordinated with graphic artists and photographers to create lobby posters and newspaper ads. He also wrote scripts for TV and radio spots and trailers.

Rapid growth in 1972 and 1973 at New World came about with a string of profitable pictures like *The Velvet Vampire*, *Night of the Cobra Woman*, and even an Ingmar Bergman release, *Cries & Whispers*, which the company had secured the North American rights to distribute. The rate of production was such that Corman had to hire a team of full-time editors, who worked in editing rooms he leased in an opticals house called Jack Rabin & Associates in Hollywood. Jack Rabin, a visual effects specialist who'd been collaborating with Corman since the '50s, provided access to good, although hardly new, cutting equipment. Prior to this, Corman and Davison had handled New World's editing needs with freelancers, whom Corman had grown very tired of having to train.

Davison's workload soon swelled to such a point that he went to Corman, imploring him to hire a full-time editor to produce TV spots and trailers. Corman agreed, and a job as a "trailer cutter" was offered to Joe Dante, who was then a magazine editor working in Philadelphia for a publication called *Film Bulletin*. Dante had graduated from the Philadelphia College of Art with aspirations to become an animator, like his hero,

Chuck Jones, and he took the job at New World—but only, though, after *Film Bulletin* went out of business.

Dante worked out of an editing room at Jack Rabin & Associates. He handled his job as a cutter well, though he had to get by as an autodidact at the Moviola. He and Jon Davison soon recognized that a second trailer editor would be needed soon. If and, more likely, when Corman agreed to a new hire, Jon wanted Allan Arkush, his NYU friend. Since returning from England, Arkush had moved into an apartment in the West Village and was driving a Yellow Cab. During the summer of 1973, Davison on a trip to New York found his old classmate and told him about New World and Corman and how movies were pumped out factory-like, cheap and fast, but they were real movies. "If you want to, come out. Live somewhere, and something will happen," he promised.

Allan listened. He'd returned from the UK with memories, not wealth. He explained to *Shock Cinema*'s Andrew J. Rausch, "I saved up all my cab money—$400—and got an airplane ticket and flew out October 9, 1973." For a month, Allan lived on Lexington Avenue in Hollywood in Jon Davison's place and later transplanted to Jonathan Kaplan's garage in Sherman Oaks, where he slept on a mattress. To stave off starvation, Allan found work "as a crew member on a couple of dental films. They were made for either the U.S. Government Information service or a dental insurance company. I was on the lighting crew as we shot gums, brushes, and teeth. I was broke." Jon Davison's predictions proved true eventually, though. In April 1974, New World offered to hire Allan on as a production assistant (PA) and "a driver for the trailer department." He would work out of El Centro, the nickname the New World editors used to refer to the Jack Rabin & Associates building, which was located at 1607 North El Centro Avenue.

In a ragged Plymouth Valiant borrowed from Jonathan Kaplan, earning $50 a week, Allan for his new job would drop off reels of undeveloped film at the MGM lab in Culver City and sound reels to Ryder Sound Services in Hollywood, with occasional trips to a screening room in West Hollywood called Nosseck's Theatre, where Corman reviewed dailies with his directors and screening copies of features near completion. Often Joe Dante rode along with Allan, who'd gotten himself his own car at that point, a "1965 white Ford Falcon with money from my father. It was a shit box with four on the floor. I bought it from a local mechanic with cash. The clutch was always breaking."

An early task for Arkush at El Centro was to find music for the trailer and TV spots then being cut for a New World women-in-prison melodrama, *Caged Heat*, which Jonathan Demme directed. John Cale, one of the founding members of the avant-garde drone-rock collective, the Velvet Underground, had composed a symphonic score for Demme that was heavy with experimental flourishes, which although great for the feature were "completely useless for a trailer." He proceeded to find more suitable music from an archive of old scores and soundtracks New World maintained at El Centro.

New World's vice president of distribution in the '70s, Frank Moreno, a tough one-time boxer from Spanish Harlem, would distribute Corman's movies through the company's transcontinental network of couriers and exhibitors. Corman was "not above buying up second-rate foreign films and trying to improve their sales potential through creative editing," explains Beverly Gray, who worked at New World as a script editor and publicist. Corman, Moreno, and the company's attorney Barbara Boyle had also discovered after the 1972 release of *Cries & Whispers* that New World could generate profit handily distributing the films of highly regarded international directors, like Fellini, Truffaut, and Kurosawa.

The days at El Centro were long. "Basically, one of us would cut the trailer. We would alternate, and then we'd all get together with Jon Davison, who was in charge," Allan told podcaster Jake Fogelnest. "And we'd talk about the ad campaign. We'd do catch lines. We'd present them to Roger. Then Jon would get the poster made, and we'd go and cut the TV spots, and we'd move on. We'd be doing *Street Girls* or *Big Bad Mama* and then Truffaut."

New World's work culture fostered creative collaboration constantly. Paul Bartel, the director of the company's *Death Race 2000*—a movie about professional race car drivers who earn points in a transnational competition by killing pedestrians—spent long hours in 1975 cutting his film with editors Tina Hirsch and Lewis Teague, for example. And Ron Howard three years later in 1978 did the same, coming to El Centro to oversee the editing of his first feature film, *Grand Theft Auto*, which Joe Dante was, as a matter of fact, assigned to cut. "Everyone who worked on New World pictures was in that editing room at some time or other, or would come by each day, even after they weren't working there," Arkush laid out for Jared Cowan at *Los Angeles* magazine.

In the second half of 1973, Joe and Allan prepared a trailer for *Amarcord*, Federico Fellini's comic quasi-fantasy of rural Italy that pokes funs at the ideals and rituals foisted upon Italy by Mussolini's fascism and at the masses who accepted and promoted it. Under Corman's orders, Allan and Joe squeezed in as many shots of female skin as possible. Allan, in an interview on NPR's *Fresh Air* program, referred to *Amarcord* as "the greatest Italian high school picture of all time." Fellini actually *preferred* the New World trailer to the original "because of its flat-out vulgarity," Beverly Gray claims. Cutting trailers for other directors' pictures stoked the two trailer cutters' ambitions to make their own movies. "One day, we were doing a trailer for some incredible turkey when it occurred to us that we could do better than this as directors," Joe Dante told Ed Naha. "One of the greatest things about doing movie trailers is that, just to reduce the movie down to its essentials, you have to learn the guts of the film," he explained to Daniel Griffith. "It's better than film school. You have to look at the movie over and over. Believe me, a lot can be learned from any movie, no matter how terrible."

Dante and Arkush on their trips between El Centro, the MGM lab, and Ryder Sound Services always with the radio dial set to the progressive rock station KROQ, would bounce ideas at one another "about what New World movie we could make." These were "a lot of strange twists on the Corman genres. One idea was a three-girl teachers movie with a teacher from Red China," said Allan. "We felt like 'Anybody can do this. We can do this.' We were always coming up with different ideas."

In 1975, Roger Corman promoted Jon Davison to head of production at New World, and Allan and Joe now had an in with the boss, who rarely took ideas for movies other than from himself. "We approached Jon . . . and fed him a storyline," Joe Dante told Naha, another three-girls plot, but about women actors this time. "Then the three of us went to Roger and hit him where he is the most vulnerable. We told him that we could make a movie cheaper than any movie he had ever made at New World. This intrigued him."

"I came right out with it and told Roger I'd like to make a bet with him that I could produce a film fifty percent cheaper than any that had been done at New World since he founded it in 1970," Davison revealed to the *New York Times*. "I said, 'Your average picture takes fifteen days to shoot, right? I'll do mine in ten days.' I saw a funny self-satisfied look come over his face, and he said, 'OK, you've got a bet. In order to win it, you'll have to do the picture for $80,000, but I'm only going to give you $60,000.'"

Charles B. Griffith, who'd written several films for Corman previously, including the black comedies *The Little Shop of Horrors* and *A Bucket of Blood*, carved out an early script for the ten-day picture. Allan and Joe didn't like it, however, so they reached out to the screenwriter who'd co-written *Night Call Nurses* with Jon Davison, Danny Opatoshu. Opatoshu (working under the pseudonym Patrick Hobby), with counsel from Allan and Joe, devised a story that had an actress named Candy Wednesday (played in the film by Candice Rialson) navigate the mad, mad, mad, mad world of low-budget motion picture production. It used a three-girl murder-mystery plot that was heavy with gags. The title of the picture, *Hollywood Boulevard*, alluded to Billy Wilder's *Sunset Boulevard*, which similarly satirized the American film industry and the manner in which it attracts and indulges psychopathic personalities. Arkush and Dante asked New York actress Mary Woronov, who'd come out to Los Angeles a year earlier to co-star with Sylvester Stallone and David Carradine in Paul Bartel's *Death Race 2000*, to play the picture's homicidal starlet, Mary McQueen.

To get *Hollywood Boulevard*'s running time long enough for commercial screenings, Arkush, Dante, and Davison had to introduce previously filmed content into the movie, a practice Corman had long promoted, as long as he held the rights to the footage. "If it was going to be the cheapest movie ever made for New World, we would have only ten days to make it. We figured, 'Well, there's no way we can make a usable movie with $60,000 unless we write it around footage from all these movies we've been doing trailers for,'" said Dante. He and Allan after a shooting day would return to El Centro and cut the trailers for other people's movies. "We were all so exhausted we can barely remember making it. We would also occasionally have to make trailers during the production, so it was pretty intense. We'd spend the whole night working, and the next day we'd be back at dawn practically to shoot chase stuff and interviews to fill out the footage." Arkush and the movie's director of photography (DP), Jamie Anderson, another graduate of the NYU film program, also shot an exuberant one-song performance that appears midway through the movie by the rock-blues band Commander Cody and His Lost Planet Airmen, portending the five-song faux-Ramones concert Allan would shoot three years later with DP Dean Cundey for *Rock 'n' Roll High School.*

"The *Ben-Hur* of Exploitation Movies" ran the tagline Jon Davison came up with for the film. Funny and smutty and heavy with what Dante referred to as "boobs and buns," *Hollywood Boulevard* ridiculed the pulpy sex-soaked films that independent low-budget outfits like New World tossed out as a matter of course. In one scene, it even tried to spoof rape with the intent of ridiculing American religious hypocrisy as the would-be rapist, a cranky, moralizing creep (played by *Daily Variety* reporter Joseph McBride) attacks the film's lead in a drive-in theater's projection booth.

Movies distributed by New World never received national releases. Rather, Frank Moreno and Roger Corman used a regional-release distribution strategy, "the tried-and-true . . . formula of opening in drive-ins in the South and then 'following the sun all the way to Canada' as the warm weather creeps slowly northward."

"The pictures would play certain areas of the country. They would inundate them with television spots, 30s and 60s. And then if the picture did well, it would stick around. If it didn't, they would just take the whole thing and move it to the next territory," said Joe Dante to Daniel Griffith.

As *Hollywood Boulevard* opened across the country, starting in Florida in February 1976, it turned a quick, if not monumental, profit since Jon, Joe, and Allan had come in under budget and won their bet with Corman. In doing so, the three raised themselves considerably in their employer's estimation, but as Corman didn't want to lose Allan and Joe as trailer editors, he was reluctant to offer them follow-up directing jobs—with one exception, a futuristic samurai-motorcycle-sci-fi actioner called *Deathsport* that had such a lousy script (another Chuck Griffith stinker) neither Allan nor Joe said yes to pursuing it.

The two friends continued cutting new trailers—one of them, *Candy Stripe Nurses*, featured a three-girl plot set in a high school—and TV spots and press kits. They never abandoned their dreams of directing, and they petitioned Corman and his story editor, Frances Doel, with ideas for movies, even though everybody knew that Roger liked to develop projects based on ideas he developed himself after scrutinizing the trends and fads that were hot at any moment in America. If a movie could not exploit a popular appetite, it would not be made.

The movie ideas Allan and Joe conceived were thick with musical elements, with titles like *High School Spirit of '76* and *Heavy Metal Kids*, the latter pinched from a Todd Rundgren song. "Joe and I gave Roger eight ideas for movies, and he turned them all down." Then, in mid-1977, Joe and Allan's diligence and loyalty were rewarded. Corman came to them with an idea to develop a "high-school picture he wanted to call *Girls' Gym*," another three-girl story, but this one would feature nubile, nude gymnasts, as Arkush explained to Kent Beyda for a piece the assistant editor placed in the *Unicorn Times*. "So Roger said, 'How about you do a high school movie for me?' I said, 'A musical?'" Allan had been toying with an idea about a high school filled with students who like rock 'n' roll—a continuation of his French class daydreams at Fort Lee High School—and whose teachers and parents regard their music as evil, like the fuddy-duddies in so many American rock 'n' roll movies of the '50s and '60s.

Allan and Joe didn't care much for Corman's naked-gymnastics concept but commenced all the same with dictating over two days a seventy-eight-page "treatment for a three-girl high school movie," Allan remembered. "In order to maximize the three-girl formula," Dante told Griffith, "which involved having three different girls who would have three different kinds of adventures and then come together at some point and spout liberal philosophy and take their clothes off, namely take their clothes off, Allan and I dictated a story for this picture into a tape recorder for five-hundred bucks, or something like that."

Top-heavy with cartoonish gags and high school hijinks, the script-treatment for *Girls' Gym* that Joe and Allan got to Frances Doel proved sufficient at some point for whatever Roger wanted, and he told the story editor to go ahead with hiring a writer to develop it into a full script. Neither of the trailer cutters had time to write a screenplay, however. Joe Dante was starting a horror movie with fish called *Piranha*—which Jon Davison was going to produce—for his first solo directing credit, and Allan as a result had more to do in the trailer department. An experienced scenarist with an understanding of teen movies and an ear for rock 'n' roll was needed.

But who?

THE PAST IS NEVER DEAD

Joseph McBride grew up in Waukesha, Wisconsin, the son of newspaper reporters, adherent Catholics both, who raised their bright and introverted and loved child in the church. Joe's years as a teenager were difficult. He attended Marquette University High School in Milwaukee, a Jesuit preparatory school twenty miles away from Waukesha, which, like Allan Arkush's high school alma mater in Fort Lee, was run by authoritarians and bullies. In his memoir, *The Broken Places*, McBride attributed the nastiness that flourished at Marquette University High School to a character named Father Boyle, the institution's official disciplinarian: "a mean old fart with a bristly gray crew cut, eyes like small steel balls, and the build of a tackle for the Green Bay Packers. . . . Father Boyle carried a sawed-off golf club fastened tightly to his fist with a leather strap twisted around the knuckles, wagging it menacingly up and down like a cold metal phallus."

The physical and psychological hostility Joe encountered daily at school, compounded by a disruptive home life—his parents were alcoholics—triggered a nervous collapse for the teen during his senior year, and Mr. and Mrs. McBride had him admitted to the Milwaukee County Medical Complex's psychiatric ward. At the hospital, Joe made a friend, "a half-Native American, half-Irish young woman" named Kathy Wolf, who was "free-spirited and helped to get me out of my shell. We wound up dating, and our relationship freed me from many of my Catholic inhibitions. She was diagnosed as schizophrenic." Kathy would die tragically in a house fire she set herself years later.

Once McBride was well enough, he returned to complete his senior year at Marquette University High School, and the next fall he started at the University of Wisconsin, where he fell in with a pack of film buffs, who included future Academy Award–winning documentary director Errol Morris (*The Fog of War*), movie critic Gerald Peary, and film historian Patrick McGilligan. Watching movies, especially ones made by John Ford and Orson Welles, aroused in Joe a desire to work in motion picture production himself, preferably as a director. He even typed out, long before copy machines became ubiquitous, Orson Welles and Herman J. Mankiewicz's script for *Citizen Kane*, in its entirety, to improve his understanding of screenwriting form.

In 1969, Joe secured a job at the *Wisconsin State Journal* in Madison, the state capital and the home of UW, working first as a copyeditor and then as a general assignment reporter. Topics he covered ranged from mentoring programs for African-American children to political demonstrations in Madison to write-ups of TV programs, among them a piece about an appearance fellow Wisconsinite Orson Welles made on *The Dick Cavett Show*. The biggest story Joe covered, probably, was a bombing incident at the University of Wisconsin that killed a graduate student. On August 24, 1970, in the early morning, a band of antiwar agitators rammed a car packed with explosives, a Ford Falcon station wagon, into Sterling Hall, the building that housed the university's chemistry department, to express their anger at the school's executive administration for permitting the US Army to exploit UW's intellectual and technological resources for wartime campaigns planned against the North Vietnamese. "That bombing was a terrible event. A graduate student was killed, and this became a big story and helped end the anti-war movement. It was one of those counterproductive acts of violence—like the Weatherman violence—that really hurt the cause."

McBride left the *Wisconsin State Journal* in 1973 for Los Angeles and within a year was writing for *Variety* as an entertainment reporter, which gave him opportunities to interact with such Hollywood auteurs as Alfred Hitchcock, Billy Wilder, Fritz Lang, Jean Renoir, Howard Hawks, and Orson Welles. Welles had known McBride before he relocated to California—Joe had been on the West Coast interviewing Welles for a book about the director he was writing when the bombers struck Sterling Hall in Madison. Welles would cast Joe to play a movie critic with the ridiculous name Mr. Pister in an independently financed movie he was making called *The Other Side of the Wind*, which starred John Huston, the director of *The Maltese Falcon* and *The Treasure of the Sierra Madre*, as a weary on-the-cusp-of-has-been director. Peter Bogdanovich, who'd worked for Roger Corman in the '60s, appeared in the picture too.

McBride's beat also included New World Pictures, which fostered his acquaintance with Corman, Frances Doel, Jon Davison, and Davison's two trailer editors, Joe Dante and Allan Arkush. When the trio from post asked the reporter to appear in *Hollywood Boulevard*, their "three-girl" send-up of New World Pictures and Corman's frugality, as a wannabe rapist who attacks Candy Wednesday in a projection booth, Joe accepted. Gaining experience as an actor, Orson Welles had counseled him, was a good way to broaden one's understanding of how movies are made.

During *Hollywood Boulevard*'s filming, McBride also got to know several members of the cast, like Mary Woronov—who'd go on to play the vindictive principal Miss Togar in *Rock 'n' Roll High School*—and Paul Bartel—the same film's kindly, Ramones-loving music teacher, Mr. McGree. Bartel had cast Joe as a reporter in his follow-up to *Death Race 2000*, a transcontinental car-race flick that New World released in 1976 titled *Cannonball*. Arkush and Dante appeared in *Cannonball* too, sharing the screen for a moment with that picture's leading man, David

Carradine, as a pair of mechanics who loan a car to the hero to complete his coast-to-coast trek. Arkush's former mentor Martin Scorsese, a friend of Bartel's, also did a short scene in the picture, playing a gangster who gnaws on Kentucky Fried Chicken, seated near Sylvester Stallone as Bartel, at a piano, plays a tune he's composed in the manner of Cole Porter.

McBride's ambitions to direct had abated since his college days, and he'd turned with increasing diligence in the mid-70s to the taxing craft of screenwriting. He was good at it. He even sold a script to New World Pictures. "In 1976, I had come up with an idea for a movie that I called *Rock City*, a takeoff on Dick Clark's *American Bandstand*. . . . I was into Elvis and Chuck Berry and a lot of the good people in the early days of rock 'n' roll, and I wanted to do a film paying tribute to the spirit and the innocence of that time. But I was being satirical, too, about how the media co-opted kids' passions and fantasies and made them into a commercial product with *American Bandstand*."

Jon Davison purchased the script from McBride for $500 and quickly passed it on to Arkush and Dante. "Allan was going to direct the musical scenes of *Rock City*, of which there were many, and Joe was going to direct the story scenes. It would have been a good match." The picture never got far in terms of development, however. Roger lived in Pacific Palisades, and one of his neighbors was Dick Clark. Having the host of *American Bandstand*'s support for *Rock City* could be useful, Corman had wagered, and he shared McBride's script with the TV host, an error as it turned out: Clark did not appreciate the parodic fashion in which he and his famous show were depicted, and that prompted Corman to kill the project.

Rock City nevertheless won for McBride a reputation as "an expert on teenagers" at New World, "which was funny because I didn't particularly like teenage movies," he told me. And in July 1977, he was approached about taking Dante and Arkush's seventy-eight-page treatment for *Girls' Gym* and turning it into a feature-length script over the course of a weekend. New World was a signatory to the Writers Guild of America West (WGA), the union for Hollywood film and television writers, to which McBride belonged. In order to pay less on script fees, Corman would often work around WGA strictures. "If he had somebody write an original script or if he bought an original script, he would have to pay the Guild minimum, which was about $8,000. . . . But if he hired somebody to do a rewrite of existing material, he could pay them half that. So his scam was he would have somebody talk a script into a tape recorder for a couple of days and have his secretaries type it up and call that a script and then hire a real writer to rewrite it for the rewrite fee." Whatever his thoughts about Corman's guile as a businessman, McBride all the same accepted the offer to work up *Girls' Gym* and went home to write.

The treatment-script Arkush and Dante had generated "was mainly a bunch of scenes of kids screwing around in a high school, misbehaving and taking over the school for their fun. . . . In one scene they had some kids in a chemistry lab mixing up drugs in a barrel. They had a pet monkey at the school, like a science pet, and the monkey drank some of the drugs, and it turned into King Kong. It was supposed to be forty-feet high, and it burst through the roof and wrecked the school, which I thought was pretty silly. But it gave me the idea 'Why not have something more serious going on that would really wreck the school?'

"As a screenwriter, I always had ideas in the back of my mind for things that might make good movies if I could figure out how to do them, and one of these ideas was a story my father Raymond E. McBride had told me. In 1927, my father was the student body president at Central High School in Superior, Wisconsin. At the school . . . a woman teacher . . . was fired for some reason. She was beloved by the students, and they responded by going on strike against the school's administration. My father led the strike. . . . They picketed for a month. . . . Eventually the strike was settled, and the teacher was reinstated. It seemed like an interesting idea for a movie, though the story was a little tame for the 1970s. But then I thought, 'Well, okay, make it a little more violent.'"

McBride drew on his knowledge of film history and remembered French director Jean Vigo's surrealist satire, *Zero for Conduct* (1933), about students who take over a school from their tyrannical schoolmasters, and Lindsay Anderson's *if...* , a 1968 British drama starring

Malcom McDowell that ends with "students taking over their school from the ridiculous adults" and turning "machine guns on the parents and the teachers." He recalled his own experience with repressive pedagogues, the rotten Father Boyle, in particular, who'd patrolled the hallways of Marquette University High School with his sawed-off golf club. The bombing at the University of Wisconsin six years earlier also guided him as he banged away at the typewriter in his apartment. "[My] memories of that got me thinking 'Let's have the students blow up the school' to give the script a more political dimension. . . . I thought, 'Oh, okay, at the end of the film, I'll have them blow up the school.' And suddenly it all came together. And when I went in on Monday, they thought this was great, so they hired me to write it."

Several meetings with Arkush, Dante, and Doel followed, and the script's title soon changed, becoming *California Girls*, after the Beach Boys' song, though the focus on gymnastics remained. McBride had calculated that Corman—a financial supporter of the Black Panthers in the '60s—would sympathize with a story about teenagers seizing their own high school and blowing it up. In doing so, he could work a political element into Arkush and Dante's original cartoonish conception of a Kong-like ape breaking through their high school's roof. Allan responded to the school's fiery destruction cautiously, however. "I, at first, rejected it," he told me. "Then, after thinking about it for a week or so, it didn't seem like we could end the movie any other way."

McBride, in a recollection of *Rock 'n' Roll High School* that appears in his *Book of Movie Lists*, explains, "The way I managed to talk Arkush into going along with my ending was by passing him the information (gleaned from a fellow journalist) that director Jonathan Kaplan was planning to end his then-filming *Over the Edge* with kids setting fire to a community center. As I correctly guessed, that whetted our director's desire to outdo a more expensive movie directed by a fellow Corman protégé."

Allan soon recognized that the idea of blowing up the school "was an image that Roger could sell. From the trailer cutter's point of view, it's a great thing. When I went to Roger and talked to him about that, it was a way for me also to get rid of the nude gymnastics, which he'd never warmed to. That was a major turn because it took it away from the smarminess that would've happened. It really pushed the script and everything in the right direction." The moral implications of having angry students blow up a school raised no qualms for Corman or his story editor, Frances Doel. "It was of no controversy to us," Corman revealed to Leonard Maltin. "We said right from the beginning, 'This is a great idea.'"

Through the summer and into the fall of 1977, McBride toiled on multiple drafts of *California Girls*. He worked with Corman's three-girl plotting strategy, filling out the lead parts, crafting intersecting stories for them. Corman and Doel subsequently pressed on the screenwriter to drop the three-girl concept and focus on just two female charac-ters instead, a nerd named Kate Rambeau and her rock 'n' roll loving best friend, Riff Randell. McBride accommodated. "I thought, 'Well, make it a female buddy-buddy film.' The only one I could think of was *Gentlemen Prefer Blondes*. . . . I modeled the two girls on two [former] girlfriends of mine. One was Laurel Gilbert, who was very sexy and pretty, but studious and reserved, and wore glasses . . . very much like the Kate Rambeau character" in what became *Rock 'n' Roll High School.* "I took the name Rambeau from Nabokov's *Lolita*, which [partly] takes place in Ramsdale. The other girl," who'd been given the name Riff upon Arkush's request (one definition of a riff is a short series of musical chords played over and over), McBride based upon Kathy Wolf, "the very lively and smart and sexy and funny" schizophrenic woman he'd met at the Milwaukee County Medical Complex. "I thought, 'I'll make her the rebel in the story.'"

Joe named the school that would serve as *California Girls'* main setting after the tough-guy coach of the Green Bay Packers, Vince Lom-bardi. "It was my idea to name the school Vince Lombardi High School and have running verbal and visual gags about him. . . . The Lombardi jokes have an important thematic function, underlining the win-at-any-cost mentality [he] typified." (One of many running gags in *Rock 'n' Roll High School* would feature photos of the coach responding to student shenanigans, one spinning like a pinwheel, one looking away, and so forth.) McBride originally hoped to name the high school after Ronald Reagan, the governor of California from 1967 to 1975, whose right-wing politics were at odds with many in the New World circle. But Corman had declined to use the name because Reagan, like Dick Clark, was a neighbor in Pacific Palisades.

As the *California Girls* script evolved, Arkush asked McBride to work a rock 'n' roll group into the storyline that would interact with the students and play songs. He told the writer to imagine the Tubes. "They were a flamboyant band, really freaky, with wild clothes and special effects when they played on stage." McBride understood that Mary Woronov, from *Hollywood Boulevard*, would play the high school film's heavy, a gymnastics coach named Miss McQueen—reviving the last name of the villain (Mary McQueen) the actress had portrayed in *Hollywood Boulevard*. Miss McQueen would carry herself with the same menace as the sinister Father Boyle at Marquette University High School. The character would have a sexual kink too. "I had a scene I liked," Joe said, "where the character Mary plays is alone at night in [a] hotel room. All the girls are in their rooms, and Mary picks up the phone, and she says, 'Is this the Dungeon of Discipline?' There's a pause, and she says, 'Do you make outcalls?' I wanted her to be an S&M character. The girls get involved with the rock group, a teacher gets fired, and I put in some other political scenes. I had a scene where they were doing war games on the school property. Dick Miller was going to play some kind of a coach, and he was going to be like a general running these games. He wound up being the police chief in *Rock 'n' Roll High School* instead."

Dick Miller, who'd played Candy Wednesday's seedy agent in *Hollywood Boulevard*, had been appearing in films for Roger Corman since the '50s, including a rock 'n' roll–themed feature of Corman's called *Carnival Rock*. A protean actor who could play dimwitted dweebs, worthy heroes, and devious heels with equal ease, Miller was a favorite at New World, appearing in *Night Call Nurses*, *Big Bad Mama*, *Dark Town Strutters*, *Death Race 2000*, and *Piranha*. Directors like Jonathan Kaplan and Joe Dante included him in their casts because his presence always made whatever films he was in better, and they considered him a good luck charm.

McBride wrote a part for Paul Bartel in *California Girls*, as well, giving the bearded and bald bon vivant, who'd played a fatuous movie director in *Hollywood Boulevard*, the role of "a beloved teacher" modeled after the teacher whose firing had prompted Joe's father to lead a student strike fifty years earlier. "I came up with a music teacher character since it was going to be a music film. This is the role Bartel plays, Mr. McGree, a very sympathetic character." The character's last name, supplied to McBride by Arkush, was intended as an homage to the Belgian surrealist painter René Magritte.

During the four months McBride drafted *California Girls*, Arkush continued to keep long hours at El Centro. As Joe Dante had gone off to prepare and direct *Piranha*, an eco-horror knockoff of *Jaws* and *The Creature from the Black Lagoon*, his influence on the high school movie's development had ebbed. Arkush, in turn, increasingly swapped ideas about the *Girls' Gym–California Girls* project with Mike Finnell, another graduate of NYU's film department, who'd worked as a production assistant on *Hollywood Boulevard*. If the script McBride was toiling on made its way out of development hell and received the greenlight from Corman for production, Finnell would come on as the film's producer to work up the budget and plan out the film's execution, seeing it through all the way to its release.

SAVING DEATHSPORT

McBride submitted his final draft for the script, which at that point still bore the *California Girls* title, in October 1977. In many ways it was outstanding, a well-written screenplay that fulfilled Corman's preferences for sex, light comedy, hard action, and a dollop of social statement. Arkush and Finnell liked many of McBride's ideas—students going on strike and rioting, the Green Bay Packers elements, the names of characters, the razing of Vince Lombardi High—but they wanted something wackier, something loaded with more gags and more surrealist effects, more like a Three Stooges short or a Tex Avery cartoon or a Jerry Lewis movie.

Arkush and Finnell passed on the McBride script to Paul Bartel for his opinion: Paul's appetite for absurdist humor matched Allan's—the two were good friends—and having him punch up the material would have been ideal, but the director-actor-writer was busy then with an original script he'd begun for a comedy about cannibalism and sex-hating murderers called *Eating Raoul*. So the script was handed on to Chuck

Griffith, whose writing tended to leave Allan unpleasantly baffled. "Chuck's script was very weird and funny," but it had nothing to do with McBride's, which was again bearing the working title *Girls' Gym*. "The original concept was jettisoned. Mike Finnell and I both agreed to the problem with it, and Frances weighed in. I remember one section—in a cafeteria lunch line a character ordered 'a little chicken, potatoes and peas,' and they were handed a plate with a miniature chicken and potato and tiny, tiny peas. Chuck gave us black-out gags with no story. He didn't add to Joe's script but dropped almost all of it, which is not what we wanted." McBride, just to note, is certain that Griffith, rather than he, was "the first writer hired for the project," but concurs "that Arkush found [Griffith's] work unsatisfactory."

Further development on *Girls' Gym* at that point stalled: New World had paid out more in terms of script fees than anyone wanted, and there still wasn't a workable script. A production office that Corman had briefly opened for Arkush and Finnell to use on North Robertson Avenue in West Hollywood shut down. Finnell became busy with a new picture called *Avalanche*. Then, in late 1977, Corman went to Arkush about taking over as director on *Deathsport*, the futuristic samurai-biker movie he'd asked him about directing earlier in the year. The picture had gone into production in the summer with another director, Nic Niciphor, intended as a pseudo-sequel to Bartel's *Death Race 2000*, but set a thousand years later in a nuclear winter, where warriors battle one another on armored motorcycles.

David Carradine was the male lead in both pictures, and his popularity as low-budget star, enhanced by the commercial success of *Death Race 2000*, was such only Carradine's name needed to be attached to the production to pre-sell it to distributors and exhibitors, guaranteeing a return, but if and only if the movie got made. Niciphor, a novitiate in terms of motion picture production and a New World outsider, had two weeks to rewrite the script and prep the shoot. Only a desperate director plunging professionally would take the job—or a hopeful naïf seeking an entry into commercial filmmaking. Niciphor exemplified the latter. He'd earned his MFA from USC's School of Cinematic Arts in 1974 and possessed no understanding of the movies New World made and the grind and intensity a New World shoot entailed.

"As I sat down to bang out the script," Niciphor explained in a recollection of the production he wrote for *Psychotronic*, "Roger set his people in rapid motion to cast the picture. Claudia Jennings was his choice. I had no idea who she was. In fact, not only had I never seen a film of Claudia's, I had never seen a film of David's or Roger Corman's either at that point! These were the days before VCR. If you missed a film at the local theater, you were out of luck. Getting a special screen from Roger to view *Death Race 2000* even was out of the question. Too costly."

Filming on *Deathsport* commenced at the end of summer 1977, and problems materialized quickly. "The script was too ambitious; the shooting schedule too tight and . . . the crew and the cast were largely sodden with drugs," Niciphor wrote. Carradine would smoke hash. Claudia Jennings was "drinking nearly a fifth of vodka a day." The motorbikes used in the film, weighted down with heavy metallic shields, were "very nose-heavy. They were very hard to ride, even for an experienced rider, which Claudia was not."

Carradine had recently starred in Ingmar Bergman's *The Serpent's Egg* and anticipated, wrongly, that international recognition of his talent as some great thespian was pending; working on a low-budget science-fiction melodrama like *Deathsport* with an untried director was thus an enormous step down for him, and he behaved horribly throughout the shoot, treating Niciphor with total contempt. "[H]is script was at times brilliant," the actor recalled in his memoir, *Endless Highway*, but "his direction seemed to me to consist mainly of hysteria and episodic tantrums."

"There was never anyone less suited to be a director in the history of the universe," Jane Ruhm, the film's costumer, said of Niciphor. "The guy was really antisocial, really didn't like people. . . . Claudia Jennings could not control her bikes. A big man couldn't control those bikes. But she had to ride them. She was a very tough girl . . . a hardcore *Playboy* playmate who'd been through it all, a really tough chick. She could not keep those bikes upright, so she blew takes. Nic, who was not an experienced director, couldn't figure out how to get what he wanted using stuntpeople and how to just punch in on closeups of her. He would get really frustrated and scream at her." After Niciphor yanked Jennings off one of the bikes, fearing she was too drunk to handle it, "David got really angry on her behalf . . . and got in a fight with Nic on the set in front of all of us."

During the confrontation, Carradine drew his belt from his waist, clenching it like a whip. "I guess I was going to beat him with it. I don't know with which end. . . . Nic jumped up and ran for his car. I ran after him." Carradine, a master of martial arts—he'd been the star of the TV show *Kung Fu*—proceeded to kick Niciphor in the shin, prompting him, as Jane Ruhm remembered, to fall down "on the ground like a dead bug, screaming, 'You broke my leg! You broke my leg!'"

Niciphor went to Roger afterward: If the producer wanted him to return to finish the movie, he would need shielding from the leading man. Corman promised Niciphor a couple of stuntmen for protection. Yet Carradine wound up breaking Niciphor's nose anyway: when the director had been discussing a shot with the film's DP, Gary Graver, and was peering through the camera, the movie star, practicing a fighting move, pivoted on the heel of one foot and smashed into the camera with the other. No one could tell if Carradine did this on purpose or by accident—he was high when it happened. But Niciphor was left badly injured in his face and was rushed to the emergency room, where he had his nose packed with "wads and wads of cotton."

At the hospital, a call came in for Niciphor from Corman telling him he had to return to finish principal photography or he would be replaced with another director, and his credits would be stripped from the production. Niciphor couldn't let this happen. *Deathsport* was going to be his first solo directing credit, so he returned. There were no serious conflicts this time, and shooting wrapped at the end of that week. Carradine, who had an acting commitment in Israel, left the country shortly after.

As *Deathsport* was assembled at El Centro by an editor named Larry Bock, Niciphor's classmate at USC, Corman reviewed an early cut. Niciphor had made a bland film, he realized, that featured too much talk, too little action, not enough skin. The job was incomplete, and Corman wanted Niciphor to shoot several action scenes in early January, when Carradine had time in his schedule for reshoots. But Niciphor this time refused, unwilling to expose himself again to the actor's craziness.

It was then Corman reached out to Allan Arkush about taking over the motorcycle samurai picture set in the thirty-first century: Needed were just four days of second unit reshoots, heavy with motorcycles, fight scenes, and explosions. He'd pay the director $450 a week. He honeyed the offer further: "You know that movie you want to make so much, the high-school movie? . . . [Y]ou can come back to it if you save *Deathsport*. And you can make your movie as a musical because *Grease* and *Saturday Night Fever* are making money. You can re-write it and make it as a musical if you do *Deathsport*." Allan said, "Okay."

The new scenes for *Deathsport*, some of which would be shot in Vasquez Rocks, a scenic land formation close to Hollywood long used by directors of westerns, and Bronson Cave, which had served as Batman's lair on the '60s TV show, under Griffith Park, and the retired Nike Missile Site in San Pedro. As Carradine's biker-warrior character was going to battle a horde of mutants in one of the scenes, a call for extras was announced, which came to the attention of Richard Whitley and Russ Dvonch.

Whitley and Dvonch were new arrivals in LA. They'd graduated from Southern Illinois University, having studied in the film department, and they wanted to become screenwriters. The casting call that day was at New World's new headquarters on San Vincente Boulevard in Brentwood, which Corman had built with New World profits and moved into earlier in the year. The new building was located closer to his home and family in Pacific Palisades. Rich Whitley told me, "When we heard Roger's company, New World, was about to go into production on *Deathsport*, a futuristic sci-fi action movie, we put our student films under our arms and knocked on New World's door. After refusing to look at our films and explaining that no crew jobs were available, the woman at the front desk said that they were looking for people to play mutants from the year 3000. The pay was fifteen dollars a day and no lunch. Even with no agenting experience we knew this was a good deal and quickly agreed. As we were being escorted out the door, we desperately asked if Allan Arkush or Joe Dante were around. As fate would have it, they both happened to be right there in the lobby. We introduced ourselves, said we were fans, and asked if they'd look at our student films. For no reason other than their exceedingly good natures, Allan and Joe agreed."

The reshoots for *Deathsport* were scheduled over four days in January 1978. Carradine still had no fondness for the movie and the people working on it and behaved in a nasty and capricious manner throughout. He greeted Arkush, his scene partner in Paul Bartel's *Cannonball*, by punching him in the chest and saying, "Welcome to the future." He also manhandled the extras Whitley and Dvonch, who'd been dressed by Jane Ruhm in rags and wore protuberant prosthetic eyes made from ping-pong balls that hindered their vision. "David hit me in the chest with a sword, and he shoved Russ against the cave wall. Then the sword went into my stomach. Then into my other arm. And he's running at me," Whitley recalled of a scene he and Russ did with Carradine. "Russ was in a contorted mess—he looked like his legs were origami. Then I'm on the ground, with the wind knocked out of me. I'm lying there, just gasping. David Carradine goes, 'Good working with you, man.'"

Arkush had liked Dvonch's and Whitley's student films—they were good comedy writers. On a lunch break at Vasquez Rocks joined by Mike Finnell, he explained to the two writers how he needed a rewrite of a script for a high school movie, a musical. He told them, still in their mutant costumes, that he'd give them a chance to try out for the job, which would entail getting him ten pages by the following Monday. He also passed on to the writers a perplexing note: "AT THE END OF THE FILM THEY BLOW UP THE SCHOOL."

The professional break Russ and Rich had come to Los Angeles seeking was here. "We went to my kitchen table across the street from Universal Studios. We did our best for making the pages funny," said Rich. The pair kept the blowing up of the school in mind but put much of their focus onto a new character Allan wanted named Eaglebauer, a huckster entrepreneur who sets up dates for high school peers out of an office he maintains in one of the restrooms at Vince Lombardi High School. "Eaglebauer" referenced a character named "Mr. Eaglebauer" in the Noël Coward-Ernst Lubitsch comedy *Design for Living*, a film for Arkush that epitomized the so-called Lubitsch Touch, with its neat skiing between eloquence and ribaldry. Whitley and Dvonch knew and admired Lubitsch's films like *Ninotchka*, *The Shop Around the Corner*, and the anti-Nazi comedy *To Be or Not To Be*, but as they wrote, they drew more inspiration from Sgt. Bilko, the grifting-motor-pool-coordinating-cigarette-smoking main character on *The Phil Silvers Show*. "We would write that dialogue for Eaglebauer and go 'Wa-wa-wa-wa-wa,' just like how Phil Silvers did it." The scene the writing team concocted had Eaglebauer meeting with a pair of potential clients: nerdy Kate Rambeau and Vince Lombardi High's starting quarterback, a doofus named Tom Roberts. While Kate is in love with Tom, Tom is hot for her sporty, rock 'n' roll loving friend, Riff. Whitley and Dvonch also wrote new material for the Mr. McGree character.

After the four days of reshoots for *Deathsport* were up and the two writers had submitted their sample to Allan, Rich Whitley worked as a tour guide at Universal, while Russ Dvonch stayed on at New World as an unpaid production assistant to help with *Deathsport* during post, working often at El Centro. Russ then took a job as an assistant editor on *Avalanche*, the combination environmental cautionary tale and disaster movie set in a ski resort starring Rock Hudson and Mia Farrow, which Mike Finnell was producing.

One day around lunchtime, Whitley dropped by El Centro to talk to Dvonch, prompting Arkush to leave his editing room to tell the two writers that he wanted to show them something. The three stepped outside and walked over "to the corner of Vine and Selma, one block south of Hollywood and Vine," to Preston Sturges's star on the Hollywood Walk of Fame.

"This is how we should be trying to do it," Allan said, gesturing to the great comedy director's star in the sidewalk. The sample scene Rich and Russ delivered had passed muster. "You do know *who* Preston Sturges is?"

"Of course! *The Lady Eve. Sullivan's Travels.*"

Allan and the writers headed next to a pizza restaurant on Hollywood Boulevard called Two Guys From Italy for lunch. "That's where he said, 'I love your pages. I'm going to give you a breakdown of what we want, right now, right here and now,'" remembered Rich.

"He gave it to us in five minutes—what the story's going to be about," Russ said. "We had to fill in all of these gaps. We never looked at Joe's script. Allan told us: 'The girl, Riff, is crazy. No one's coming to the school. They burn it down.' That was basically it," Whitley recalled. The writers were given a ten-page document to work from, "A beat sheet," Arkush told me, "which was an outline based on what we were keeping from Joe's script and what we were changing."

The two writers would have to invent new scenes and new characters and add copious dialogue, but "Allan made us promise . . . not to change the names of the characters because Roger Corman had already okayed the script." The pair would have several months for the rewrite. "I was a tour guide during the day at Universal Studios," said Whitley. "We would write at night, and Russ would type up everything that we did at night during the day. Sometimes I tried the jokes out on the tours, but they didn't usually play well."

The challenge for Dvonch and Whitley was to make the students at Vince Lombardi High School and their destruction of the premises amusing, not worrisome. They revered *Horse Feathers*, the college-themed Marx Brothers movie that ends with an extravagant football game, where all involved, despite experiencing terrific physical violence, avoid permanent injury; so, too, with *Duck Soup*, which ends in a kooky war. Violence stripped of its capacity to terrorize and cause lasting pain is also the basis of every physical joke in the Three Stooges short subjects played constantly on American TV. They laced the story with double entendres, references and allusions to other movies, and sight gags. "We got paper airplanes in people's ears," said Rich. "We set out to make the kids lovable characters, but in a cartoonish, fun kind of way." They drew inspiration from their favorite television comedies. "We would watch *Monty Python Flying Circus*," Dvonch said, "but what we really looked forward to every day was *Green Acres*. We thought that was the best written show on TV at the time."

"*Green Acres is* a really funny show," said Whitley. "Everyone is in a weird bizarro world. It's that whole sense of what is real and what isn't I think that shows in our writing of *Girls' Gym*, which, of course, became *Rock 'n' Roll High School*." New characters to occupy the bizarro world were created, including a pair of evil hall monitors named Fritz Gretel and Fritz Hansel, some sexy friends for Riff and Kate, Shawn and Cheryl, and a gym teacher, Coach Steroid, whose gender is regularly misidentified (a nod to the then-current trend of snickering at Olympic athletes, most notoriously those from East Germany, whose use of human growth hormone left them with bulked-out physiques). They typed up small parts for themselves too. Russ would wander through the film as a harried freshman student, the subject of multiple pranks, while Rich would appear in several shots hoisting unwieldy piles of books. A fixed starting date hadn't been announced for the production, but the two guys from Illinois were all the same quite happy. "We'd gone from mutants to screenwriters in less than a year," Rich said.

The future of *Deathsport*, on the other hand, was fixed. Arkush had saved the picture, and Frank Moreno and his staff in New World's sales office had committed, firmly, to releasing the motorcycle-samurai picture in April 1978. Allan had written and cut the trailer and supervised the feature's editing with Larry Bock. He'd share an onscreen credit co-directing the picture with Henry Suso, a pseudonym New World invented: Nic Niciphor's contributions to the movie were not going to be acknowledged.

MAKE IT DISCO

Corman followed through on his promise to Allan to revive the high school picture after *Deathsport*'s redemption. But he wanted a change in the film's thematic concept. Having high school students blow up their school would stay, but he had some concerns about a film with a female coach as the lead. Crown International Pictures in March had released a movie titled *Coach*, starring Cathy Lee Crosby as a sexy sun-bleached high school basketball coach, and it had flopped: The heavy in *Girls' Gym*—the Miss McQueen part McBride had created for Mary Woronov—could lead to impeded sales. So, now, rather than a nude gymnastics team led by a sadomasochistic coach, Corman wanted to exploit disco music. Six months earlier Paramount Pictures had released *Saturday Night Fever*, starring John Travolta as an anguished paint salesman from Brooklyn who finds his raison d'être on the lighted dance floor. The receipts from *Saturday Night Fever* by the spring of 1978 had already surpassed $100 million. A dance-music theme, Roger insisted, could be dropped into Allan's high school picture as simply as an olive into a martini. "Make it disco," he said.

"*Grease* and disco movies like *Saturday Night Fever* were big at the time," Allan told Harvey Kubernik, "and he could have added *Thank God It's Friday, Car Wash, Disco Godfather*. I said, 'Absolutely.' On the telephone he says, 'We'll call it *Disco High*.' 'That sounds great!' In my mind, it was never going to be called *Disco High*."

Dropping the nude-gymnastics hook was enticing, but Allan and Mike couldn't get away from it completely. They'd begun already coordinating several musical set-pieces, including a scene in a gym auditorium that would feature high school students dancing as female gymnasts flung themselves acrobatically through the air. Mike, who was now planning out the film at an editing bench at El Centro and sometimes over at the production office on North Robertson Avenue again, had been approaching gymnastics teams around LA about appearing in the movie, and he'd managed to persuade the owners of a club called Arcadia Arabians to send over some of their team members in return for a $15 donation and a mention in the film's closing credits.

Corman's frugality prevented Finnell from hiring a location manager to scout for potential shooting sites for *Disco High*, so he took to roaming around Los Angeles in a Plymouth Valiant he'd won in a church raffle back home in Connecticut. "I wanted as much time as possible, especially since I was pretty much doing everything by myself. . . . I used to go out on the weekends and drive; literally just get in my car and drive around. I remember spending all day, like on Sundays, doing this. Drive around with hardly any idea of what I was doing or where I was going," Finnell told journalist Jared Cowan.

On his journeys in the Valiant, Mike, whom Allan sometimes accompanied, searched for schools that could serve as the picture's main setting, along with a house where Riff Randell lives and numerous outdoor locations, including a scenic overlook on Mulholland Drive that would do as the Lovers'-Lane locale where Eaglebauer schools his clients Kate and Tom on the art of necking.

Finnell hewed a tentative budget together, as well. "So, we'd convinced Roger to let us make this movie, and Roger had decided also that we could make this movie for $165,000. That's what he's going to give us. Mike Finnell and I are horrified. Mike is a great producer: does all this diligence, figures everything out, does a budget in terms of what else Roger had made for $165,000, which was *Summer School Teachers*. And that movie didn't have any music in it," Allan noted.

With a promise of a budget, though, even one that was agonizingly low, the producer and the director could now get on with casting *Disco High*'s principal roles: Eaglebauer, Tom Roberts, the hall monitors, Fritz Hansel and Fritz Gretel, Coach Steroid, Kate Rambeau, and Riff Randell; Mary Woronov and Paul Bartel were still on to play Miss Togar and Mr. McGree.

The film's lead part, Riff Randell, went to P. J. Soles, who'd had big parts in two of the '70s' best horror films, *Carrie* and *Halloween*, beating out Daryl Hannah and Rosanna Arquette, and by doing so gaining punk-rock immortality. Soles was twenty-eight in the spring of 1978. Even so, Finnell and Arkush were certain she could convincingly and appealingly present herself as the rocking and rolling teen leader of an insurrection. They had seen "a sneak preview of *Halloween* on Hollywood Boulevard," Allan remembered. "And she was so good in that movie. . . . I remember thinking I would love to have her *and* Jamie Lee Curtis [the lead in *Halloween*]. Jamie Lee Curtis could play the part of Kate."

"In those days, obviously, they tried to see as many kids as they could for a part. They narrow it down maybe to six, and then you'd go in," P. J. recalled for me in a 2021 interview. "I think I was on my third audition when I really thought the part was mine. I knew I could make it happen. I walked in, and Rosanna Arquette was sitting there. Only she and I. And she goes, 'What are you doing here?' I said, 'Well, I'm up for the role of Riff Randell.' And she goes, 'Well, they already told me the part's mine. So you're wasting your time.' I go, 'Oh, don't be silly,' I said. 'This is my part.' I could see why they'd like Rosanna, but I had more of a wholesome look that they probably were looking for. I read another scene probably. I think Allan Arkush and Mike Finnell were both in the office, and Roger Corman came in. He looked at me, and he said, 'You know what? Make your hair a little bit more blonde, and you've got the part.' So then I went out and said, 'Oh, Rosanna. Good luck. We'll see who's on set.' Just some friendly rivalry. Rosanna did get to ultimately star, with Madonna, in *Desperately Seeking Susan*, which she was perfect for. So we all get the roles truly meant for us!

"I felt pretty confident. I went out that day and started buying some wardrobe pieces because I had my idea for how I wanted to have Riff look onscreen—very bright and colorful. I knew the clothes were really important. For *Halloween* and *Carrie*, I'd used my own wardrobe. This was going to be my last teenage role, and I had a very specific look in mind: I wanted her to pop off the screen, like a comic book, almost. I went to Fiorucci, I went to Fred Segal. I got the jacket that I wear in the opening scene, where I'm saying to Kate, 'I'm getting a lot of static' and I'm dancing on top of the table—a red satin jacket with musical notes on it. It was at Fred Segal, three-hundred dollars. I'd put it on hold, and the day that I got word that I got the part, I went over there and bought it. 'I have a jacket on hold for me,' I said. And Rod Stewart was there. He wanted the jacket, too. When they brought it out, he said, 'Yeah. I want that jacket.' I told him, 'No, no, no. You don't understand. I put it on hold. I got this part in this movie.' In any event, we had a tug of war, and finally, he let it go, and he let me have it. I got Converse sneakers, too."

Now that Corman's support for the high school movie was secure, Mike and Allan could proceed with finding a musical act to supply the songs for the student uprising that was going to cap off their quickly-coming-together film. A disco group like the Village People or KC and the Sunshine Band or Boney M. or the Spinners would be ridiculous. Disco was for hedonists, for escape and sensuous pleasure, not civil disobedience. The band Allan wanted for the raging kids, the "children of the revolution" as Marc Bolan might have called them, would have to play rock 'n' roll. The act would need to be popular or, at least, display a potential to connect with the movie's targeted teen audience. Tom Petty surfaced as a possibility briefly and also songwriter-producer Todd Rundgren. Rundgren's "Heavy Metal Kids" from 1974, with lyrics about creating peace with a hydrogen bomb, had guided Allan's thinking when he and Joe Dante first spitballed movie ideas in Allan's Ford

Falcon on their runs between the MGM lab, Ryder Sound Services, and El Centro, with the radio always on, the dial set to KROQ.

Allan and Mike headed up to San Francisco and met with Rundgren, who, they learned abruptly, was wary of the ways Hollywood depicted rock 'n' rollers in movies and TV, too often making them look like goofs, shallow and dumb. He'd have been interested, Rundgren told Allan, if the movie were more serious—more like Lindsay Anderson's *if. . . .* "He didn't like our story because it was funny." Having a title like *Disco High* didn't help. After the meeting with Rundgren, "We never let anyone know it was called *Disco High*. It was on the title page that Roger got, but every time we sent the script to a band, or anyone we knew, we changed the title page to *Rock 'n' Roll High School*," Arkush told filmmaker Robert Nuñez.

Allan and Mike then approached Cheap Trick, the power pop quartet from Rockford, Illinois, who hadn't yet cracked mainstream radio but soon would with the massive success of their *Cheap Trick at Budokan* LP. Cheap Trick's longtime drummer, Bun E. Carlos, when I asked him, confirmed that New World offered the band $15,000 to appear in the picture, which was too low an offer for the time commitment the movie would entail. Cheap Trick had countered with a request for $50,000, to which Allan, wincing at the price, said that he would see what he could do.

An attorney named Paul Almond, who in 1978 served as New World's head of business and legal, aided Allan and Mike at this point in their efforts. Before joining New World's legal staff, Almond had been director of business affairs at Warner Bros. Records. He'd left on good terms and had negotiated for the use of two Warner Bros. songs for the soundtrack on Ron Howard's *Grand Theft Auto*. Almond, in June, set up an appointment for Allan and Mike to meet with Warner Bros.' PR department. There, in Burbank, Devo and Van Halen were offered up as possibilities, but Devo, the experimental art rockers from Akron, Ohio, didn't fit Allan's concept for what the band he wanted crashing Vince Lombardi High School would look and sound like, and as LA's Van Halen had a reputation for being unmanageable, he passed on them too.

Then an A&R rep in the meeting named Carl asked, "Well, you do know Sire Records?" Warner Bros. Records had struck a recent distribution deal with the independent New York City label, whose stable included several "punk" acts that had come up out of the Lower Manhattan music scene in the mid-'70s playing gigs at clubs like CBGBs in the Bowery and the more upscale Max's Kansas City on Park Avenue near Union Square. Sire bands included Talking Heads, the Dead Boys, and Richard Hell & the Voidoids; they were all quite good, Allan thought— he'd read about them in the rock 'n' roll magazines, and KROQ's Rodney Bingenheimer often featured New York punk on his Sunday night show, Rodney on the Rock. Still, none of these groups felt right for what Allan thought the movie needed.

Then the A&R rep, Carl, suggested the Ramones. The band had released three albums so far—*Ramones*, *Leave Home*, and *Rocket to Russia*—and had a fourth one about to come out, *Road to Ruin*, along with a live album, called *It's Alive*, in the works. Allan was a fan. He told Jake Fogelnest, "I used to read Robert Christgau's column in the *Village Voice*. I'd started reading about the punk scene in New York, and Robert Christgau gave this album an 'A' called *Ramones*. I went out and bought it and put it on and listened to it, all the way through."

The hard-fast drone pop of *Ramones*, the band's first LP, released by Sire in 1976, baffled Allan's seasoned ears at first. Songs like "Blitzkrieg Bop," "Beat on the Brat," and "Today Your Love, Tomorrow the World" all sounded the same to him—crude, jarring. The Ramones' second album, *Leave Home*, similarly failed to rouse the blood. But in 1977, the band had released *Rocket to Russia*, which Allan right away recognized was a great album, with knock-out tunes like "Rockaway Beach," "Locket Love," "Teenage Lobotomy," and "Sheena Is a Punk Rocker," all gritty and lovely and endearing and heavy at once, like the Archies in a firefight.

The Ramones looked great too. The four original members— Tommy, Johnny, Dee Dee, and Joey—who pretended to be brothers and shared the same fake "Ramone" surname—all wore cheap leather jackets, torn blue jeans, skinny-boy T-shirts, and busted sneakers. The

Ramones were like a band that wrote novelty songs without meaning to. They managed to project lovableness and threat at once—perfect for a movie in which rock 'n' roll music and the people who make it are regarded as dangerous and subversive by anyone over thirty. Carl the A&R guy's suggestion "just struck me as funny. . . . I started picturing high school girls worshiping Joey."

The Warner Bros. Records PR people pointed Allan and Mike in the direction of the Ramones' co-managers, Linda Stein and Danny Fields, who were both in Los Angeles. Fields had helped the Ramones get their recording deal with Sire Records. Fields lived in New York City, but Linda Stein, semi-estranged wife of Sire co-founder Seymour Stein, kept an apartment at the Hotel Bel-Air. Fields and Stein together owned Coconut Entertainment and oversaw most of the Ramones' business dealings. They were eager to hear the pitch. American radio had all but rejected their clients, so maybe a part in a movie, even a low-budget one, could help the band in their unrelenting pursuit of a hit.

Allan and Mike rushed to Bel-Air from Burbank in Mike's Plymouth Valiant and met Linda and Danny in the groomed garden on the hotel's grounds. "Tell us the story," the co-managers asked, between puffs on a joint. *Rock 'n' Roll High School* would be about repressive school administrators and cops who try to prevent a rock 'n' roll–loving teen-aged songwriter named Riff and her friends from listening to the kind of music they like, which precipitates a student revolt. "They just loved it. When we told them that the school blows up while the band plays, they jumped up and down, saying, 'We wanna do this!' They were really excited about it," Allan told writer Zack Carlson, for his book *Destroy All Movies!!! The Complete Guide to Punks on Film.*

Now, though, the Ramones had to be approached and convinced to appear in the picture—there'd been similar offers before, which they'd declined, much as Todd Rundgren had, over the way movies and TV shows depicted rockers as morons. And Allan, who'd only seen the Ramones in photographs, needed to watch them play live and to interact with them personally to assess if they'd be controllable on the movie set and if the ferocious but at the same time endearing sound they made on

Rocket to Russia had any likelihood of connecting with movie audiences. There were no upcoming shows scheduled for the Ramones in Los Angeles that summer, however. If Allan wanted to catch the guys playing live, his best chance would be back in New York, the band's hometown. But they'd have to get a show booked first. That would work, Allan told the co-managers. New York in a way was his hometown too.

ENTER THE RAMONES

The Ramones would never have a breakout single during their twenty-two-year run as a band, but in 1978, four years since they'd first formed in Forest Hills, Queens, they still believed they had hit-making potential. For more people to hear their music, they needed radio programmers to add their songs to stations' playlists. They'd been branded in the press as a "punk-rock" band, an epithet they never wanted. They only wanted to be pop stars, "to be a bubblegum group," as Johnny, the band's guitar player, explained to Monte A. Melnick, for Melnick's memoir, *On the Road with the Ramones: Bonus Edition*. Melnick was the Ramones' tour manager from 1974, the year the band formed, to 1996, the year they broke up. "We looked at the Bay City Rollers as our competition. We thought we were a teenybopper group." They despised the overwrought corporate-rock acts like Styx, Yes, and the Eagles, whom they blamed for leaching from rock 'n' roll and radio all its fun. "We decided to form our own group because we were bored with everything we heard," said Joey, the band's singer, for the *Irish*

Times. "We missed hearing songs that were short and exciting and good. We wanted to bring the energy back to rock 'n' roll."

The Ramones had brought in 1978 playing a New Year's Eve gig at the Rainbow Theatre in London. The concert was recorded for a live album, which everybody in Ramones-world hoped could raise the band's profile, just as the concert album *Alive!* had for another New York City–based band with a novel look, KISS, back in 1975. Handling the concert's recording that night was Ed Stasium, a young engineer and producer who'd previously collaborated with the Ramones on *Leave Home* and *Rocket to Russia*. The guys jetted home to New York from London soon after, and after a show January 7 at the Palladium (very close to NYU), they headed out on the road for several shows, paired with the Runaways—the pop-punk teen act featuring Joan Jett, Jackie Fox, Samantha West, Lita Ford, and Cherie Currie. In his abrupt and harsh way, Johnny recalled in *Commando*, his memoir: "We started 1978 on a tour with the Runaways, a band of dykes. At least a couple of them were. Dee Dee was friends with them. It went well, and we travelled through the middle of America in the dead of winter. The tour lasted three months."

When the Ramones came off the road in the spring, Tommy, the band's drummer, informed the others he was quitting. Tommy liked cigarettes, and Johnny had banned smoking in the van that the band's tour manager, Monte A. Melnick, used to carry the guys, and often their girlfriends, from show to show. "Tommy couldn't stand it in the van for ten hours, not having a cigarette, and everybody giving him an attitude about it," Dee Dee, the Ramones' first bass player, wrote in his memoir *Lobotomy*. "Tommy was starting to fall apart and have a breakdown," Johnny said. "He was becoming catatonic and having trouble dealing with everything. He couldn't take the road." Tommy's own reasons for leaving the band were less histrionic in tone; as he revealed to Ramones biographer Jim Bessman: "I was having a very good time and enjoying making records and feeling that with every album we made we were making progress and doing something valuable. But, I started to get claustrophobic about touring, and since I loved the studio, I decided to just produce albums and quit the road."

The search to replace the drummer had commenced quickly because the Ramones were due to return to the studio to record their fourth album, *Road to Ruin*, in May. Blondie's drummer, Clem Burke, had come up as a possible replacement. So did the Heartbreakers' Jerry Nolan and Paul Cook from the Sex Pistols. But the person the Ramones wanted most was Marc Bell, who kept the beat for Richard Hell & the Voidoids, one of the artier bands to emerge out of the Lower East Side scene. "We knew Marky because he was the drummer of the Voidoids, and we thought he was too jazzy and was wasted in that group," Johnny said. "We didn't want to steal the drummer from another band, but he was much better with us."

Persuading Marc Bell to jump from one band to another was easy enough as he didn't like Richard Hell. He auditioned as a formality and got the job, adopting the band's tough look and the Ramone surname, also changing his first name to Marky, which sounded more casual, more street, than Marc, while at the same time nodding to Marky Maypo, the cartoon mascot for the popular hot-cereal brand. The Ramones all used the same last name because it underscored "the unity of our group," Johnny told the *San Francisco Examiner* in 1978. Dee Dee had been the one who came up with the surname; his inspiration was Paul McCartney, who, during his Beatles years, had checked into hotels using the moniker "Paul Ramon."

After several weeks of practicing with Marky, the reconstituted Ramones returned to the studio to record *Road to Ruin*, with Ed Stasium and T. Erdelyi producing. T. Erdelyi was actually Tommy, the Ramone's ex-drummer, who'd always been more interested in working as a producer, like Brian Wilson in his twenties and thirties, than touring. *Road to Ruin* was going to take the band's hard-fast-sometimes-sweet sound in a more commercial direction, with the intent of getting the rockers on the radio. At the end of the '70s, explained Andy Shernoff, bass player and main songwriter for another great CBGBs band, the Dictators, who refers to himself, justifiably, as the Christopher Columbus of punk: "You wanted to be popular, you wanted to tour, you wanted to make records. And there was one way of doing that. There was no internet. No MTV. There was radio, and that was it."

The Ramones on *Road to Ruin* took the minimalist thumping sound that permeated the first three LPs more self-consciously in the direction of power pop, with all new songs the band had been writing over the previous months, among them "She's the One," "I Just Want to Have Something to Do," "I Wanna Be Sedated," and even a country-rock song—in the same manner as the Stones' "Dead Flowers"— titled "Questioningly." There was a world-beating cover of the Searchers' "Needles and Pins" too. Seymour Stein had pressed on Stasium and Erdelyi to get the guys to record material that would help them pry themselves free of the "punk" sobriquet and its violent and prurient connotations, and *Road to Ruin*, so went the hope, was going to do it. Monte A. Melnick in his memoir, *On the Road with the Ramones: Bonus Edition*, noted: "While the 'punk' tag was helping bands like the Sex Pistols and the Clash sell a lot of records, it seemed to be holding us back and preventing us from getting on the radio."

"We're just middle-class kids from the suburbs. We wanted to be a rock group like the Beatles, but people were always saying that we were punk. We're not punk. We're no more punk than old Presley or the Beatles were. Punk makes me think of some guy who just hangs out and never does anything or who's always giving people a bad time. We really care about our music," Johnny complained to the *Indianapolis News*'s rock 'n' roll music columnist, Zachary Dunkin, in 1979.

Seymour Stein had no problem with the punk tag, he wrote in his memoir, *Siren Song*, when it "got kids to run and buy our records, fine," but the "problem was radio, especially in America where the word *punk* sounded about as appetizing as *jerk* or *scumbag*." "Punk" had once been slang for a female prostitute, but its meaning had morphed and jumped genders and become a prison-house term for someone "kept by an older man as a (typically passive) sexual partner, a catamite," explains the *Oxford English Dictionary*. "A man who is made use of as a sexual partner by another man, esp. by force or coercion."

Sire in 1978 launched a marketing campaign to replace the "punk" handle with "new wave" instead. "I stumbled on the idea of 'new wave,' pilfered from the French cinematic movement *Nouvelle Vague*. I don't know if I first read it somewhere or heard it in a conversation, but it popped into the air and became my standard telephone spiel to win over every plugger, program director and hippie jock."

Stasium and Erdelyi kept the new songs as clean-and-clear sounding on *Road to Ruin* as possible—no sludge, no fuzz, and nothing too fast, too punk, with the exception of a few tracks, like "I Wanted Everything" and "Bad Brain." Recording, at Media Sound in Manhattan, took a month, and, afterward, as the Ramones always did, they returned to touring. Through the summer of 1978, they had a chance to introduce several of their new songs as they played shows with the Patti Smith Group, the Dead Boys, and Marky's old band Richard Hell & the Voidoids.

Danny Fields and Linda Stein, through their management company, Coconut Entertainment, had followed up on the promise they'd made to Allan Arkush and Mike Finnell at the Hotel Bel-Air in June and secured a booking for the Ramones at Hurrah, a nightclub on the Upper West Side that billed itself as the city's only "rock discotheque." They'd be headliners for a three-night weekend stint, August 11, 12, 13. Allan was delighted. He could fly in on Friday, the 11th, and get back Sunday, only missing a day of work. His dad, Jacob, was living now in an apartment in Lower Manhattan (the Arkushes had divorced while Allan was in college). He could crash on his dad's couch.

Corman would never cover the airfare to attend a rock concert, so Allan bought his own ticket and took a redeye flight, steerage-class, back to New York. Seated in the rear of the cabin, near the toilet, he didn't sleep much and used the time in transit reading through the most recent copy of the Dvonch-Whitley script for *Disco High*. The writers had done what he'd hoped for, adding gags and dialogue and building up several storylines, having taken the girls' gym coach character Joseph McBride invented, Miss McQueen, and transforming her into a fascistic high school principal named Miss Evelyn Togar.

The writers worked up the Riff Randell character in a way he liked quite a bit. Allan had given the character the name "Riff," an allusion to the leader of the Jets street gang in *West Side Story*. His concept for the middle-class suburban female high school student whose heart throbs for rock 'n' roll arose from his memories of three women he'd known in New York. "When I was working at the Fillmore, and I was in college, the Stones had a big tour coming to promote *Let It Bleed*. This is 1969. They're coming to America, and it was a big deal, that tour. There was a big article in the newspaper about these young girls who had cut school for three days to get in line for the Stones tickets. A picture of them ran in the *Daily News* or whatever it was. Gail, Diane and Janice. That was the inspiration for Riff.

"Then, being part of the Fillmore staff, we all got choice of tickets, and I got third row tickets to the Stones. But I didn't have a date. All of us from the Fillmore go to Madison Square Garden, and I'm planning to just sell the ticket—to scalp it. And there, we run into Gail, Diane and Janice. 'Oh, my God! This is great,' I say to them, and then: 'Where's your tickets? You were first in line.' They go, 'We're in the fuckin' hundredth row. They give people in the business all the good tickets. Where are you sitting?' I said, 'I'm in the third row.' 'The third fuckin' row?' I said, 'Yes. I have an extra ticket.' Gail goes, 'Give it to me! Give it to me! I'll do anything. Give it to me!' I said, 'Gail, it'll be a pleasure.' She's next to me during the whole concert. Now, you've got two Riff Randells side by side in the concert and another one next to me. You've heard *Get Yer Ya-Ya's Out*, the Stones album? That's the concert; you can see parts of it in *Gimme Shelter*.

"It's an incredible show, and they go into 'Honkytonk Woman.' Everybody is standing and screaming, and Mick Jagger has these roses in his hand. He's singing, 'She covered me in roses' and 'She blew my nose and then she blew my mind.' He throws the roses in the air. Gail launches herself like an Atlas rocket, grabs me by the shoulder, jumps on the chair, hurls herself up, grabs for one of the roses and rips my shirt, but she got the rose."

ONE! TWO! THREE! FOUR!

After his plane touched down at LaGuardia Airport, Allan took a bus up to the Port Authority and then the subway down to the stop at Union Square, walking the rest of the way to his father's apartment, where he napped on the couch before getting back out on the street and starting up to Hurrah on West 62nd and Broadway. The nightclub, located in Central Park West, was just a "coke spoon's throw," as Blondie's Gary Valentine described it, "from Lincoln Center," and far enough away from the Lower East Side to feel like another planet.

Hurrah had opened in November 1976 for the New York disco crowd, years before the synth-and-strings dance pop had its heyday, when it seeped like syrup across the linoleum floor of American popular culture. The young and beautiful would visit Hurrah to drink, to do drugs, and to dance to records selected by a house deejay. But by 1978, discotheque competitors in NYC, like Studio 54 and Paradise Garage, had sprung up, siphoning away customers, forcing Hurrah to adapt—or die. The club started booking live acts, like the Village People, and the female impersonator star of John Waters's *Pink Flamingos* and *Female*

Trouble, Divine, in a one-person burlesque mystery show called *The Neon Woman*. Hurrah started to schedule punk and new wave acts, too, many of them who'd fledged in CBGBs, like Talking Heads and Suicide.

Merrill Alighieri, Hurrah's longtime staff videographer, told me that after the Divine show finished its run in July 1978, the club "made the transition from disco to rock 'n' roll. It was really the beginning of the whole new wave thing. Hurrah had a great sound system, with good sound engineers and a bigger dance floor than some of the small clubs. It was still a small club: they could cram a thousand people in there, illegally. I think it was supposed to hold only two-hundred, maximum. It had a very chic look. The interior had this sweeping kind of S-curve of faceted mirrors that you almost felt like you were walking inside of a prism. They had TV monitors hanging off the ceilings like stalactites. There was no signage on the outside of the building. On the interior of the entrance door, though, someone had painted 'Hurrah.' You went up a couple of staircases, which winded a little bit, that had a little landing in-between. There was one doorman-bouncer, named John. A huge guy. He would tell everybody, 'Watch the steep steps going down. You miss one—you miss them all!' You walked up those stairs, and then there was another guy, who stamped your hand when you walked in. There was a dance school in the building, and there were some really cool dancers who would come to the club all the time. It attracted the downtown crowd by bringing in downtown musicians."

The doors opened at Hurrah each night around nine. Allan was on the Ramones' guestlist for both the Friday and Saturday night shows. Once he climbed the stairwell and had his hand stamped by the door guy and got inside, he was greeted by Danny Fields, who led him backstage to meet the band. The Ramones took craft seriously—they were no stragglers—and they liked to run through songs to warm up before shows, playing without electric hookups and amps. Marky in *Punk Rock Blitzkrieg* wrote that Allan "was a little surprised to see us rehearse a few of the songs unplugged before the show, but that's what worked for us." Allan watched and listened to them running through numbers like "Pinhead" and "Sheena Is a Punk Rocker."

Once they were done, he proceeded to lay out the concept of the film. *Rock 'n' Roll High School* was going to be a musical comedy filled with dancing and singing teenagers, with appearances from all kinds of radio personalities, like LA jocks Rodney Bingenheimer and the Real Don Steele, just as Alan Freed had in *Rock Around the Clock*. The soundtrack would be thick with Ramones songs, and so, too, if Sire could let it happen, an accompanying tie-in soundtrack album. The four would have to learns some lines and act a little, but not too much. They'd spend more time on screen performing material from their records. He was hoping they would work up some new stuff too. There'd be a concert in the movie, a fake one but with real fans, and a couple of musical numbers performed with the cast. He told them about his time at the Fillmore East, how he'd lit shows for The Who. Joey loved The Who and that made him like Allan. The conversation backstage at Hurrah started to soar. "When I described the ending, how they'd show up at the school, and be playing as the building went up in flames, they all went, 'We're in! We're in! We're doing this!' They totally got the whole wish-fulfillment aspect of it," Arkush explained to journalist Jon Zelazny. To Zach Dunkin, Johnny clarified that "The idea of the movie was good for us because it meant we could play ourselves, rock stars, and didn't have to play something that wasn't us. We also wanted to make sure it was a good picture and that someone like Roger Corman was behind it because we had a lot of offers to do other films, but we never took them."

During the conversation backstage, Allan was handed copies of the most recent issue of *Punk*, an illustrated pop-culture magazine, heavy on satire and confrontational humor, which profiled and interviewed figures from New York's vanguard music scene, bands like the Dictators, Blondie, the Patti Smith Group, and the Ramones, and musical subversives Lou Reed and Iggy Pop. The guys directed him to a *fumetti* in the magazine, a comic strip comprised primarily of photographs rather than drawings. Titled "Mutant Monster Beach Party," the photo-story featured Joey as the surfer-boy love interest of Blondie's singer, Deborah Harry. Several figures from the CBGBs set showed up in the panels, including Scott Kempner (the Dictators), Jonathan Paley (Mong, the

Paley Brothers), David Johansen (New York Dolls), John Cale (the Velvet Underground), Joey Ramone's brother, Mickey Leigh, music writer Lester Bangs, and pop-art maven Andy Warhol.

Punk Magazine had been co-founded by John Holmstrom, a graduate of the School of Visual Arts in Manhattan, and Roderick "Legs" McNeil, a writer. They had developed the script for "Mutant Monster Beach Party," poking fun at beach-party movies, like American Independent Pictures teen-exploitation films *Beach Blanket Bingo* and *Dr. Goldfoot and the Bikini Machine*, and low-budget science-fiction movies of the sort Roger Corman made in the '50s, like *Not of This Earth* and *War of the Satellites*, the types of movies Holmstrom and McNeil and the rockers in the photos had grown up watching. Roberta Bayley operated as the project's director of photography, with contributions from Chris Stein and Bob Gruen. Joey received a creative credit, too, for contributing to the storyline bits of lyrics sung by the kids in the photos, like "The girls out there knock me out you know / But we can't go surfin' 'cause it's twenty below," which Joey would rework and include in "Danny Says," one of the tracks on the *End of the Century* LP the Ramones recorded with Phil Spector in the spring of 1979. Joey was the only Ramone in the strip. The Ramones' 6'6" front man was never handsome, but Bayley and her photographers made him look good anyway, snapping his spindly physique as he clasped a beat-up surfboard, wearing shorts, smiling shyly like Mona Lisa, with his long legs carrying him along the Manhattan streets and the Coney Island shoreline.

Allan hung around long enough backstage to witness Joey engage in one of many pre-show rituals the singer obsessively observed, in this instance drinking a shake made with Hemo-Tonic (a medicinal syrup used to treat iron-deficiency). Then the director walked from the dressing room back to the dance floor. He realized at that point the Ramones *were* cinematic, very much so, and ideas for gags featuring the four nudged into consciousness, a good sign. He positioned himself away from but close enough to the stage to study the band and simultaneously monitor the audience's responses. Amalgams of abstract images, kaleidoscopic and ceaselessly moving, streamed across the TV screens that dropped down from the nightclub's ceiling. Stacked amps rose from the sides of the stage like Moai heads, onyx monoliths bathed in hot light. Punks and students and artists, the backs of their T-shirts tacky with sweat, glanced expectantly through the gray-purple cigarette haze toward the array of guitars and drums and microphone stands gleaming under the hot lights.

The evening's opening act, Klaus Nomi, was a rubber-band thin opera singer dressed like a commedia dell'arte clown, whose voice sounded like wind shooting over alpine mountaintops. Next came the Mumps, fronted by Lance Loud, one of the stars of *An American Family*, an early reality TV show about an affluent family from Santa Barbara, which ran on PBS in the early '70s. The Mumps were like the Screamers in LA—never signed but should have been. Lance Loud that night prowled around the stage, shirtless and handsome, as his bandmate, and the Mumps' songwriter, Kristian Hoffman—who'd also appeared in *An American Family*—thrashed at his keyboard. Hoffman's songs combined manic pacing, splintering melodies, and self-effacing camp lyrics. They'd rouse crowds with an anthemic tune called "I Like to Be Clean," which could have been written for Dee Dee Ramone, who liked to take showers four times a day.

Around eleven o'clock, the Ramones scrambled onto the stage. In that moment between the band's manifestation under the lights and the start of their playing, the crowd in Hurrah constricted along the front of the stage, strangers standing within inches of one another, each clutching a bottle of beer or a cigarette or both. Then Dee Dee lurched toward his microphone and shouted "One! Two! Three! Four!" and the band stormed into "Rockaway Beach," their New York City surf song, followed by "Teenage Lobotomy" and "I Don't Want You," a new one from *Road to Ruin*. The overhead lights streaked the shoulders of their black jackets and their scalps. Joey's fingers around the microphone were pale like melted vanilla ice cream. Johnny and Dee Dee stared out over the pogoing punks and slam dancers with the concentration and toughness of steelworkers as Marky worked the drums like the pistons in a muscle car. The influences of Jack Nitzsche and the Bay City Rollers

and the Ronettes and the Stooges and Slade swept through every song
at once. Allan—who at the Fillmore East had lighted Neil Young, Miles
Davis, Brian Wilson, Pete Townshend—knew he was beholding something grand, something great.

The Ramones sped through their set in about forty minutes, ending
the night with "Pinhead," a song Joey delivered from the point of view
of someone living with microcephaly, a condition that leaves skulls mis-
shapen and the brains inside them undersized. As the song neared its
end, the emaciated singer hoisted a sign that read "Gabba Gabba Hey,"
a line repeated over and over in the song. They'd written "Pinhead"
after seeing Tod Browning's cult horror film *Freaks*, which has several
people with microcephaly starring in it, each one's cone-shaped head
shaved clean except for a curlicue of hair held in place with a bow on top.
"We were in Cleveland . . . in 1977, and our show was rained out. We
went to see the movie *Freaks* and wrote a song about pinheads," Johnny
told Monte A. Melnick. "Gabba Gabba Hey" was the Ramones' take on
the cry of the grotesques in Browning's startling film, "Gooble-gobble.
One of us! Gooble-gobble. One of us!" The "one of us" in the chant is
the movie's villain, whom the titular personae turn into a pathetic half-
chicken-half-woman monster.

Allan was excited as he returned backstage following the show. He
wanted to chat with the guys more about the film, about when it would
likely start shooting, how long they'd be needed in Los Angeles if they
came on, and what they could probably expect in terms of pay—$25,000.
But before any sort of substantive conversation got underway, "This guy
came in; very drunk, very loud . . . and I realized it was Lester Bangs,"
Allan recalled for Jon Zelazny. "I'd read everything he'd written; he was
like a god to me. He was just giving the Ramones a hard time, y'know,
being really funny. The Talking Heads walked in . . . and he started pick-
ing on [bassist] Tina Weymouth!"

The Ramones took Allan to CBGBs that night, a grotty hole set
amidst wrecked sidewalks and stumblebums, where the owner, Hilly
Kristal, allowed his pet dogs to shit on the floor. Then all headed off to
Joey Ramone's loft apartment around the corner, which he shared with

Arkush's professor Martin Scorsese (center).
Courtesy Allan Arkush

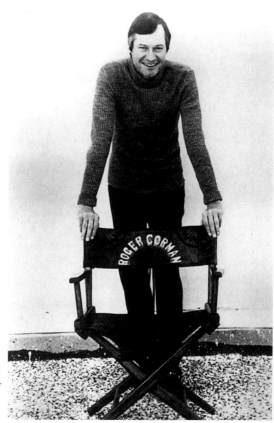

Roger Corman, founder-owner of New World Pictures.
© New World Pictures

Allan and Joe at El Centro (l–r: Allan Arkush, Joe Dante).
Photo by Paul Bartel / Courtesy Wendy Bartel

Sign for Elvis Costello's show at Hollywood High, June 1978.
Courtesy Allan Arkush

Joseph McBride, who drew heavily upon personal experience and knowledge as he provided the film script's earliest drafts.
Courtesy Joseph McBride

Screenwriter Russ Dvonch (l), the Freshman, with Joey Ramone (c) and Allan Arkush (r).
Courtesy Richard Whitley

Screenwriter Richard Whitley, with P. J. Soles and the Ramones.
Courtesy Richard Whitley

Nyuck-nyuck-nyuck: Arkush (c) and writers Rich Whitley (l) and Russ Dvonch (r).
Courtesy Richard Whitley

The director and his stars: (l–r: Allan Arkush, P. J. Soles, Joey Ramone).
Photo by Carin Abramson / © New World Pictures

First day of shooting: Clint Howard (l) and Vince Van Patten (r) on Mulholland Drive.
Photo by Richard Whitley

Big goof on campus: Tom Roberts may be a klutz, but Vince Van Patten was a ranked professional tennis player at the time of shooting.
Photo by Carin Abramson / © New World Pictures

Best friends Kate and Riff (from left to right: Dey Young and P. J. Soles).
Photo by Carin Abramson / © New World Pictures

Dee Dee getting clean.
Photo by Carin Abramson / © New World Pictures

Working out with the laundry cart.
Photo by Carin Abramson / © New World Pictures

Riff leads the parade through Vince Lombardi High.
Photo by Carin Abramson / © New World Pictures

Miss Togar (Mary Woronov)—mean to students, meaner to mice.
Photo by Carin Abramson / © New World Pictures

Arturo Vega, where the air smelled like cigarettes and emulsion remover. Vega, a graphic artist, had designed the Ramones' logo—an American eagle clutching a baseball bat, encircled by the names of the guys in the band (recently updated to include Marky's), with the slogan "Hey Ho Let's Go" printed on a banner streaming over the bird's bald head. Vega also worked the merch tables at the Ramones' shows, selling T-shirts and Frisbees with the band's name and insignia printed on them. Vega and his assistant, David "Moon" Davis, created all the band's promotional goods in the apartment, a Bowery imitation of Warhol's Factory.

Arkush got back to his dad's apartment some time before sunrise, exhausted but certain he'd found the band for the high school movie. He was going to tell Mike Finnell that the Ramones displayed a kind of power and fury—and nuttiness—that would complement the antics and gags in the Dvonch-Whitley script. But he had to sleep, knocked flat on his father's couch from the one-two punch of a redeye flight and a Ramones concert. When he woke up, he walked down to the Village "to my favorite record store, Bleecker Bob's, to hang with Bob and go through the racks," where he bought an Animals LP that he brought back to his dad's apartment before heading back out.

Allan planned to attend the second night of the Ramones' three-night stint as well. He and the Ramones had been invited to a pre-concert meal at Seymour and Linda Stein's Central Park West apartment, a quick walk to Hurrah. The Steins believed in the Ramones, recognized them as rock 'n' roll revolutionaries, believed still they could break nationally. To celebrate what looked like was going to be, hopefully, a mutually beneficial collaboration between Sire Records and New World Pictures, the Steins laid out a feast that night. "Seymour Stein ordered a fabulous Italian meal, brought up to his beautiful . . . apartment," recalled Allan on a DVD commentary he recorded with Mike Finnell and Rich Whitley. "We're sitting around with all this beautiful Italian food on plates and silver trays, and all takeout. And the Ramones looked at it, and all of a sudden say, 'Where's the pizza?' Seymour had to call up and have a pizza brought up. No one was eating the soft shell crab, the osso buco."

NOOSE ENDS

Upon his return to LA, Arkush asked for a meeting with Corman, who believed in the value of meticulous planning during preproduction and consented. Mike Finnell and New World attorney Paul Almond were invited too. Allan had to persuade his employer of two things. First, that the band he'd just seen, heard, and eaten pizza with in New York, the Ramones, should play the band in the high school movie. Second, the title, *Disco High*, needed a change. As he presented his case, Allan showed Corman the "Mutant Monster Beach Party" *fumetti* from *Punk Magazine* and directed him to the photos of Joey with his surfboard and a list of "Inspirations," which appeared in the strip's credits, thanking *MAD* magazine cartoonist Jack Davis, American-International-Pictures, and Roger Corman. He also explained that only two bands were in consideration for the movie's featured musical act: Cheap Trick and the Ramones. But while Cheap Trick was asking $50,000 to appear, the Ramones could be secured for half that, which prompted the tycoon, seated behind his desk, to declare, "This is our band." But he then had to be disabused of the notion that the Ramones were an Italian-American disco band, which he presumed they had to be. Roger may not have been hep to punk, but his reasoning was far from preposterous: What other type of band could he expect, after all, to appear in a movie that had the title *Disco High*?

Allan then explained, like a with-it kid to his square father, that the Ramones made hard, fast, raucous rock 'n' roll, and the disco idea for the movie had to be shelved if the Ramones were going to be in it. "That's where my Fillmore East experience came in. Because I saw The Who many times destroy their amplifiers, I got up on Roger's couch," Arkush explained to Robert Nuñez, "and I did Pete Townshend's arm swings. I basically sang 'My Generation' and showed him how you smashed the guitar, and that feeling was what rock 'n' roll was about."

Arkush also addressed the visual style he wanted to implement in the movie. A disco film would look one way, a rock film another: In June, he'd gone to see Elvis Costello and the Attractions perform a show in the gymnasium at Hollywood High. "I took photos of the concert," Arkush told Nuñez, "and I took photos of the outside of the school and the crowd and brought them in to Roger and showed him what I was talking about, and what the kids would look like in the movie." Corman, almost convinced, looked over to Paul Almond. "What do you think, Paul?" The attorney answered, "He's absolutely right." His recommendation carried weight with Corman. "He knew I knew music." The title *Rock 'n' High School* was formally fixed to the script at that point.

Allan had stood up to authority, just as he had at NYU during the student strike, and won. Corman soon after granted the film a $300,000 production budget, up from $165,000. As the story goes, Corman wound up cutting $20,000, however, from the final budget to cover the cost of new shutters for his home in Pacific Palisades. The guarantee of a budget, albeit a fluctuating one, permitted Mike and Allan to proceed with formally offering the Ramones their $25,000 fee for appearing in the film. The terms seemed okay for a working band that hadn't pierced the American Top 40 with any of their singles. Principal photography would start November 27, 1978, the Monday after Thanksgiving. They could also count on, Marky wrote in his memoir, "free rooms, all we could eat and drink and royalties on the soundtrack."

Allan now told the writers Russ and Rich, who'd been attached to the project for eight months now, they could finally write gags with a specific band in mind. To help them, "Allan gave us cassettes and vinyl copies of Ramones' music," said Whitley. "I was listening to '70s hippie music at the time. Russ and I put this music on, and it was, like, 'Wow, rock 'n' roll!'—but they called it 'punk.'"

P. J. Soles was notified, too, about the Ramones' casting. "In the early version of the script I was given, the Ramones are never named. There was only 'THE BAND.' I wouldn't have known the Ramones anyway. Allan gave me a cassette, and he said, 'Go home, and listen to this, and try to sing along, and get to know their songs, because you're their number one fan.' And I put it in our old cassette player. My boyfriend then was Dennis Quaid. He played guitar, and I played too. We were very much into music, although we were listening to the Eagles, at the time, and Jackson Browne and Joni Mitchell. When I first played it, Dennis and I looked at each other. He actually liked it right away, and I just said, 'Oh, my God. What is that?' I couldn't believe that I was hearing something that I didn't relate to at all. I'm an actor, so I was going to obviously be their number one fan regardless of what it sounds like. Now, I love their music. But it took me, probably, a couple years to actually warm up to it."

Playing Riff, Soles noted, was not going to be an extension of her own personality but rather an act of pure invention. In "Staying After Class," a filmed conversation she had with castmates Vince Van Patten and Dey Young, P. J. said: "I spent my money on my wardrobe because that was important, to me, to look really weird. Because that character was not me in high school. I went to high school in Brussels, at the International School of Brussels. I was learning French. I was editor of my school paper. I was a straight-A student. I was not the Ramones." The actress drew creative inspiration from them at the very same time. "Above anything else the Ramones had energy. They had pure energy. And as their number one fan, I wanted to translate their musical energy into my acting energy. So, I wanted to talk fast. I wanted to move quickly. I wanted to pop off the screen with my wardrobe, with my energy, with my enthusiasm, with my joy," she told me. "That really was the guiding principle, as well as that I wanted her to be a really quintessential American teenager."

Filling out the remaining cast in the summer of 1978 fell to Mike and Allan and casting director Lynn Farrell—a friend of Allan's he'd gotten to know while taking a class at Jeff Corey's school of acting. Farrell gave herself the part of Angel Dust in the picture—a groupie who contends that she, rather than Riff Randell, is the Ramones' number one fan. Finnell notified Mary Woronov and Paul Bartel that the high school picture had been greenlighted by Corman, that its title was now *Rock 'n' Roll High School*, and they had parts waiting for them. Loren Lester and Daniel Davies also tested, respectively, for the roles of Togar's hall monitor henchmen, Fritz Hansel and Fritz Gretel.

Loren Lester, curly-haired Fritz Hansel, told me in 2021: "Sadly, I am the only surviving hall monitor." Dan Davies, who played Fritz Gretel, died in 2017. "I was very excited to possibly get this part, and I had been working for a number of years already. I started when I was sixteen, so I'd been working in the business for about four years. I had done a number of commercials and other movies, but when you're kind of at that level, you're not a star: you take whatever job comes your way. You don't always get excited about doing a particular job, but when I got the script for *Rock 'n' Roll High School*, I was, for the first time, really excited about doing something that I had a chance to audition for . . . I had just started at Occidental College. I had had an agent since I was fifteen. . . . I went in, and I read, and I don't remember if I got a call back or if they just cast me from that first audition, but I went in, and I hit it off with Allan and got the part."

The director and the producer also needed to cast Tom Roberts, Eaglebauer, Kate Rambeau, and the P.E. teacher, Coach Steroid. With the promise of a budget, they could also proceed with planning the concert sequence that would act as *Rock 'n' Roll High School*'s musical centerpiece. The arena the Ramones would play, the fictional Rockatorium, was going to be modeled after the Fillmore East. Early on, they considered the Starwood Theatre on Santa Monica Boulevard and the Greek Theatre on North Vermont Avenue but, in the end, cut a deal with Lou Adler and David Geffen, the co-owners of a pair of West Hollywood rock clubs, the Whisky a Go Go and the Roxy, to shoot at these establishments over two nights, one after the other. A softcore adult theater downtown called the Mayan would provide the concert hall's exterior; the Mayan's recessed proscenium-like entrance made an ideal space for Riff in the film to camp out in front of for concert tickets for three days, just as Allan's friends from his Fillmore East days, Gail, Diane, and Janice, had outside Madison Square Garden in October 1969.

Allan and Mike decided, as well, as the summer proceeded, that the bulk of the movie's school-set scenes should be shot at a retired Catholic high school in riot-scarred Watts. Built in the '30s, Mount Carmel High School—with sloping tiled roofs and high red-brick walls—had also served as the locale for the 1956 musical drama *Rock Around the Clock*, one of the biggest of the early rock 'n' roll movies. But the school had been closed since 1976 due to slumping enrollment numbers; Mount Carmel had also been condemned "because it wasn't earthquake proof." A Carmelite priest named Fr. Robert L. Boley oversaw Mount Carmel for the Archdiocese of Los Angeles. He granted Finnell "unfettered access" to the building and grounds for ten shooting days for a scanty $50 daily fee. Father Bob, as he liked to be called, reminded Allan of "the hip young priest in [a] bad-boys-in-the neighborhood movie," as he told Jared Cowan. He may have been hip, but he was an easy mark: Allan and Mark slipped "an innocuous version of the script" to the priest—with the sham title *School Days*—which they'd stripped of gags and scenes that could worry him, including the climactic school-inferno sequence. Allan confessed to Daniel Griffith: "We swore we wouldn't harm the high school. Mike [told] Father Bob, 'I promise you, we will not damage this high school.' As we're walking back to the car. I said, 'That was great, Mike.' He says, 'Yeah, now I'm going to hell.'"

Mike and Allan also negotiated with the Los Angeles County School District to film at Van Nuys High School in the San Fernando Valley, fifteen miles north of Hollywood. Opened in the 1924, the school had a spacious patio adjacent to the cafeteria, a grassy quad, and a gymnasium that would work well for the girls'-gym musical scene that had been planned, now with Riff set to sing the movie's yet-to-be-written theme song as gymnasts whirl around her, the last remnant of Corman's original concept for the film. Unlike Mount Carmel, Van Nuys was a fully-functioning school, and the production could only plan to shoot there during the school's winter break.

The guaranteed production budget allowed for Finnell and Arkush to hire the film's technical crew too. Cinematographer Jamie Anderson—who'd shot *Hollywood Boulevard*—was considered at first for DP, but union restrictions prevented him from working on a non-union production. An offer to Dean Cundey followed. Cundey had a long record of working on independent low-budget movies, including *Halloween*: he relied on three camera assistants (Krishna Rao, Paul Elliot, Thomas Vanghele) and a boom operator (Rhonda Baer) with him through the shoot. An assistant editor named Kent Beyda working at El Centro would get footage ready for delivery to the MGM lab and assemble the rushes for Arkush, Finnell, and Corman to review. For hair and makeup, Gigi Williams was secured; Linda Pearl would oversee set dressing and decoration; Marie Kordus would head the art team; Jack Buehler had costume design; Terry Soda would aid Mike Finnell with his planning as production coordinator; two assistant directors were assigned to the production, too, Gerald T. Olson and Caren Singer; and Rob Bottin, who'd created the murderous fish for New World's *Piranha*, would provide the movie's special makeup effects. As Sire and Warner were giving Allan and Mike access to several songs for free and others at cut-rate prices from their catalogues, there were no plans to hire a composer. The film's score would be created by Allan in an editing room at El Centro after principal shooting wrapped in the third week of December.

With *Rock 'n' Roll High School* a go, set by Corman to start November 27, the head of New World Pictures—always as much the teacher as the businessman—summoned Allan to his office on San Vincente. He reminded the director, with the gravity of a college professor keeping office hours, that once the four-week shoot (twenty shooting days, three weekends in-between) proceeded, Allan could expect not to get much rest. "I have a little talk I give first-time directors," said Corman to Robert Nuñez. "And I gave that talk to Allan before shooting. And he was sitting there, and he was taking notes. He was listening to everything I said. And at the end, I said, 'And, Allan, be sure you have a chair with your name on it. It is more tiring work than you think. You will be exhausted.' And I could see he took no note on that, and I could see he just brushed that one off."

LOS TACOS AND THE TROPICANA

When Sire Records released the Ramones' *Road to Ruin* in September 1978, the band's deliberate pivot toward a more commercial sound—the "big Radio move" as *Sounds'* Jon Savage described it—was received by critics often more with praise than censure. A review in the *Boston Globe* argued: "The Ramones' fourth album continues the trend of *Leave Home* and *Rocket to Russia* toward a more melodic pop sound, although it still contains a good number of hard-core blitzkrieg boppers. New drummer Marky (Bell) Ramone . . . has added a new level of instrumental expertise, and the band seems more confident in its new direction." *Rolling Stone's* Charles M. Young, considerably less enamored of the aural sheen and improved musicianship, nevertheless regarded the LP favorably: "*Road to Ruin* is a real good album. It isn't as funny or as powerful as their debut, *Ramones*, but this does not mean the band is losing its grip. It means they figured out that the nigh-pure power chords and satire of their first three records—though enormously satisfying to smart people like myself—was too threatening to dumb people like you. So the Ramones compromised. They decided to meet you halfway and cut some slow songs, some guitar solos, some stuff that sounds like it uses twelve-string and pedal steel."

When Allan Arkush had had a chance to hear *Road to Ruin*, his thoughts turned to which songs he could pull from it for *Rock 'n' Roll High School*. "I Just Want to Have Something to Do," the opening track, was clearly a keeper. So was "I Wanna Be Sedated," a sick-joke song about going crazy that was super-catchy, perfect for the picture. Joey had written "I Wanna Be Sedated" after having had his face come close to being permanently injured by an exploding tea kettle he used as a vaporizer to help open his sinuses before shows, his horror and worry surfacing in lines like "I can't control my fingers, I can't control my brain."

None of the songs on *Road to Ruin* came close enough, however, to sounding like the music Allan wanted for a pot-induced daydream scene he had started planning out with Russ Dvonch and Rich Whitley, which would have the Ramones visit the teenaged Riff in her bedroom and serenade her. So Allan approached Sire producer Ed Stasium about getting a new song from the guys, a love song that was hushed and pretty and filled with longing, something like Todd Rundgren's "Hello, It's Me," but with the Ramones doing it.

"Ed Stasium and I were talking about a slow song for the bedroom scene in the movie. He brought up 'Questioningly,' but I didn't really like the song that much. I may have mentioned the Ramones' version of 'Needles and Pins' as closer to what I wanted. I love that cover." Allan's reservations were understandable. Not only was "Questioningly" on the mopey side, its thematic focus on a ruined love affair didn't match the upbeat concept of the scene. Dee Dee had another song available, though, that was more optimistic—a sweet pop ballad called "I Want You Around." He'd written it for his girlfriend, Vera Boldis, whom he'd met at Max's Kansas City earlier that year. Vera worked in the Garment District as a secretary and occasional model. "We still weren't married yet," Vera told me in a 2021 conversation. "He'd had a lot of crazy girlfriends before me, so I was more reserved and fun. I had a regular nine-to-five job."

Allan also asked Stasium for a theme song that would exploit the film's title, just as "A Hard Day's Night" and "Help!" had for the first and second Beatles movies. The task went to Joey, who wrote songs on a four-string guitar that he brought on the road with him—he liked writing in motel rooms. The theme song Joey came up with copped the speedy sound of '60s hot rod tunes like the Beach Boys' "Fun, Fun, Fun!" and Ronny & the Daytonas' "G.T.O.," with jokey lyrics about hating teachers and principals, and a simple refrain—the repetition of the title "Rock 'n' Roll High School" over and over.

Dee Dee married Vera at the Church of St. John Nepomucene on the Upper East Side over Labor Day weekend 1978, and the following Tuesday, September 4, the Ramones left for a European tour. When they returned to the States in October, they shortly after reconnected with Ed Stasium to tape the earliest versions of the two new songs. "Sire had a little basement studio. It had an eight-track. We recorded the demos for 'I Want You Around' and 'Rock 'n' Roll High School' without Joey because Joey didn't like going down in the basement. Who knows why? He just didn't like going down to that studio." Joey's basement phobia was such he even wrote a song about it that appeared on the debut record, *Ramones*, called "I Don't Wanna Go Down to the Basement." "So we recorded the boys—Marky and Dee Dee and John— in the Sire basement. Then I had to find another eight-track studio in Manhattan. We went to Moogy Klingman, who had a studio on West End Avenue—he was associated with Todd Rundgren, and the Utopia people [Rundgren's band]. Joey and I went over there for our afternoon-evening session to do the vocals. I did some guitar overdubs, as well."

Road to Ruin, sadly, but predictably, wasn't getting much airplay outside of big cities and college campuses in the weeks following its release. The Ramones' booking company, Premier, without any sense of irony, scheduled a series of concerts that had the guys open for Toto and Foreigner, two bands that exemplified the tasteful corporate rock sound the Ramones had been waging a sonic campaign against since 1974. But the Ramones didn't have a choice. They lived off their gigs. They had to play to stay solvent. The band's steadiest source of revenue didn't come from record sales, nor even ticket sales, but rather from the sale of merchandise, the T-shirts, stickers, Frisbees, coffee mugs, key chains and so forth stamped with the band's name on it.

Usually the Ramones traveled by van, with their tour manager, Monte A. Melnick, behind the wheel, while the road crew rode in a rented yellow Ryder truck they used to haul the band's gear. In November, the Ramones began their westward migration. "We set out to drive to Hollywood . . . and on the way we opened for Foreigner in St. Paul, Minnesota. The next day, we drove nine hundred miles to Denver, and the day after that we drove one thousand miles to LA," Johnny remembered in *Commando*. November 20, a Monday, was the date of the band's arrival, three days before Thanksgiving, with shooting on *Rock 'n' Roll High School* scheduled to start in a week.

Monte had booked the rooms for the guys and their cortège—girlfriends, wives, roadies, and techs—at the Tropicana Motel, on 8585 Santa Monica Boulevard, for the next several months out. The band's commitment to *Rock 'n' Roll High School* would only last about two and a half weeks, but they were going to start recording their next record, *End of the Century*, with producer Phil Spector, in the spring of 1979 and had several concerts scheduled throughout the western states in the months between.

The Tropicana Motel served as a magnet for touring bands that weren't rich. Trudie "Plunger" Arguelles-Barrett, a member of the art collective the Plunger Sisters, an LA punk insider who'd followed the Ramones from the first time she'd heard *Ramones* in 1976, told me that the Tropicana "looked like a hotel from a '60s teen movie [with] a lazy summer-in-LA vibe [and] a black-bottomed pool. . . . Bands were always welcomed at the Trop, and it was affordable, so that was where everyone stayed."

Andy Shernoff stayed at the Tropicana Motel whenever his band, the Dictators, came through Los Angeles. "It used to be owned by Sandy Koufax. Originally, he was signed by the Dodgers, and he played in LA, and he was one of the greatest pitchers of all time. It was a very cool looking hotel, with a good location. It had a restaurant called Duke's. It had a pool. It was a mid-century modern-looking motel right in the middle of LA. People hung around the pool. There were parties. Tom Waits was hanging out living there." Art and danger kept close quarters at the motel, as borne out by a story told to me by Craig Leon, who produced the Ramones' eponymous first album for Sire Records. Waits had snuck a piano into his room, which he used for writing songs. "Once on a visit to the Tropicana, Tom taught me that the ceilings were made of something where you could flick matches into them. He'd come in the room and lay down in the bed, and he'd flick lit matches up, and they'd stick to the ceiling. That's how he would concentrate."

The Ramones' rooms were equipped at the motel for long-term stays, each with a bed, a kitchenette, a sitting area with chairs, and a TV. Once everybody got settled in their rooms, Allan Arkush and Mike Finnell headed over from the production office on North Robertson Avenue to meet up with Marky, Dee Dee, Joey, and Johnny to discuss the script and hopefully rehearse a little. Mike introduced himself to the band with a letter of greeting, dated November 22, 1978, which read: "The cast and crew as well as Allan and myself are very excited about your involvement in this project, and we all want it to be FUN. We're aware that this is a new experience for you and encourage you to ask us any questions you may have. The hours will be long and hard, therefore anything that we can do to ensure your comfort will be done—just ask."

Arkush and Finnell had understood the Ramones were not actors. And Allan had seen how dynamic and explosive on stage they were, but in person an awkwardness distinguished the four, an almost neurotic reticence, and handling them in any sort of normal fashion as a director, he realized, like asking them to read the script, learn their parts, and rehearse, was going to be fruitless. Dee Dee seemed barely literate, while Joey got stuck trying to correctly pronounce the name "Mr. McGree," the music teacher Paul Bartel was going to play in the movie. Instead of "Mr. McGree," Joey could only muster "Mr. McGloo." The singer's inability to speak in a manner that wasn't weird, however, seemed funnier than getting the sought-for pronunciation, and Arkush later told Dvonch and Whitley to write "Mr. McGloo" into Joey's lines. "I had the ridiculous idea that we would do a rehearsal of the lines. I had assumed that they could be treated like actors. I was so naïve. We sat in one of the hotel rooms of the Tropicana and painfully read the script out loud, which was useless because, first off, they're not great readers. Dee Dee really almost could not read. Johnny read really well without much inflection. I knew that Johnny could carry more scenes than Dee Dee. Marky and then Joey was reading the line, and he got 'Mr. McGloo.' He got it wrong, and I said, 'That's funny.'"

The Ramones, Allan soon learned, as well, were not comfortable about having to lip-synch to prerecorded versions of their songs once the cameras were rolling. They didn't want anybody mistakenly thinking they didn't actually play their own music. Everybody had to know it was them on the records they made, and faking on the screen could get the fans thinking the other way around, which had unraveled the Monkees. Allan attempted to reassure the guys that lip-synching was routine in movies; it was only in music documentaries like *Woodstock* and *The Last Waltz* where the musicians were actually playing what the audience hears.

To make his point, he asked Marky, Dee Dee, Johnny, and Joey to come up to his place on Lexington Avenue to watch a movie he thought could be helpful, *A Hard Day's Night*, the best rock 'n' roll comedy ever made. That evening at the apartment didn't start off well, though, as Allan shared with Grant Hermanns at Comingsoon.net. While Allan was setting up for the screening—he had his own movie projector in the apartment—the Ramones killed time browsing through their host's mammoth record collection. "Johnny all of a sudden says, 'What the fuck is this?' He pulls out this section of Grateful Dead records and goes, 'You like this hippie shit or what?'"

No other rock band was probably less similar to the Ramones in terms of style, delivery, and purpose than the Grateful Dead, and Johnny was not a Dead fan. For the moment, Allan had lost the guitar player's respect. Once again he took a stand, explaining to Daniel Griffith: "I said, 'You guys are like the Grateful Dead. And you're both auteurs. If you played a Grateful Dead song, it would not sound like the Grateful

Dead. It would sound like the Ramones. So when you sing 'California Sun,' it doesn't sound like the original. It sounds like the Ramones. And if the Grateful Dead played, 'I Wanna be Sedated,' it would be thirty minutes long, and it would sound like the Grateful Dead." Allan's rhetoric wasn't enough to assuage the hippie-hating guitar player, however.

Russ Dvonch and Rich Whitley had swung over to the apartment on Lexington Avenue that same night, as did Mike Finnell. Whitley recalled in an essay he wrote with Dvonch about their experiences on *Rock 'n' Roll High School*: "We met the Ramones at Allan's house, where, hoping to inspire us, he screened a 16-millimeter print of *A Hard Day's Night*. . . . Allan wanted everyone to know that this was the tone that we were going for—a manic blend of comedy and rock 'n' roll. Since this was before the MTV music-video boom, Allan explained how the Ramones would be lip-synching their songs, just like the Beatles. The Ramones became confused, saying John and Paul would never just mouth the words. . . . They thought they were really singing up there on film!" Rich told me, "So we started to watch *Hard Day's Night*. My memory is that it got to the scene very early in the movie where the Beatles are on the train, and the girls are trying to put their hands to the wire mesh to touch the guys as they were playing on the train. Allan was saying, 'See, they recorded the songs first. And then they lip-sync to it.' And my memory is that the Ramones go, 'No, no, that's John and Paul, they're really singing.' Allan stopped the projector and said, 'They recorded the songs first, and then they lip-synched to it.' Allan to make his point started referencing movies, whether it was Gene Kelly movies, *Singing in the Rain*, Fred Astaire. That's when I first found out, maybe all of us found out, that Johnny was a film fanatic. He had three-hundred movies on tape, so he knew all those references." Johnny's faith in Allan had fully revived by the end of the night; they couldn't like all the same bands, but they connected over the movies.

"Russ and I were so inspired by *A Hard Day's Night*: It's one of my top ten favorite movies. We went home, and we wrote all this dialogue and these scenes for the Ramones because we were inspired by the Beatles being in the bathtub and shaving on the mirror and all that stuff. We were so excited. I remember we wrote these things, and we gave them to Allan. He goes, 'These are terrific, but they'll never be able to say any of this dialogue. . . . They'll never be able to say anything of this.'"

Thanksgiving that year fell on November 23. Jerry Heiner, the well-heeled chief of the investment company that owned the Tropicana Motel, invited the Ramones over to his home for dinner. Johnny that night brought along his girlfriend, Roxy. Joey, though he was going steady with a woman named Cindy, came along with a new friend, Linda Danielle, whom he'd just started talking to at the Tropicana. If Marky showed up that night, too, he probably brought his wife, Marion, along. The newlyweds Dee Dee and Vera, on the other hand, had been "invited to heiress Dana Magnum's house," according to Vera in her memoir *Poisoned Heart*. "Her family owned the Magnum department store chain, and Dana herself had just married a prince, who'd bought her an island as a wedding gift. . . . Upon our arrival at her mansion in the Hollywood Hills, Dana was very gracious. . . . The place was filled with all sorts of celebrities," including Jackson Browne and the Tubes—and Mick Jagger, who "started hitting on me in full view of the whole party. Despite the awkwardness of the moment, Dee Dee was flattered, and he held on to me even tighter."

Following their evening at the Magnums', Dee Dee and Vera returned to the Tropicana and were visited in their suite by Marky Ramone and a drug dealer named Velvet, who were there "to smoke some marijuana." The pot was laced with PCP, and soon after Marky and Velvet left, "Dee Dee began to freak out and proceeded to trash the hotel room as well as me," wrote Vera. Fearing for her life, she fled to San Francisco, and when she came back to Los Angeles, a week later, shooting on *Rock 'n' Roll High School* had already begun.

Allan spent a quieter Thanksgiving at Jonathan Kaplan's house in Sherman Oaks, where he'd slept for a month in the garage five years earlier, eating dinner with Kaplan and his sisters and the cameraman Jamie Anderson, who'd been unable to shoot *Rock 'n' Roll High School* due to union restrictions. P. J. Soles and Dennis Quaid got married that day, on a ranch, in faraway Texas. P. J. told me, "We said 'I do' under a big tree out in a field while a friend strummed the guitar and sang 'Love Me Tender.' Then we had a big turkey feast and rode horses. My mom made a three-tiered heart shaped carrot wedding cake. It was really special. So 70s!"

Friday, November 24, nearly everything was about as in place as it could be for principal photography to begin. The shooting schedule was all planned, but two roles still needed filling, Kate Rambeau and Coach Steroid. Late casting was a norm for low-budget productions, and auditions weren't always needed. Only the week before, the great news had come in to Mike and Allan that Vince Van Patten would play Tom Roberts, Vince Lombardi High's "star quarterback," who's a dolt. Van Patten, who'd just turned twenty-one, recalled that "Roger Corman contacted me and knew of me, and said to my agent, 'Would Vince be interested in this part?' I had started acting as a kid actor at age nine, and I never stopped working. I was doing all kinds of TV series and shows and strange little movies. I thought it might be interesting. I'd kind of heard of the Ramones and read the script, and I kind of liked the part. Roger told my agent that he'd love to meet me. And I met with him. I didn't read or anything like that. He knew my work. And he said, 'Here's the script. Do you want to do it? It starts next week.' And I said, 'Yeah, why not?'"

Clint Howard had been secured to play Eaglebauer, the Cupid-for-hire, who mentors Tom Roberts through the film, helping him find his way to Kate Rambeau. Scenes featuring Coach Steroid could all be done at Van Nuys High School three weeks away, so the need to fill the part was not hugely pressing. The Kate character, on the other hand, was to appear in the first shot the crew had scheduled Monday, a scene in which Kate and Eaglebauer drive up Lovers' Lane for Kate's schooling on high school dating with her training partner, Tom Roberts. The Kate part had been cast at one point, but the now forgotten actress who had the part was forced to step away due to a scheduling conflict with another picture she was on. Allan and Mike were eager to test someone who could play Kate in the brilliant-but-awkward manner they wanted, and they agreed to meet with an actress named Dey Young. "I'd come out to California, and almost before I even got an agent, I was at a party and was speaking with a casting director named Valerie Marsales, who said, 'They're looking for this one character in this movie called *Rock 'n' Roll High School*. They're pretty desperate, and they start on Monday.' Then the next thing I knew, I was meeting with Allan Arkush, and it was Friday. I was pretty much cast immediately. They had tried to find this character for a while, and they couldn't, from what I understood. Allan had me wearing big geeky glasses to complete my look. It was my very first job in Hollywood and my very first movie ever. I was twenty-three playing a seventeen year old, and it was just really very exciting. It was just kismet, being-at-the-right-place-at-the-right-time and having the right look: the girl next door, the science whiz, Kate Rambeau, sidekick to Riff Randell."

That final weekend before shooting the Ramones met up with Ed Stasium at Cherokee Studios on North Fairfax Avenue in Hollywood to record the final versions of "I Want You Around" and "Rock 'n' Roll High School." Ed was chagrinned to find that Tommy Erdelyi wasn't going to work the control board with him this time. "Once I got to Cherokee," Ed Stasium recalled, "I expected Tommy to be there because Tommy had worked on all the previous records with me, going from *Leave Home, Rocket to Russia* and *It's Alive*. Tommy and I were very proud of *Road to Ruin*. When I got to Cherokee and saw the band there, I'm like, 'Where's Tommy?' And John was like 'He won't be here. He's not coming.' I was shocked and dismayed. I don't know why they cut him out of the project. They'd cut him out of the Ramones."

Stasium kept notes from the two-day recording session. Saturday would be given to "I Want You Around," Dee Dee's love letter to Vera, who was now hiding from him in Frisco. Ed remembered, "We did more guitars and more vocals and percussion, and then I mixed the stuff. We always recorded the tracks very quickly. Johnny wanted to get in and out. They were always well-rehearsed, and usually it was in a take or two that we would get the backing tracks. Little Matt [Mathew Lolya, Johnny Ramone's guitar tech] was friends with Joan Jett, and for 'I Want You Around,' I actually borrowed Joan's Les Paul to do the power chords."

Allan Arkush dropped into the studio on Sunday when the Ramones were recording the movie's titular theme. Earlier in the fall, he'd been given copies of the demos by Ed, which he'd thought were wonderful. "I Want You Around" he liked right away—perfect for the bedroom scene. But the theme song Joey had written had a line in it he didn't like, a reference Joey put in to a "therapy pool" that was there to rhyme with "principal." A therapy pool's association with hydrotherapeutic treatments for mental patients bothered him. "The 'therapy pool' lines didn't fit at all and read like a cliched Ramones lyric. Ed suggested that if it didn't work I should explain all this to Joey. Joey accepted the criticism graciously. We talked and came up with 'Don't wanna be taught to be no fool,' which, with its bad grammar, was both funny and appropriate."

P. J. Soles came into Cherokee that day, as well, to record her vocals for the version of "Rock 'n' Roll High School" she would sing for her classmates in P.E. She sang with the basic tracks the band had cut earlier, but the key they'd played in didn't work for her voice. "Ed worked with the Ramones to transpose it to a more comfortable key for P. J.," Allan said, "but we were running out of studio time, so the band went to Los Tacos on Santa Monica Boulevard for lunch. Ed kept Marky's drums and played all the guitar parts in less than an hour."

"I'd made a safety copy of the Ramones version, to have her sing on, a copy of the multitrack so she could do her vocals," Ed remembered. "It was too low for her, so we had to change the key. I had to basically re-record everything. I kept the drums and then re-recorded bass and guitars. Dennis Quaid sings backing vocals with me. Dennis and I were drinking some cognac and got a little plastered during that session."

IN DREAMS, BEAUTIFUL DREAMS

On Monday, November 27, 1978, principal photography on *Rock 'n' Roll High School* commenced. Motion picture production companies rarely have feature films shot in sequence: The availability of locations, people, and equipment determines the order in which a movie's shots are filmed, not the script. Through the morning, Arkush, Finnell, and Dean Cundey would be filming a quirky parody of a sex-ed lesson led by Eaglebauer for his virginal clients, Kate and Tom, a scene that appears nearly an hour into the released version of the film. The lesson, as the script specified, would take place on a Lovers' Lane. The production crew showed up before dawn at an undeveloped roadside overlook on Mulholland Drive in the Hollywood Hills, which peeked out at the San Fernando Valley. Clint Howard and Dey Young arrived for makeup and wardrobe first, coming in at 6:15 a.m., as the sun began to lift over the Valley's eastern edge. Vince Van Patten was due a half-hour later.

For the day's first scene, with Eaglebauer driving Kate in a convertible up to his outdoor classroom, a tow car pulled the vehicle (its top up) along Mulholland. The scene has Kate fretting to Eaglebauer, "This will never work. Tom will never like me. I don't know who I'm kidding. What possible reason could there be to put myself through all this? *Sex.* I must admit, as far as reasons go, it must be one of the best." To which, with dubious sincerity, Eaglebauer replies: "Kate, I've known Tom ever since he was a freshman when I sold him his first touchdown. You're just the type of girl he goes for."

Eaglebauer had been first imagined by Allan Arkush as a nerd with entrepreneurial acumen for a character actor named Eddie Deezen to play; Deezen had played an obtuse dweeb, Eugene Felsnic, in *Grease.* The actor passed on the Eaglebauer role after landing a part in Steven Spielberg's war comedy, *1941*, which started shooting in late-October 1978. "We contacted Eddie Deezen's manager, who said, 'Well, Eddie can't do this movie. I mean, he's got *1941* coming out.'" Allan had gone to the actor himself, trying to nudge him, he recollected for Robert Nuñez, saying, "'Eddie, this movie would be out and gone before *1941* is finished shooting.' But to no avail. We didn't get Eddie."

Arkush had then approached Clint Howard about his interest in playing the Eaglebauer part. Clint knew Allan, who'd shot second unit stunts and chases for *Grand Theft Auto*, his brother Ron Howard's first feature film—Clint had played a mechanic character in the picture. "I got a phone call from Allan," Clint told me. "It was probably a month before filming, and he laid it out, like any director would. He said there was a wonderful part that he thought I'd be right for. He wondered if I'd be interested in doing it. The caveat is that when you work for Roger, you're working for scale. So there was no negotiating."

Allan employed a light touch as a director—his instructions to actors could be scant, and he lauded improvisation. When Clint asked him about the direction for Eaglebauer he should take—with Deezen uninvolved no one any longer thought the character should be played as a nerd—Allan told Clint simply to make Eaglebauer "a wheeler dealer. Be funny."

"How Eaglebauer was going to dress was important," Clint said. "And doing that on a Roger Corman scale, it's creative. It wasn't until I got the wardrobe that I really felt like Eaglebauer was within my grasp. I think that it's costumes that give you the first time to really get any tangible stuff in your hand. When the wardrobe supervisor started talking about wide lapels, she had a vision of what Eaglebauer was supposed to look like. . . . That's part of the process. Sometimes it's even the props, the jewelry. That was a real fun thing to do every day, to put on the Eaglebauer uniform. I'd come into work as Clint, and I'd put the wardrobe on and then put the Superman chain on, and I'd be Eaglebauer."

Clint in the press kit New World prepared for the film's release said that he "had never done a character like this before—nothing so outrageous as Eaglebauer. I realized what was necessary: I would really have to pull out all the stops on this guy without sacrificing his humanity. I think if you get to the heart of the character you find that's he's very serious despite all his off-the-wall showmanship. Eaglebauer, being a salesman, never gives up. He will make a success out of a situation or somebody's problem, no matter what. There's lots of energy in the character, which attracted me to the role in the first place. What it comes down to is this: Eaglebauer loves life. And no matter how grim things look, he remains an optimist. I like that sort of person."

Clint was nineteen years old in November 1979 and already had spent most of his life acting. As a character named Leon, he'd appeared several times on *The Andy Griffith Show*, in which his brother, Ron, played the program's child lead, Opie. "I was just a toddler on the set," Clint said. "I'd show up in my cowboy outfit and. . . . really enjoyed being around the people and action. . . . I ended up doing five episodes as Leon, the little guy who handed Barney [Fife] peanut butter sandwiches." When he was six, Clint appeared in the feature film *Gentle Ben* with his dad, Rance Howard, and later had a recurring part on the *Gentle Ben* TV series. He'd appeared on episodes of *Star Trek* and *Night Gallery* too. Playing Eaglebauer "was one of the first jobs I did where I was on my own as an actor. As a child actor, my dad was always with me. Slowly he let me travel from the nest," the actor recalled for documentarian Robert Nuñez, "but *Rock 'n' Roll High School* was one of the first films where I was driving to the set by myself, and I was on my own, and it was rock 'n' roll, baby."

Once the scene in the towed convertible finished, the actors and the shooting team returned to the pull-over on Mulholland. The cluttered San Fernando Valley glimmered under the morning sun. Vince Van Patten had arrived and stood on the shoulder, dressed as Tom Roberts: Jack Buehler in wardrobe, working out of a trailer, had given him a cream-colored letterman's sweater and parted his hair parted down the side like Robert Redford's in *The Great Gatsby*. Van Patten, playing an insufficiently nimble star athlete, was, in truth, a ranked professional tennis player. The publicity materials New World prepared for *Rock 'n' Roll High School* noted that "When he whistles a forehand crosscourt, one might at first glance take the athletic figure with long blond hair to be Bjorn Borg himself. Not necessarily because the physical resemblance is that close—but because he plays the game so damn well. Vince Van Patten is a young and very popular actor and he's also ranked #2 in Mens' Singles in tennis-crazy Southern California." Vince had gone three sets with the sixth-ranked player in the world, Raúl Ramírez, six weeks before shooting on *Rock 'n' Roll High School* commenced, at the 1978 Hawaii Open in Maui. He'd played in Wimbledon earlier in the year too.

The actor-athlete would draw inspiration for his take on the dim-witted self-doubting star quarterback from writers Russ Dvonch and Rich Whitley, who came to the set every day—Arkush kept the writers on hand asking them to work up new gags when he thought they were needed. "They loved Bob Hope," Van Patten said of the writers. "They would walk around the set and do impressions of Bob Hope. That rubbed off on me in my performance because the guy had to be very insecure and shy. I threw in the Bob Hope because of them," he noted in the filmed reunion he and Dey and P. J. shot in 2009.

Vince and Clint felt at ease around each other. "I loved Clint when I was growing up in New York. We used to watch *Gentle Ben*, and he was a big child actor. We never got to work together until then, and I was just kind of a fan. And I knew Ronnie [Howard]. Clint and I bonded. We liked our roles. He was funny in it. He was this real dealer to my naive kind of guy who just wanted to get action, and we had a lot of laughs. Clint and I bonded really well," Vince told me. Van Patten, by the way, had been offered the part of Richie Cunningham for the pilot for the TV sitcom *Happy Days*, but his parents, actors Dick and Pat Van Patten, according to a piece in *Sports Illustrated*, "wouldn't let him take it because the script included a scene in which Richie fumbles with his date's bra strap at a drive-in." The part, of course, ultimately went to Ron Howard.

As the warm California sun poured onto Mulholland Drive, the actors took their places. Clint, wearing a suit, his button-down shirt open, his chest hair and his Superman necklace on naked display, stood before the same convertible his character had just been driving. In his excitable manner, Eaglebauer addresses his pupils, who sit side by side in the convertible's front seat, the car's top now down, with a chintzy Liberace-like candelabra rising from the car's hood. A production assistant hoisted up a broad, black sheet stretched around a frame, which had been airbrushed with a streak of lights to simulate the romantic sight of a city at night. After addressing some basic techniques about getting to first base, the businessman announces, "This next step can either make or break a successful date," and with a teaching prop, a female blow-up doll girded by half a dozen brassieres around her chest, he explains how to get to second base, unsnapping bras as he speaks: "A one-handed approach, strap unfastening is a basic skill that must be mastered. Now watch closely as I demonstrate. There's the hook. The snap. There is the double hook. There is the dreaded mini hook. And, if you play your cards right, the easy, open, frontal assault."

Clint reflected: "I might have snapped a bra or two in my life, but I wouldn't consider myself a pro. Every one of those bras, they were all breakaways. So I could look fast, and of course, sound effects. You bring in the sound effect of the hook and the snap and the button and the illusion is 'Oh man, he's really doing it.' My fingers aren't that fast." How did Dick and Pat Van Patten respond to this scene, one wonders, given their previous reluctance to having Vince appear in the much less salacious *Happy Days* pilot?

Once shooting for the sex-ed lesson was complete, actors and crew rushed down to Los Feliz, a leafy residential neighborhood just east of Hollywood, ten miles from the Mulholland overlook, for a scene in which Eaglebauer continues his training of Tom on the methods of modern dating. Mike Finnell had rented for the day an outrageously gaudy customized van, the Warlock, that featured a bearded wizard zapping electric bolts at dinosaurs from his fingertips air-brushed against its side. And on the inside, there was a bar and a telephone. The van was parked on Hillhurst Avenue, on the street outside the house where P. J. Soles was going to do the musical daydream number with the Ramones in Riff's bedroom the next day.

In the van scene, the dating coach and his pupil continue their conversation with Tom exploring the vehicle's sumptuous insides. It's the afternoon just before the Ramones' concert at the Rockatorium, and Miss Togar has confiscated Riff's and Kate's tickets. Tom, under his tutor's counsel, wants to ask out Riff now that she no longer has plans. He doesn't see yet that Kate's the gal for him—one of the major dramatic questions driving the film is "Will love at last find Tom Roberts?" In the phone call to Riff, Tom says, "Listen, I'm just lying here in my new van, on my beautiful waterbed, listening to the Ramones' brand new album on this fantastically expensive stereo, wondering if you'd like to maybe go out tonight and get drunk." Emboldened by a slug of Jack Daniels, the quarterback reclines, quite serene, his awareness of his ineptness as a suitor for the moment forgotten.

Corman had a custom of visiting productions on the first day of principal photography to observe the crew at work and assess the degree to which the director needed his attention, if any. Clint recalled that when Corman dropped by that first day of shooting, he "told Allan that everything looked fine . . . and this helped inspire us all." On these first-day visits, Corman reminded his directors of three sacrosanct rules to follow as they got through the production, which Arkush summarized for journalist Michael Goodwin, a freelance journalist who visited the production on several occasions for a feature he was writing for the men's magazine *Penthouse*: "[O]ne, get lots of coverage, lots of angles; two, sit down on the set as much as possible; three, don't congratulate the crew when you get a good shot, 'cause it'll take a minute, and if you get thirty setups a day, you'll lose half an hour of shooting time."

For the second day of shooting, Tuesday, Dey Young and P. J. Soles were both due at 6:45 a.m. at the two-story house in Los Feliz on Hillhurst. Using the house's garage as a staging area, the crew shot upstairs most of the day in a bedroom and an adjacent bathroom. P. J. couldn't help but feel on-guard. Her scene with the Ramones called for her to walk around in various stages of undress, and the guys in the band, to her, looked really strange, really far out. A sense of relief came when she saw who the DP was going to be: Dean Cundey, who'd filmed her in *Halloween*—she'd played a supporting character named Lynda Van Der Klock, who's hideously murdered in the picture by the serial killer Michael Myers. "The first day on set, I see Dean, and he looks at me. He goes, 'What are you doing here?' I said, 'Hey, I'm Riff Randell, rock 'n' roller.' And he was so excited. Then I knew I was going to be in good hands and well taken care of. Dean had already worked with me on *Halloween* and knew how to treat me cinematically: I felt in a very trusting place."

The film's art team, led by Marie Kordus, had converted an inauspicious and tight upstairs nook into a rock 'n' roll temple, with photographs of rock gods, including The Who's Roger Daltrey and a guitar player who could be Jeff Beck, spackling the walls along with posters for Sire Records bands like the Pirates and Talking Heads, as well as Black Sabbath's *Never Say Die!* Ramones swag filled the room, too, like a *Road to Ruin* record-store poster pinned to the wall above Riff's bed and a black-and-white cardboard cutout display of the band's original lineup— Dee Dee, Joey, Johnny, and Tommy—leaned up against a window sill.

As the bedroom scene plays in the film, Riff burns a joint, dressed in a tomato-colored outfit listening to *Road to Ruin* on her record player. The opening notes (D-G-D-G-D-G-D-G) of "I Want You Around," a song that, of course, doesn't appear on the *Road to Ruin* LP, sift through the tight room. Joey then appears, crouched in a plush chair, as Johnny, his face uncharacteristically placid, sits nearby, playing an acoustic guitar. Angular and lean, as if made out of drainpipes and chopsticks, Joey under Allan's direction crawls onto P. J., lip-synching into her face about how "he'll be good to you."

Arkush and Cundey struggled with the lack of space in the bedroom in the Los Feliz house all day. The DP was obliged to work with "this really old Mitchell . . . a giant camera that looks like it's made of cast iron." Such was the tightness in the upstairs room that "I had to find a place for all four Ramones, and all I could think of was to put Marky out the window," Allan remembered for Daniel Griffith, and this entailed having the drummer set up his kit near a tree in the house's backyard. Before Cundey could get out to shoot the drummer, though, he had to finish several interior shots for the daydream scene first; and by the time the crew could set up, the late-November sun had set. Hence in the finished cut of the film, the Ramones in Riff's daydream, despite playing the same song all at once, are doing so not only in different spaces but also different times of the day. Riff's weed must be really strong! The joint on the set, though, was a prop, rolled with rosemary.

For Dee Dee's appearance in the daydream, Arkush had P. J. enter the bathroom adjacent to the bedroom, wearing only a towel. She draws the shower curtain and finds a clothed Dee Dee standing in the bathtub playing a phallic bass guitar as water blasts at him from a phallic showerhead. The idea for the gag had come to Arkush when he learned about Dee Dee's real-life compulsion to bathe one-two-three-four times a day.

One of Arkush's inspirations for the "I Want You Around" sequence had been Frank Tashlin's *The Girl Can't Help It*, a glossy rock 'n' roll sex comedy from 1956 starring Jayne Mansfield, Edmond O'Brien, Julie London, and Tom Ewell. Tashlin had been a cartoonist before he moved on to film directing, and he liked to exploit the impossible physics and surrealist potential of animation in his movies. Riff's daydream alluded to a scene in *The Girl Can't Have It* when a spectral Julie London sings the bluesy "Cry Me a River" to the film's drunken-talent-agent male lead, Tom Ewell. Riff welcomes the Ramones in her fantasy, but the stewed Ewell trembles at the sight of his ghostly but beautiful singer. P. J. recalled: "It's probably my most favorite scene in the movie because it's just really lovely, such a fantasy. It was so much fun to film, although when Joey was leaning over me I had my mouth open, and he was singing so hard that he was spitting in my mouth. Not having known them,

I remember just jumping up afterward and going to the bathroom and rinsing my mouth out. I thought, 'Oh, my God.' They looked like creatures to me, especially Joey. I really loved when Johnny cracks a smile because he didn't smile much. I think he thought it was just so funny that Joey was getting to be romantic with me."

P. J. could sense that the Ramones weren't comfortable, however, on and off the set. "I thought of them as being shy—they were. Johnny and Marky were huge fans of Roger Corman movies, so I think that there being in a Corman movie was exciting to them. They didn't really know how to be when they were on set. They had never done a movie before. They had to get up early in the morning. They weren't crazy about that. They just really kept to themselves."

Dey Young, like so many who worked on the movie, had never been aware of the Ramones before the shoot. "They all looked like they were in a stupor. I was just in awe around them, just going, 'Oh, my God. What is this about? Who are these guys?'—literally just watching and observing this phenomenon in front of me."

P. J. and Dey clicked right away. "Allan let us improv a lot of that scene in Riff's bedroom when Tom calls," Dey said. "'I don't want to be happy, I want to be with Tom.' That was just totally me; it was not part of the script. In that scene, Riff's teasing me . . . we're throwing pillows at each other. The amazing thing for me was that P. J. had been in this business, and she was such a pro. I was the newcomer to the whole thing. She just took me under her wing." The dialogue between Riff and Kate focuses heavily on boys, on the reasons why Kate likes Tom, and why Riff likes Joey Ramone: "All he eats is pizza," the rock 'n' roller says. "I just love the way he just holds the pizza. All he eats is pizza. I just love the way he just holds the pizza dripping above his mouth. He just slithers and slides it into his mouth. It's so sexy." Just as P. J. and Tom were playing characters with personalities quite a stretch from their own, so, too, was Dey. The Kate character, Dey explained to Robert Nuñez, "was very different than what I was in high school. I was a little rebel, and I looked like I was this straight girl, but I was really more of a rebel, like Riff."

Rich Whitley and Russ Dvonch spent the day at the house in Los Feliz often hanging around in the garage staging area. Grady Sutton, an elderly comic actor who'd been cast in *Rock 'n' Roll High School* to play a fusty school board president, came by, though the scene he was going to shoot wasn't scheduled until Friday afternoon at Mount Carmel High School. The writers were enamored of the Kentucky-born character actor: He'd played W. C. Fields's blockhead son-in-law, Og Oggilby, in *The Bank Dick*, and they approached him, saying, "We loved you in *The Bank Dick*." To which the old man replied: "Was I in *The Bank Dick*? I can't remember."

THE KIDS ARE ALL RIGHT

On Wednesday, the production moved to Mount Carmel High School on South Hoover Street in Watts. The Ramones weren't going to be needed that day, but Dey, Vince, and Clint were, this time to shoot Kate's and Tom's scenes with Eaglebauer in the restroom head-quarters of his company, Eaglebauer Enterprises. One song Arkush knew he would have access to for the movie's soundtrack, thanks to New World's negotiated arrangement with Warner Bros. Records, would be Brownsville Station's 1973 school-themed redneck-blues hit "Smokin' in the Boys Room." In addition to filming the dialogue scenes between Eaglebauer and Tom and Kate in his office stall, the crew were going to shoot a spate of gags featuring male extras sucking on cigarettes and other burnable products in the bathroom—toilet humor of a literal sort. The paralleling scenes of first Tom and then Dey coming to visit Eagle-bauer's office were shot in tandem, having each actor filmed walking through the smoky boys' room one after another and having in both instances the actors cut to the front of a preposterously long line, where they receive an assist (due to the direness of their romantic needs) from a secretary functioning as Eaglebauer's gatekeeper named Norma. The actress playing Norma was Allan Arkush's second cousin, Terry Soda, the movie's production coordinator, who'd been a student at Fort Lee High when he studied there.

The shooting crew filmed Tom's and Dey's in-person dialogues with Eaglebauer one after another, as well, each set in the bathroom stall that Eaglebauer inhabits like a manic Bilbo Baggins in his Hobbit-hole. An actual stall wasn't used, however. Rather, an empty room was transformed into an office, with a desk, telephone, and piles of high school contraband, like answers to tests and fake hall passes, a graph on the wall, and clocks set for different time zones. For the exchange between Clint and Vince, Eaglebauer tells Tom, who's come to him for help "getting laid," that he will have an easier time scoring if he pursues Kate Rambeau. And as he promotes Kate to Tom, the exuberant operator draws open curtains that have covered the wall behind him, revealing a hanging photographic portrait of the beautiful science-loving gal, just as if she were a prize for a game show contestant to bid on. To play out the gag further, Eaglebauer entreats an offscreen pitchman named Johnny to "tell Tom how happy he'll be with Kate." To which Johnny, his voice provided by longtime quiz show announcer Jay Stewart, answers, his golden pipes booming: "Kate Rambeau, age seventeen, attends Vince Lombardi High, where she majors in nuclear physics. This perky gal-on-the-go's hobbies include protons and checkers."

Silliness and goofy gags permeate the exchange between Eaglebauer and Kate, as well:

EAGLEBAUER: Tell me, have you had much experience with boys?

KATE: Well, once I played nurse with a boy next door and got sued for malpractice.

The next day, Thursday, at 7:00 a.m., forty extras, many of them LA punkers, convened at Mount Carmel to spend the morning in the school's barren corridors rioting to the Ramones' take on "Do You Want to Dance?" The song had been a top-five hit in 1958 for Bobby Freeman and charted again as a Beach Boys single in 1965 and again in 1972 for Bette Midler. The Ramones' version, recorded for *Rocket to Russia* with the spelling "Do You Wanna Dance?," had sunk like a brick in a swimming pool when Sire released it as a single in March 1978. But for Arkush, the song's unhappy commercial performance meant nothing. He wanted dancing in the movie to serve as an expression of resistance, and the song with its revved-up pacing sounded like a call to action in 4/4 time.

Today would be Mary Woronov's first on the set. The actress hadn't yet decided on the approach she'd take with the Miss Togar character. She'd considered playing the principal in a somewhat reserved manner, doing a take on Eve Arden's amiable TV heroine Miss Brooks, but the crazy energy emitted by the dancing extras rollicking through the corridors of Mount Carmel to the Ramones prompted her to reconsider. "I saw the kids . . . and they were all punk rockers, and even my make-up lady was a punk rocker. She was on roller skates, and she'd come at me with those pointed brushes," the actress told Zack Carlson. She realized she needed to play Miss Togar in a broader, campier, crueler fashion. "I had lots of freedom, and the role was pretty funny. It gave me lots of room to stretch."

Born in 1943, Mary had grown up in an affluent home in Brooklyn. "It was a very 50s home life. I went to a private girls' school, my mother was a housewife, my father was a doctor, and everything was very *Ozzie and Harriet*," she said in an interview she gave to Terry Gross. She'd gone to college at Cornell but quit and later fell in with Andy Warhol and his entourage of shimmering superstars, appearing in his underground film *Chelsea Girls* and performing in his touring music-art act, the Exploding Plastic Inevitable, to songs like "Venus in Furs" and "Sister Ray" performed live by the Velvet Underground. "I danced with Lou Reed . . . I did a nice bunch of boot-licking and whip things. . . . I was tough, hard," she boasted to *Interview*'s Donald Lyons.

Mary later joined the outré independent theatrical group Play-House of the Ridiculous, performing in transgressive stage productions around New York City that exploited Grand-Guignol-type gore and gender-fluid dramatis personae. For a 1967 Play-House of the Ridiculous science-fiction farce called *Conquest of the Universe*, she'd created the part of a depraved, sexless psychopath named Violet, which became the character template for Miss Togar in *Rock 'n' Roll High School*. Gigi Williams's handling of Mary's hair at Mount Carmel, taking the long honey locks and pulling and pinning them into a masochistically tight coiffure, gave the actor a look at once puritan and hyper-sexual.

Woronov had left New York for Los Angeles in 1974 after Paul Bartel, an acquaintance since the late '60s, asked her to come out to play a murderous racecar driver named Calamity Jane in *Death Race 2000*, the science-fiction action-comedy he directed for New World. Bartel had told her, as she revealed to *A.V. Club*'s Will Harris, "I can get you in on this movie, and I need you," to which Mary had replied, "'Fine, I'd *love* to drop everything I'm doing in New York.' I'd just finished a play, *In the Boom Boom Room*, and I was doing a soap opera, of all things, to make money. So I said, 'Yeah, I'll go out.' And then he said, 'I'll just introduce you to Corman—he'll look at your legs, so wear something that shows your legs off—and he'll hire you.'" The ploy worked; Mary got the part.

Allan had worked closely with Dvonch and Whitley on shaping the Togar character as they'd crafted their script, finding inspiration from the cavalcade of creeps he'd squared off against at Fort Lee High School during his time there. He drew upon a conflict he'd had with one teacher named Mr. Kelly, in particular, over the United States's involvement in Southeast Asia. "I was reading the *New York Times* one Sunday. This was my senior year. There was an ad against the war in Vietnam. Now, I had not seriously thought about the war until I saw this ad. The ad had been taken out by Peter, Paul and Mary, Bob Dylan, Joan Baez. Everyone in whom I had an interest was on this ad, and it really struck me. It wasn't something that was in the forefront of my mind, but these people were against the war. That really struck a chord with me.

"Co-incidental to that, in my world history class, the teacher was Mr. Kelly, who'd been a Marine. He was also the varsity basketball coach. Mr. Kelly had a lot of juice because we were a big basketball school. He wanted to have a debate about Vietnam in the class—I think he was pissed off about all this antiwar stuff going on. He asked who wanted to be for it in the debate, and, of course, being no fools, most of the guys on the basketball team in that class raised their hands. Then he said, 'Who will take the side against it?' Nobody stuck their hand up. Then, I remembered that ad, and I put my hand up. Mr. Kelly looked at me, and he goes, 'Oh. Arkush. It figures.' Then he assigned two of the cheerleaders to me.

"I go to the school library and start to look up Vietnam. There are no books about the topic or the history of Vietnam, only *Time* magazine and *Newsweek* and that stuff, which was insufficient. But, by then, I had already become frustrated with the school library. The *New York Times* had had an article in 1965 about the ten greatest American novels since World War II. I looked at that list, and I realized I had only read one of those books and that was *The Catcher in the Rye*. I go to the school library and start looking through the card catalog for these books, and they don't have them. I go to the desk and I say, 'I'm looking for *The Naked and the Dead, Herzog, Invisible Man, Go Tell It on the Mountain.*' I don't remember all the books. The librarian said, 'We don't have those books.' I said, 'Well, why not?' Then she says, 'Well, we're not allowed to have those books. Those books are banned from our library.' I go to the town library. It's the same thing. Certainly, it was known to some degree that *Catcher in the Rye* was not allowed to be read. Then I realized that none of these books were. So that was the opening for me to go to downtown New York to Greenwich Village and go to bookstores and start reading those books, buying them.

"I went down to an Eighth Street bookstore, or maybe it was Sheridan Square, and asked them, 'Do you have any books about Vietnam?' expecting what the school library had said. But the clerk goes, 'Oh, yeah!' They had the history of Southeast Asia, American colonialism, all of that. I buy a couple of those books. They give me the *Village Voice*. They give me a magazine called *The Realist*. I had all this material, and I read up on Vietnam. I did not know that the French had taken it over. This was the first I learned about napalm.

"I came into the debate really prepped. The two cheerleaders didn't want to read any of this stuff. The other team had just read *Newsweek* and *Time* and came in with a bunch of phrases like 'Domino Theory,' but no historical perspective. We started the debate. Whatever they were saying, when it came time from my side, I just undercut them with historical analysis. Nobody, including Mr. Kelly, had even thought about the French being there and taking over the government, and this was the fate of Vietnam: to be taken over by other people. It was the history of the country. To the Vietnamese, we were just another version of those people. Whereas to us we were the savior.

"When I started talking about napalming, and I maybe showed a couple of pictures, it got ugly in that class between me and Mr. Kelly. When it came time for my summation, he started actually debating me. I remember finishing and the class . . . It was clear: I had wiped out everybody. But there was anger toward me because I was talking back to Mr. Kelly. Remember, he's the basketball coach, so he's got six-foot-tall guys. I remember he looked at me as I left the room like a sniper looks at the victim. That was one thing that really struck me, and it ended up being part of Togar.

"Another part of Togar is this: I was supposed to do a book report. I did it on *Franny and Zooey* by Salinger. I wasn't stupid enough to do it about *Catcher in the Rye*. It's *Franny and Zooey*, it's the nice one, the nice Salinger book. When it came time to hand in the report for grades, the teacher said, 'This is unacceptable. The book is not from the school library.' Thus I had to re-do the whole report with a different book because 'You had to have a book that was in the school library,' which as a rule I could never have possibly known, and I rejected that. I said, 'That rule was never stated, and I did the work. I wrote the full report. I read the book. So here, take it back.'

"She gave me a warning, and then we ended up marching down to Mr. Raimondo's office. Mr. Raimondo is Togar to me. 'What's going on?' he asked." Mr. Raimondo was the principal at Fort Lee High School. "By now, they knew I was an intellectual troublemaker. Mr. Raimondo said, 'Well, it's obvious that you have to redo the report; that's in the rules.' I said, 'Look, there's a lot of books that you don't allow in the library.' I got heated. I claimed that the school was turning into *Fahrenheit 451*. You can imagine this skinny high school kid talking about this shit to them. They don't know what I'm talking about.

"Then, finally, I said, 'Okay, what in the book is objectionable? Show it to me, and then I'll know.' It was then that it came out that neither of them had read the book. They just said, 'Well, it's in the rules.' I said, 'Okay, that's not fair. I'm not going to compromise on this. Just flunk me *for doing the work*. How about if you read the book? Because I've read it. Twice.' Silence . . . That was when Mr. Raimondo said, 'Okay.' He wasn't going to read *Franny and Zooey*, and that's it. I got a B+. I deserved an A."

Allan always knew that any way Mary played Miss Togar would be right for the picture. And as she came out of makeup that morning, her bizarre appearance validated his convictions. In the scene they led off with, Mary was to be joined by her brown-shirt flunkies, the vile hall monitors, Fritz Hansel and Fritz Gretel, in a conversation that starts in her office and moves to a hallway. During her first week as principal at Vince Lombardi High School, the first week of 1980—a new week, a new month, a new year—Miss Togar has grown frustrated over her inability to exert control over the student body. "Look at me when I'm talking to you," she barks at her cronies. "You're supposed to be my eyes, my ears, my nose! If this school is going to get back on the winning track, we have to start cracking down immediately!"

Woronov imbued Togar with a surfeit of confidence; her upbraidings recalled the exaggerated manner in which Colonel Klink addressed the obsequious and moronic Sgt. Schultz on *Hogan's Heroes*. The actress also shot the principal full of psycho-sexual depravity, with hints of Shirley Stoler's vicious, albeit morbidly obese, detention camp warden, who rapes that film's eponymous anti-hero in Lina Wertmuller's *Seven Beauties*. As Mary said of Miss Togar to Daniel Griffith: "That kind of Nazi principal . . . she's obviously really cold, but she really wants to get laid."

The day of shooting in Mount Carmel's drab, urine-colored hallways continued with Arkush and Cundey and crew filming Vince Van Patten as he strolls by himself along a locker bank, letting out his thoughts about his stultifying sex life, a spoof of the wimpy nebbishes Woody Allen played in *Manhattan* and *Annie Hall*, but with a low IQ. "What's wrong with me? I'm captain of the football team, my complexion has cleared up, and soon I'll be going to the college of my choice." What's wrong with Tom is his lack of self-awareness, which he reveals, a moment later, when Shawn (Chris Somma), a pretty student with a chest-hugging top—this is a New World picture, after all—approaches him. "Nice weather we've been having," he says, thrusting at her waist, scaring her. "A little dry lately, but I hear it's raining cats and dogs in Idaho." He does the same thing to Shawn's friend Cheryl (Marla Rosenfield).

The production had two additional shooting units also working Wednesday, one helmed by Allan's dependable friend, Jon Davison, and another by a young writer from Wisconsin named Jerry Zucker. Davison and Zucker were about to make their first major studio feature film, *Airplane!*, a parody of aviation disaster films like *The High and the Mighty* and *Airport*. Jon, after producing both *Grand Theft Auto* and *Piranha* for New World, two of Corman's most profitable releases, had gone to Paramount, attached to *Airplane!* as its producer, and since the film's three-man directing team—Jerry Zucker, David Zucker, and Jim Abrahams—needed experience, he'd asked Mike and Allan to permit them, as well as himself, to direct some second unit content for *Rock 'n' Roll High School*.

Jerry Zucker was to shoot a scene that appears toward the end of the movie but before the school bombing when the two hall monitors hide themselves in a laundry cart from rioting students. The Ramones seize the cart, roll it down a hallway, and shove it out a window. "Paramount had just bought *Airplane!*," Zucker said to Chris Nashawaty. "Jon suggested I do a day of second unit, because I had never directed a movie before, and we were going to direct a movie. He thought it would be a good idea just to see what it was like. And I said, 'Sure.' And I talked to Allan Arkush, who explained to me what they were looking for."

"The good thing about it for me was I got the feel of what it's like to be on a set, directing a scene and with the crew, and just what that feels like. It was really helpful, and it was the exact reason why Jon wanted me to do it. I felt like they were doing me a favor more than I was doing them a favor. David and Jim, were there, too, for part of the day. I think they were observing to see what it was like. It was someone else's material. It's not like we all could sit, like we did on subsequent movies, and discuss how to accomplish our vision. It was just like, 'Okay, shoot the hamper moving down the hall. Shoot it coming at the camera. Shoot it going away.' I was never what you'd call hip—I didn't even really know who the Ramones were. But I had a blast. It was the first time I was actually on a set with cameras and actors, and I loved it," Zucker told me. He would enjoy a great career, excelling as a director of both comedies, like *Ruthless People*, and dramas, most notably the supernatural super-hit *Ghost*. He and his brother David Zucker and Jim Abrahams would also develop the *Naked Gun* film series starring Leslie Nielsen, O. J. Simpson, and Priscilla Presley.

"It was just a regular-sized laundry cart," Loren Lester told me. "We fit into it just fine. They had one where they had cut out one of the sides of it, so that when they shot that interior of the two of us praying, that was an interior shot. We were not physically in the actual cart when they were pushing it around down the hallway or through the window, obviously. So we had the scene where we're climbing in, and then they pushed the cart around all over the place, and then the cut to the interior where we were inside of it, but we never had to actually do a stunt or anything like that."

Marky in *Punk Rock Blitzkrieg* remembered: "[W]e were filming a climactic scene where the four members of the band push the two SS-like hall monitors in a laundry cart down the hall and out a second-story window. We were looking forward to it, since none of us ever liked Nazis or hall monitors very much." The Ramones also appreciated the exercise. They'd been confined for much of the day in a teachers' lounge, which would serve them through the Mount Carmel portion of the production as a dressing room. The experience of hanging around with nothing to do for hours at a time demolished their happiness and sense of well-being, it seems. "The filming of *Rock 'n' Roll High School* was torture, sitting around all the time," Johnny complained.

They had their girlfriends and wives often with them, but they suffered together as only voluntary prisoners can—consternated, yet complicit, in their own misery. A rash of problems much worse than boredom faced them, too, making the hours in the teachers' lounge more desperate. Danny Fields had hepatitis and was recuperating back in New York. Vera Ramone was sick with hepatitis, too, forcing her to stay sometimes at the Tropicana to rest. Johnny's girlfriend, Roxy, would drink through the day, it seems, which Johnny did not like. And Joey's girlfriend, Cindy, was showing signs of frustration, almost like a prisoner locked up too long in an isolation facility. Dee Dee's drug habit, which would kill him twenty-four years later in 2002—in Los Angeles—bedeviled the poor bass player all through the shoot. "It was good that we got to do the movie, but it wasn't the most pleasant experience. In fact, it was horrible, real low-budget. . . . During the entire shoot, I was very unhealthy mentally; I was too soggy-brained from alcohol and barbiturates to concentrate."

Marky has a clear recollection of himself and Dee Dee leaving the school building just after the band completed work on the laundry cart scene and scoring free dope on the perimeter of the Mount Carmel grounds. A chain-link fence blocked off the school from South Hoover Street, and there, according to Marky, fans passed on packets of drugs to Dee Dee. The gift-giving wasn't exclusive to this day. Moon Davis, the merch guy, noted in a self-published memoir, "Everyone wuz always givin Dee Dee pills, joints, booze. Shit, methadone."

The Ramones' awkwardness and emotional distress, their collective breakdown in the cell-like teachers' lounge, troubled others. Michael Godwin, in his profile of the production, observed, "There's a tense, uncomfortable relationship between the movie people and the Ramones. . . . [T]he filmies are threatened by the rockers' doomsday deadpan style." Arkush went to the guys, to help them, to assuage their anxieties as best as he could. He told Zack Carlson, "They wanted a TV set, so we got 'em a little black-and white one, and set 'em up in the teachers' lounge. . . . They just sat and watched TV and ate pizza, and that was that."

Drugs, illness, and dissatisfaction aside, the Ramones managed to remember on occasion the old kindergarten directive to "Be kind to others." Loren Lester recalled that during shooting he "still wasn't driving, so my mother drove me to the set. One day I was trying to find her. I was going to lunch or something—or dinner. I found her sitting in the classroom the Ramones were using, and they were all eating pizza together. Joey said, 'Hey! Fritz's mom is here.' I talked to her after that, and she told me, 'Oh, they were such cool guys. I was walking down the hall, and they said, 'Do you want some pizza?' And I said, 'Sure.' So she went in there, and she had pizza with them."

Jon Davison that same busy Wednesday directed an extended gag reminiscent of a Sunday paper comic strip. For the scene, Dan Davies as Fritz Gretel folds a paper airplane out of a note Miss Togar has written for Mr. McGree, an invitation to join her in the school's "animal room" for a meeting. The hall monitor launches the plane with a jab of his chubby hand. It soars down a hallway and through a bank of lockers, crossing Vince Lombardi's campus and into the open window of a classroom, where Mr. McGree is seated before his students, slamming into the music teacher's right ear. He unfolds the airplane, glances at the message inside, and announces to the class, "Ear mail!" Bartel in a recollection for *Film Comment* revealed that he got "a kick every time I see this scene, and it isn't the clever cutting or the special effects. It's the memory of the excruciating pain the scene caused me, take after take. . . . This paper airplane was really a fairly heavy *cardboard* airplane. and it wasn't sailing through the air, but sliding along a piece of invisible monofilament, one end of which was anchored to a plug which had been *glued* into my right ear."

On Thursday, the crew filmed primarily in a cloistered board room at Mount Carmel for a scene featuring a batch of repressive school officials who want to see Vince Lombardi High School's recalcitrant student body stomped into submission by the jackboot of school administration. These officials have tasked Miss Togar, as the school's new principal, on her first day in this role, with executing their stern objectives. Restrained in a wheelchair across the room from her sits Togar's predecessor, Professor Webb (Jim Lawler), whose attempts to tame the students have reduced him to a mental invalid fed cold, gooey oatmeal by a pair of hospital orderlies. Should she fail, presumably, she'll wind up like him (and she does!).

Present also in this mean-spirited meeting are a morose school board member played by screenwriter Joseph McBride (tall, thin, glasses) and Grady Sutton (tall, stooping, gray) as the president of the school board who introduces the new principal. "Never before has the school board seen a student body such as this," the old fatuous chieftain laments, reading from a prepared statement rather than speaking extemporaneously (Sutton had had trouble remembering his lines). "But, starting today, things will be different. May I present to you an administrator who has promised to carry out her duties with an iron hand!"

Arkush first approached Joe DeRita about playing the part of the school board president. DeRita, a later member of the Three Stooges comedy team, had recently received approval to stay at the Motion Picture & Television Country House and Hospital, an assisted-living facility for indigent movie professionals, on Mulholland Drive. And he'd passed on the role because a paying job could cost him access to his benefits. Using the Screen Actors Guild Directory, Arkush, who specifically wanted an elderly actor to play the autocratic school board president, had found that Grady Sutton was available, and the actor accepted the offer to play the part. *Rock 'n' Roll High School* would be Sutton's last picture. He was seventy-three at the time of shooting, and he'd soon, in fact, become one of Joe DeRita's neighbors at the Motion Picture & Television Country House and Hospital.

Rich Whitley knew from the shooting schedule that Sutton would be on set that day, and he'd brought a copy of W. C. Fields's autobiography for the comic actor to sign. Fields had been a hip icon for Vietnam-era college kids, who'd latched on to him as a symbol of defiance and subversiveness. Arkush during his year at Franklin & Marshall had had a poster of W. C. Fields hanging from his dorm wall. Sutton's memory, fortunately, was working better now than it haa d at the Los Feliz house. He signed the book: "To Rich: Don't Buy Beef Steak Mines"—a reference to a plot point in *The Bank Dick* that has Sutton's bumbling character, Og Oggilby, under his father-in-law's influence, buy shares in a shady mining operation.

In the address Mary delivered as Miss Togar to the school board, the sadism of her Play-house of the Ridiculous character Violet returned, sharp and brilliant like a switchblade. "As we stand on the threshold of a new decade, we must face harsh reality," the character growls. "Our educational system has become far too permissive. Today's students lack the discipline to take advantage of the studies offered them." Togar's delivery is disrupted, however, when Fritz Hansel (the one with curly hair) hands her a salacious letter he's penned for her, not the second page of her prepared remarks, which, caught off-guard, she reads aloud before catching herself: "My darling, Evelyn, how I long for the feel of your luscious thighs wrapped around my—"

The hall monitors, described by Whitley and Dvonch in the script as being dressed "in a style similar to the Hitler Youth," are as ludicrous as they are evil, wearing uniforms deliberately, Arkush let on in the DVD commentary he recorded with Whitley, "made too small, so the buttons would stretch, emphasize their girth." As ridiculous as they looked, the actors complemented Mary's performance, and she valued them for this. She told Robert Nuñez: "You know, there're two of them—Tweedledee and Tweedledum—and they got giggly when I wanted them to. They were very instinctive and very good."

After lunch, Dey Young joined Mary Woronov and Dan Davies and Loren Lester and worked through a series of shots in Miss Togar's office in which Kate presents several handwritten excuse notes for Riff's absences from school. Riff in the film story has left the suburbs that surround Vince Lombardi High School for the dirty city sidewalk outside the Rockatorium, where the Ramones will have their concert, to buy one hundred tickets for herself and ninety-nine friends. Each note provides a different reason for why Riff can't attend school—death in the family, death of her pet goldfish. To augment the sense of evil in this enclave, Dean Cundey lighted the set like a chiaroscuro painting, with high hats striking Dey's face and heavy shadows draping the room around her. Michael Godwin said of Cundey's handling of the interrogation scene that it was "an expressionist exercise for two lights and Woronov, featuring menacing shadows and a crane shot that starts up near the ceiling. . . . The camera swoops down on Miss Togar, catching flashes of her scary, spinsterish beauty as she paces past the lights. 'I've made a list of school policy,' she says smiling with evil anticipation. 'First, I think it would be tidy if all the students wore neckties. Also, lunch hour is cut in half, because I am *doubling*,' she bellows, savoring each word, 'silent study hall.'"

Arkush and Cundey and crew rounded out the day getting cutaways and filler shots, like having Vince and Dey do the hustle in a hallway to the Ramones' "Do You Wanna Dance" blasting from the speakers of the production's mobile PA system. The music the Ramones make is so hip, evidently, even kids into disco, like Tom and Kate, can shake-shake-shake to it. A dry-ice fog was pumped onto the set as candy-colored lights dappled the linoleum, evoking the electrified floor John Travolta cavorted on in *Saturday Night Fever*. Under the dancers' feet, the set decorators had laid out several dance-step decals taken from a disco self-instruction book Tom carries sometimes.

Moon Davis, the Ramones' merch guy, would later sneak off the set with these dance decals, pasting them to the tour crew's egg-yolk-yellow Ryder truck. "Moon got into a prop room or a prop truck and found those footprints and grabbed a bunch of them," Matt Lolya remembered. "And then he put them all over the side of our Ryder truck." The decals stayed stuck to the truck for quite a long time. Matt said that a couple of weeks after the Ramones had finished their commitment to *Rock 'n' Roll High School*, they'd toured several states in the Mountain West. It was in January 1979 when "We were going to play in Salt Lake City, Utah. There was a snowstorm, and I was driving in the left-hand lane, gingerly. A semi passed me in the right-hand lane and because of the suction of the semi passing, I lost control of the vehicle, and we went down into the median. The tires were completely immersed in snow. There was no damage. We were just stuck."

The Ramones' white tour van, with Monte A. Melnick behind the wheel, moments later shot past the stranded Ryder truck. "They knew it was our truck because of the footsteps on the side. Monte had thought, 'I better stop,' because we had to get to Salt Lake City by a certain time. He told Johnny, 'I better stop and make sure they have enough money to get out of this situation.' And Johnny was like 'Don't stop. Don't stop. Don't stop.' But Monte insisted and they stopped, and he gave me money. It cost us about $300 to get towed out of the median."

Why was Johnny okay with the crew stranded and the equipment separated from the band like that? "It didn't make sense. Regardless of whether he cared about us, he was not going to be able to do the show in Salt Lake City because the equipment was with us. And John was always very much 'Do the show—get the money—run.' If we couldn't get there with the equipment, they couldn't do the show, and that would basically be a cancellation, screwing up everything. But that was John. Don't walk next to a cliff with him, I learned; you don't know if he'll push you off."

As days at a time would pass at Mount Carmel when the Ramones were not needed, and Saturdays and Sundays the cameras didn't roll, the band's booking agency, Premier, scheduled concerts for Joey, Dee Dee, Marky, and Johnny during the first week of December—the second week of principal photography—in San Bernardino, Stockton, Long Beach, and Phoenix. Being separated from the confines of the Mount Carmel teachers' lounge and the endless swathes of time between camera setups was welcomed, yet the concerts were hardly relaxing getaways; they were work, and sometimes work for rock stars can be dangerous.

When the Ramones played San Bernardino on Friday, December 1, for example, at Swing Auditorium, opening for Black Sabbath, promoters billed the concert as "The Kings of Heavy Metal vs. The Kings of Punk Rock." The guys in Black Sabbath were friendly enough people, the singer, Ozzy Osbourne, in particular, but their fans often brought weapons to shows; and the Ramones that night in San Berdoo could only get six songs into their set before they had to flee the stage as the audience, screaming "Ozzy! Ozzy!" hurled whisky bottles and batteries at them—even an ice pick. "Black Sabbath has a slightly different crowd than ours," Joey joked for Crispin McCormick Cioe.

Over that first weekend, Arkush, Finnell, and Corman reviewed the footage—five days' worth of dailies in a single sitting. "Roger did all his screenings at Nosseck's screening room on Sunset Boulevard, which was walking distance from the original New World office, right next to Tower Records. It was very cheap," said Allan. Corman liked what he saw in the footage, but he cautioned his hard-working employees about giving too much time on the screen to the Ramones: They looked strange and lacked sex appeal.

Mark Helfrich, one of three production assistants assigned to *Rock 'n' Roll High School*, had become the person tasked with transporting reels of film back and forth between the MGM lab in Culver City and the editing rooms in Hollywood, once and a while dropping off screening copies of films at Nosseck's too. Mark had come out to Los Angeles earlier in 1978, taking a break from the University of Wisconsin to find out for himself if a career in motion picture production was something he truly wanted to pursue as a professional. In LA, he'd wound up crashing on a friend's couch for several weeks, unable to find work at first. But as he was perusing *Daily Variety* one day, Mark had come upon an announcement for an upcoming film project, a Lily Tomlin comedy called *The Incredible Shrinking Woman*, which John Landis at that time was attached to as director. Mark decided quite boldly to call Landis and ask for a PA job on the movie. He got through to Landis's secretary. "This is Mark Helfrich calling for John."

The secretary replied, "What's this in regards to?"

"Put me through to John."

The forceful request worked, and Mark was connected to Landis. The pair shot the breeze for several minutes before Mark asked, "Is there anything I can do on your film?"

"I'm up to my eyeballs with help," Landis answered, "but give a call to Roger Corman's New World Pictures. They'll probably have something for you."

Mark then called New World Pictures' main office on San Vincente Boulevard. When a receptionist answered, he said, again being direct, "This is Mark Helfrich calling for Roger." The receptionist wasn't moved. Mark called three more times before he got through to one of Corman's assistants, who asked him, "What's this in regards to?"

"His next picture."

"You mean *Rock 'n' Roll High School*?"

"Yes!"

The assistant gave Mark the telephone number to the production office on North Robertson Avenue; when he called, Allan answered.

"John Landis told me to contact you," Mark said.

Allan, a longtime friend of Landis's, answered, "Then come on down."

Mark rode the city bus— he didn't have a car—and at the production office, it was Mike Finnell who interviewed him.

"Do you have a car?" Mike asked. To work for New World it helped to have wheels.

"No," Mark admitted. "But I have a van," which wasn't true. There was a van for sale across the street from where he was living. "I had about $600 left to my name. I had brought $800 to California when I moved here. That was the rest of my nest egg. But I bought that van and got the job as a PA. I was a PA on *Rock 'n' Roll High School* for the entire shoot. I drove the Ramones all around in the van.

"Because I had that van, I was sent to places like furniture warehouses to pick up fifty school desks and bring them to the schools for such-and-such a set. Anything that needed large transportation, I was asked to do. I'd pick up the Ramones and bring them to the set and take them home to the Tropicana, which was a very low-rent operation. The Ramones would be at the Tropicana, and I'm driving this beat up old van. Then, we'd go to this abandoned high school Mount Carmel to shoot the movie really early in the morning. You know the budget of the film, but for me, I was in Hollywood. I was making a Hollywood movie that was being shot 35-millimeter. It was my first job in the film industry—this was the big time. I didn't know any different. I was having the time of my life. I loved it.

"One time we were shooting at Mount Carmel, and Mike Finnell said, 'We're going to run into meal penalty unless we get the meal, our dinner, to the cast by 6:02 p.m.'" New World, though itself a non-union company, used actors who were in the Screen Actors Guild (SAG) and had to honor the union's strictures. "'Go to the McDonald's,' Mike said. 'It's several blocks away. Get our order. I already called it in. It's one hundred hamburgers or cheeseburgers. Make sure you're here no later than 6:02.' So, I get in my van, I drove over to McDonald's. I went in there. I said, 'I'm here for the order, one hundred burgers.' And they said, 'Oh, we haven't started that yet.' I said, 'I need it now. I need it now. I have to get back.' Mike Finnell had impressed on me that it was a matter of life or death: get these burgers back by 6:02, or else there'd be meal penalty. I had no idea what meal penalty meant. But it sounded really serious! The way he spoke to me was like, 'This is your mission.'

"They started doing burgers, and then they said, 'Do you want to help?'

"So I hop over the counter, and I start making the burgers too. We make them all. I've got them in the van. I'm pulling up to the school, and it's 6:02 as I'm pulling in, and Mike's running toward me with his hands out. I give him a couple burgers, and he runs. He had to take them to a couple of the actors who *were* in the union. They had union rules that they had to be fed exactly after a certain interval of time. So he ran, and he got them in their hands. A meal penalty was avoided, and everything was fine. It was crazy like that every day. I mean, I was slinging burgers and wrapping them in paper just as part of the job."

On Monday, the second week of principal photography proceeded. None of the shots scheduled for the day called for the Ramones. They were opening for Black Sabbath in Long Beach that night, and Tuesday they would do the same in Phoenix. The concert at the Long Beach Arena in Orange County, a forty-five-minute van ride from the Tropicana, passed without incident. This time it "was just a normal show. Ramones fans came and left after the Ramones played, I assumed. Sabbath fans probably stayed while the Ramones were on stage, but they were not unruly." The Ramones the next day set off for Phoenix, and there they learned, painfully, again, that unlike the kids in Vince Lombardi High School, who embrace the band heart and soul, the disciples of Ozzy did not. "The second ten rows loved us, but the first ten rows hated us. One guy just missed me with a bottle. They didn't start throwing garbage until 'Surfin' Bird'—that seemed to provoke them," Johnny remembered.

During the Ramones's absence, Arkush oversaw the shooting of several shots in which students spontaneously spring up from their desks in their classrooms and dance after Riff and Kate seize the high school's PA system and drop the tone arm on "Sheena Is a Punk Rocker." A second unit working simultaneously filmed the establishing shot of Vince Lombardi High campus that appears in the film's first frame, with the most famous utterance attached to the Green Bay Packers' revered coach spelled out across a sign sitting out front: "Winning isn't everything . . . It's the only thing."

Several shots that day with Paul Bartel, the effete Mr. McGree, were filmed inside Mount Carmel. Dean Cundey used an old Mitchell 35-millimeter, with its Mickey-Mouse-ear design and tripod stand, to shoot the portly actor tearing his sports jacket open to reveal a Ramones T-shirt underneath as he dances with the lithe Riff Randell. Bartel also delivered for the camera a goofy-dumb joke with sonorous panache, standing in a classroom before a crowd of apathetic students, gesturing to a portrait of the immortal Beethoven, and in his glib, but likeable, way, says, "Here we see Ludwig Van Beethoven, who, as you all know, wrote his greatest symphony when he was deaf—which was practically unheard of at the time."

Cundey and Arkush got a shot of Mr. McGree mispronouncing the Ramones' name, too, just as Joey mispronounces his backstage at the Rockatorium. Riff has returned from the concert hall's box office with a hundred tickets for the upcoming concert, which she's passing out to anyone who's interested in going. When she moseys up to Mr. McGree, the one kind adult in the film, and offers him a ticket to the Ramones concert, the teacher begs her, "But who are the Ramonies?" "The Ramones," she corrects him. "They're the best group in the world, Mr. McGree."

Bartel, of Montclair, New Jersey, enjoyed playing the part of McGree very much. "It was, of course, a satirical role. I tried to play him more realistic in the beginning so he wouldn't come off as a complete caricature. The transition the character makes is more amusing that way, I think: You have this square, bookish professor and lover of classical music who in the end evolves into a sort of punk dilettante. . . . I enjoyed the role and the chance to work with people I like. It was great fun. I never danced so much in my life." He thought the Ramones were wonderful, comparing them to "a breath of fresh amyl-nitrate. Fresh, intoxicating and full of life. It was great fun shooting the picture."

Following their evening performance in Phoenix on Tuesday, the Ramones were due back at Mount Carmel Wednesday in the early afternoon. The morning would be given to shooting the moment in the film that triggers the student uprising and the subsequent bombing of Vince Lombardi High School, which brings down the Togar regime: when the malicious principal and her goons burn a pile of records confiscated from Vince Lombardi students. Arkush planned the scene as an homage to the book-burnings depicted in Ray Bradbury's novel *Fahrenheit 451* and the movie Truffaut adapted from it. The crew positioned the day's extras around Mount Carmel's schoolyard, separating them by age, forming two groups of onlookers: students and their parents. Also present were P. J., Dey, Tom, Clint, Mary, and Paul—and screenwriter Joseph McBride.

The Ramones showed up at Mount Carmel at their announced time, 1:00 p.m., but the bonfire scene still had not been shot. As the guys started toward Mount Carmel's front entrance, bound for the teachers' lounge to wait for their call, they saw a plastic tarp Marie Kordus and her set decorators had stretched over the pile of records. Joey didn't think the joke about burning up records was all that funny and made an effort to save the ones he could. Arkush said, "[W]hen we were going to burn all the records . . . we went through the pile and couldn't find a lot of classic records we wanted in there, like Dylan, The Who and the Stones. We found out that Joey had gone through all of [them] and kept the ones he liked. 'You can't burn these! These are good albums!' We said, 'Joey, we'll buy you the albums, but we have to burn these ones!'" The well-meaning thief, reluctantly persuaded, turned over the missing platters, and shooting

THE KIDS ARE ALL RIGHT

commenced a short time later, with the extras and the main cast assembled on the schoolyard, and the Ramones watching on, outside of view.

Arkush during the shoot more typically shouted "Roll camera!" than "Action!" to start a scene, and when he did so, standing beside Dean Cundey at the Mitchell, Mary Woronov, the worldly and thoughtful Ivy Leaguer who liked sculpting and painting, transformed herself again into the demented Miss Togar. "This high school is a failure!" the brittle despot snarls. "Our overall grade point average is the worst in the state." Every Nazi has a scapegoat, and Togar's is Riff. "Why, in the last three days student Riff Randell alone . . . banded the students against me to attend a concert by the Ramones, where they played that awful rock 'n' roll music! Before me you see my first major step in putting this school back on the winning track. I give you: the final solution!" (This "final solution" Miss Togar refers to hearkens back to the euphemism the Nazis used for a series of decrees and policies that resulted in the mass deportation of European Jews to death camps in World War II. Allan Arkush in fact lost a family member in the Holocaust, his grandmother.) The hall monitors in response to their commandant spray lighter fluid on the mound, and flames spring up, scorching cardboard covers and warping vinyl.

Dean Cundey filmed the fire partly in closeup, aiming his camera at copies of *Highway 61, Who's Next, Sticky Fingers*, and the Ramones four Sire albums, *Ramones, Leave Home, Rocket to Russia*, and *Road to Ruin. Road to Ruin* had been the band's most recent release and the cartoon cover that *Punk Magazine*'s John Holmstrom and graphic designer Spencer Drate created for the LP jacket surfaces regularly in *Rock 'n' Roll High School*. Johnny Ramone and Linda Stein had asked Holmstrom for his creative opinion in May 1978 about a drawing they were considering for *Road to Ruin*'s LP jacket. *Punk* had been promoting the Ramones since before the band had even released its debut album, *Ramones*. He'd drawn the cartoon that appeared on the back cover of the *Rocket to Russia* LP, a rendering of a pinhead character riding on an ICBM bound for the USSR. A fan named Gus MacDonald had passed on to Johnny and Linda a sketch, which had the original four Ramones—Tommy,

Dee Dee, Johnny, and Joey—performing as monstrous animals (a lobster and a snake) press themselves through a pair of amplifiers, with
the New York City skyline stretching behind them. "Everyone liked it
and thought it was a great idea for a cover image," Holmstrom told me.
"It was just a bit amateurish and needed a few changes. But the basic
design—the placement of the Ramones within a circle, their legs splayed,
New York City in the background—was awesome. When I was asked
who should redraw the sketch, I said: 'Wally Wood!'" Wood had been
a comic book artist, famous for his contributions to EC Comics releases
like *MAD* magazine, *Weird Science*, and *Weird Fantasy*. "Unknown to
me and everyone else, since people tend to keep health problems private,
Wally Wood was in poor health and handed the job off to his assistant,
Paul Kirchener. . . . For whatever reason, Paul didn't want to follow
Johnny's orders and was apparently either obstinate on not stealing
another artist's idea or unable to deliver what they wanted.

"I was summoned to a meeting at 157 West 57th Street—Coconut
Entertainment's HQ—the management company for the band. I didn't
know why they asked me to be there. Paul's sketches were all hung up
on the walls of a room, and they asked me to check them out. I could see
that he was avoiding their very simple request: 'Redraw the Gus Mac-
Donald drawing, but replace Tommy with Marky, remove the lobster
claw and snake, and make the buildings in the background more like the
real New York City: bombed out and destroyed.'"

Amidst the extras and the equipment set up outside the Mount Carmel school building for the bonfire, Arkush and Cundey also squeezed
in a shot of another parent who's been attending the rally—a giant mouse
wearing an apron with lettering printed across the front that reads:
"I Hate Mouse Work." Allan had Rob Bottin, who'd designed the
costume and was inside it, wobble back and forth, nervous over news
made moments earlier, as the students, outraged by the bonfire, rush
the school building that Miss Togar plans to call in the National Guard.
(Only blocks from Mount Carmel, in 1965, the National Guard quelled
the Watts Uprising using tear gas to disperse rioters. The National Guard
had notoriously killed student demonstrators on Kent State University's

campus in May 1970, as well.) Arkush thought mouse gags were funny and wanted them woven throughout the movie, further adding, like Eaglebauer's physics-defying office, a surrealist quality to the story. Bottin would return the following week when the production moved to the Roxy Theatre for a scene as a punk-rock-loving giant mouse, who wants to get in to Rockatorium for the Ramones concert.

The first encounter between the Ramones and Miss Togar was filmed that afternoon. The Ramones, in the film story, have come to Vince Lombardi to tell Riff Randell they plan to record "Rock 'n' Roll High School" as their next single, which she's written for them in Mr. McGree's music class. Their arrival coincides with the students' initial assault on the school. "Things sure have changed since we got kicked out of high school," reflects Johnny as the four in their leather jackets and shag hairdos traipse amidst the bedlam. At first, the principal mistakes them for students, which prompts Johnny to clarify: "Hey, we're not students—we're the Ramones." To which Mary deliver the most often quoted line from the film: "Do your parents know you're Ramones?"

Arkush kept himself open to suggestions from the band through the entire shoot, and while "many of Miss Togar's dialogue lines were taken verbatim from things said by my high school principal, it was John's idea to put the 'Kick Me' sign on her back," Arkush explained to the *Village Voice*. As written by Whitley and Dvonch, Johnny was to have pinned a button of some sort on to Miss Togar, but now it was Marky who creeps behind the principal and sticks a sign that reads "KICK ME HARD" to the space between her pinched shoulder blades. Of course, Togar's line in the scene when she asks "Do your parents know you're Ramones?" couldn't have been taken verbatim from Mr. Raimondo or Mr. Kelly or any of the other autocrats at Fort Lee High School, though the paranoia and belligerence that distinguished Mary's delivery, encouraged and shaped by Arkush's direction, seem all the same to reveal their lasting influence.

Joining the cast that day also was Dick Miller, the star of Roger Corman's *War of the Satellites* and *A Bucket of Blood*. He'd be playing Chief Klein, an autocratic police official simpatico with Miss Togar, concurring in her repudiation of rock 'n' roll music and punk couture. When Togar declares, for instance, "Those Ramones are peculiar," the Chief replies, scowling at them like a schoolyard thug, "They're ugly: ugly, ugly people," a line that Miller allegedly improvised. Los Angeles Top 40 disc jockey the Real Don Steele came over to Mount Carmel that day to play Screamin' Steve Stevens, an all-rounder media guy in the movie—afternoon radio show host, concert emcee, TV news reporter. Steele's part in the film would function like the chorus in a Greek play, providing witness to the actions of the story while filling in gaps in the narrative. The deejay-actor possessed an odd, braying manner of speaking, a consequence of hearing damage wrought by years of listening to music too loud through the headphones he wore in the radio booth.

Mike and Allan had decided that Mount Carmel, announced for eventual demolition as it was, would serve best as the site Vince Lombardi High School's students blow up. Filming the climactic explosion wound up taking two nights, Thursday (December 7—Pearl Harbor Day) and Friday (December 8). Arkush had planned early on to have Jack Rabin & Associates, the opticals house on North El Centro, provide a miniature model of the school to detonate. But the idea was quashed by Corman, who expressed emphatically to Arkush and Finnell, "This is not going to work. This isn't going to look good," Arkush said on the DVD commentary he cut for the film. Corman then pointed the director toward Roger George, a pyrotechnics specialist, who'd done the explosives work for *Grand Theft Auto* and *Deathsport*. Roger George wanted to use a combustible powdery substance called naphthalene to create the illusion of blowing up the school building without inflicting any actual damage to Mount Carmel. "Naphthalene is the kind of stuff that often shows up in terrorist bombs. But it's not the thing that does the damage. It's this thing that gets the whole thing going. Now the size of your naphthalene explosion . . . is directly related to the temperature: the colder the temperature, the bigger the explosion."

The main players in the film—Mary, Paul, Tom, Clint, Kate, and Dey, and once again the screenwriter Joseph McBride—spent several hours waiting in classrooms and trailers for the call to the outdoor set as

Roger George and his assistants took longer than anybody expected setting up. A group of high school students from Mira Costa High School had been brought out to Mount Carmel in buses to appear in the scene too and were left to wait around with nothing to do.

The sun set that afternoon a few minutes after half past four, and the temperatures dipped deeply as darkness settled. A series of chain-link panels rising around the edges of Mount Carmel kept fans and gawkers—and some protestors—away from Roger George and his assistants as they set up around the school's illuminated entrance. Members of the Los Angeles Police Department showed up, uninvited, to monitor. "The whole area was fenced off and [neighborhood] residents were all hanging around, looking in. You felt like you were an animal in a cage. They were yelling things at the kids and ruining some of the takes," Johnny told *Trouser Press*'s Jim Green.

Many of the Mira Costa students Finnell had recruited for the night were scheduled to take the SAT two days later on Saturday. They wanted to feel rested before they took the test that would determine the range of colleges they could apply to. As the night wore on, to discourage the kids from re-boarding their buses and leaving, Mike Finnell adjusted the clocks inside Mount Carmel. "We got way behind," Arkush explained for Daniel Griffith. "And there's all these students in the school who are extras, and they're supposed to be out by 10:30. So Mike goes, 'When we are doing other stuff with them?' Mike goes into the room where the students are sitting and moves back the clocks—that's good producing. So they keep thinking, 'Well, it's only nine.'"

Joseph McBride spent hours inside the Mount Carmel teachers' lounge with the Ramones. They didn't talk much. To kill time he read a biography of Douglas MacArthur he'd brought along. He found the guys to be pleasant enough. "I liked them right away," he recalled. "Allan was kind of surprised because he was thinking they'd be like the Beatles in *A Hard Day's Night*. The Beatles were charming, verbally witty and good actors. When these guys showed up, though, they were monosyllabic and withdrawn and weird. It was a little disappointing that they were not more talkative. But I found them sympathetic. I had read an interview with them in *Rolling Stone* around the time we were making the movie. They were talking about growing up in Queens, where they were considered very geeky, and the 'nice' ordinary girls wouldn't go out with them. So they had to break into the grounds of the local mental hospital and date schizophrenic girls, which I thought was sweet." McBride was empathetic due to his own experience dating a "schizophrenic girl," Kathy Wolf, whose memory had guided him as he created the earliest versions of Riff Randell in his drafts for *Girls' Gym* and *California Girls*.

Vince Van Patten in New World's press kit for *Rock 'n' Roll High School* recalls staying up late with the Ramones: "I remember . . . when we were working quite late—it was around 2:30 A.M., and I had to do this dance scene. We were all sitting around. The Ramones were there with their little group—and somebody brings in several six packs of beer. So we're all sitting there in school chairs in a circle drinking beers, talking and stuff, and I suddenly thought, 'How strange it is that we're shooting a film.' This was really the most relaxed and informal set I'd ever seen." Bizarrely, Dee Dee took a moment in *Lobotomy*, many years later, to defame Van Patten. "I didn't like Vince Van Patten or the other extras in the movie. They weren't bad people or anything but they just came from a totally different world than the Ramones. They were a bunch of tennis players, and we're not like that." But Van Patten wasn't an extra, nor were there any other professional tennis players in the cast.

When Roger George at last gave the go-ahead for the explosion, the outdoor temperature had fallen forty degrees. The film's leads, the extras, and the Ramones gathered round the high school's flagpole. "It's 2:30 in the morning," Godwin wrote in his eyewitness account. "Fatigue cracks [Allan's] voice, but his eyes are burning; on some level, this is *his* high school he's blowing up. People emerge dreamlike from the school, crossing the lawn in sleepy silhouette against a blaze of spotlights. Four automatic, high-speed cameras are placed up close, focused, anchored with sandbags."

The Ramones picked up their instruments and took their places, and on Allan's cue, P. J., wearing a leather jacket (as much to keep herself warm as to signify Riff's status as an honorary member of the Ramones), appeared. The actress cried out, "Hit it!" and pressed down the plunger on a detonator box. The band pretended to rip into the song Riff's written for them, with Joey lip-synching as the prerecorded version of the tune surged from the mobile PA system's speakers. Then a massive burst of chemical fire unleashed by Roger George with firepots, mortars, and naphthalene blasted from the front of Mount Carmel.

Mark Helfrich remembered, "I was there on the set because I was a production assistant. It was a really, really cold night. Roger George, the effects supervisor for the film, had calculated the explosion for a certain temperature that was a lot warmer than what it ended up being. I don't know what time we actually shot it, but it was very late, like two or three in the morning. Roger George was quite a character himself. He was missing a finger because something exploded in his hands on some film. We were going to embellish the explosion. We had gas canisters that we were supposed to turn on at the exact moment of the explosion and after, so the fire would keep burning. But it ended up that we really didn't need that much because the explosion was five times larger than what Roger George said it was going to be. It was so hot the extras dancing behind the Ramones around the flagpole got their hair singed."

"They let off the explosion, and it was huge," said McBride. "We had five cameras. It was a gigantic fireball, and windows were blown out, and sprayed glass all over everybody. The trees caught on fire; the American flag caught on fire. And they had a great shot—I saw it in the rushes—this slow-motion shot of the American flag tumbling in flames. I said to Allan, 'Wow, great shot.' And he shook his head and said, 'Too symbolic.'"

"I was there," Kent Beyda said. "I remember it was very dark, and all of a sudden it was really bright. The heat, too. I was the only assistant editor, so I didn't have a lot of time to go to the set in general, but I definitely had to be there when they blew up the high school. . . . It was a great moment and made for a grand climax to the film."

"Mount Carmel was going to be torn down anyway," said Loren Lester, "and so all of the hallways were filled with stuff that the students had left, that had been pulled out of their lockers. The library books were spilling out of the library into the hall. The place was ready to be demolished. So it was the perfect place to light a bomb at the end of the movie, I guess. It was in a very dangerous area." The fury of it all thrilled Clint Howard. "I don't think any of us even imagined how awesome the explosion would be. It was incredible! That night, everybody got sunburned."

Johnny recalled for Jim Green: "They say, 'We're gonna blow up the school' and I figure it's gonna be some kind of trick thing. So we're playing on the grass in front of it, and it really blows up! All of a sudden I hear this big explosion and I look back and see this huge ball of fire over my head. I thought, 'If it comes any closer I'm running!' But it sort of faded out." Joey said: "It shook the whole place, the flames shoot out, a lot of the kids got burned. But they said it wasn't anything to worry about, the burns were like sunburn."

The naphthalene blast startled nearby dogs, prompting a cacophony of agitated woofing, and rattled windows, frightening locals who remembered the fiery riots that had brought the National Guard into Watts thirteen years earlier. "We got in so much trouble. The neighborhood was furious, and the police were furious because we had broken the [shooting] permit," Arkush told Jared Cowan. The damage to nearby residences was greater, it seems, than to Mount Carmel. P. J. Soles said: "I don't think the school had any damage. I think they were in front of the school, not in the school: it was made to look like we blew up the school. Mount Carmel was set for demolition, which is why they let us film there. But if there was really any damage to the school . . . I don't know. The boom and the look of it were so much bigger than they expected."

The police shut the production down immediately, denying the crew from getting reaction shots to the explosion and shots of the extras with flames flickering around them. They needed more with Don Steele addressing his TV news–viewing audience from the campus of Vince Lombardi, too, and kids dancing to "Rock 'n' Roll High School," and a shot of Kate and Tom kissing amidst flames. To get all this, they were going to have to return to Mount Carmel to re-stage the school's destruction. Father Bob, fortunately, didn't back out of the arrangement

Arkush and Finnell had secured with him, though their promises about not damaging Mount Carmel had been ignored—even the shrubs on the school grounds were burned. "So Mike talks them into letting us come back." But the production was told: "No more explosions." "In the eighteen or twenty hours Mike had left before we have to come back," recalled Arkush, he had to find a fresh horde of extras to play students. Many of the kids who'd danced under Roger George's big bang weren't coming back: They had the SAT to take the next day, and the pool of extras Friday night was significantly smaller. The scenario presented the filmmakers with a logistical conundrum. "We can't even match the clothing. They're different kids. We get all these flame bars. That's how we do it the next night—with the flame bars because we can't use naphthalene."

Several shots and scenes tangentially related to the student uprising and the bombing were also filmed outside over those nights in Watts. One had the hall monitors swaddled in bandages, injured from having been thrust out the window earlier by the Ramones, in the laundry cart. "The funniest gag for me was [when] we wind up in the clothes hamper, and they push us out the window," said Loren. "We go flying out the window and then next time you see us, we're all bandaged up. You know, Dan in the bed, and his leg is up, and I'm on crutches, and my arm's in a sling." Also filmed were the Ramones again pretending to play "Rock 'n' Roll High School" and a final shot of Miss Togar, doddering and nearly catatonic, led off in a wheelchair by the unctuous hall monitors.

The Real Don Steele was back at Mount Carmel, too, following his afternoon radio show, to shoot some takes in which Screamin' Steve Stevens, with microphone pressed up to his flexile mouth, blurts out expository quasi-political observations and injunctions to the audience. One shot had Screamin' Steve cover the calamitous events at Vince Lombardi in a safari jacket, with a yellow scarf tied around his throat and an expansive pair of glasses held in place by the isosceles triangle of his nose, describing the dispute between the school's administration and its students as "a classic confrontation between mindless authority and the rebellious nature of youth—or is it rebellious authority against naturally mindless youths? Either way, the moment of truth is at hand." A shot of Joe Dante dressed up like a cop, sunglasses over his eyes, standing beside Dick Miller, was filmed on one of these nights as well.

Monday, December 10, should have been a great day for the Ramones—it was going to be their last at Mount Carmel. They would pretend to play their cover of "Do You Wanna Dance?" in the school's hallways, swarmed by a mix of cheerleaders, football players, and punks, all rocking around them. After breakfast that morning, the band herded toward the van to get to Watts for the day's shooting. Before Joey's girlfriend, Cindy, could board, though, it seems that Johnny swatted her in the face: She had been complaining that she couldn't take another second of the terrible boredom that came with sitting in the teachers' lounge at Mount Carmel. The guitar player climbed into the van and told Monte to get them all to Mount Carmel, leaving Cindy behind, banished and alone, in the parking lot. Marky tells the whole story in full detail in *Punk Rock Blitzkrieg*.

Joey, apparently, responded to this awfulness by ignoring it, sitting in the rear of the tour van not saying anything. He wasn't that much committed to Cindy any longer, anyway. He'd been falling in love with Linda Danielle, his Thanksgiving date from two and a half weeks earlier. Matt Lolya explained to Monte A. Melnick for *On the Road with the Ramones: Bonus Edition*: "Linda was a big Max's Kansas City chick . . . always hanging around the scene." Linda had been dating Justin Strauss, the lead singer of the Long Island power pop band Milk 'N' Cookies, who'd brought her out to Los Angeles earlier that fall, but she'd stayed on in West Hollywood after Strauss had gone back to New York. "That's when the romance between Linda Danielle and Joey Ramone began. It started as a casual friendship."

Any hole Cindy's expulsion left in Joey's emotional life Linda swiftly filled. She started crashing with the singer at the Tropicana Motel, unbothered by the enormity of his obsessive-compulsive disorder and the constricting anxiety that pushed him to count and tap in precise patterns repeatedly in order to feel secure enough to get through his day.

He had smelly feet, too: His OCD kept him from taking his socks off and washing them when he was on tour, and the Ramones were almost always on tour.

Joey and Linda both fell hard for each other. Jaan Uhelski, a friend of the band, told Monte A. Melnick: "Joey might have been a little obsessed by Linda. That was the one great love of his life." They liked watching the same TV shows, especially the sitcom reruns that played late at night. "Los Angeles was like New York: it had TV all night. In a lot of the cities that we traveled to, like in the Midwest, TV went off 1:00 in the morning," said Matt Lolya. "In LA, you could be watching the *Mary Tyler Moore Show* at 2:00 in the morning, 3:00 in the morning *Gunsmoke*, all the old shows."

One of the programs Joey and Linda liked watching in the Tropicana was *Get Smart*, the James Bond lampoon in which Don Adams played bumbling secret agent Maxwell Smart and Barbara Feldon costarred as his better-looking, brighter, more self-aware second, Agent 99. (Joey and Linda recognized parts of themselves in the TV characters, maybe?) The experience of watching *Get Smart* would get a mention in the song "Danny Says," which the band recorded with Phil Spector in May. A reference about hanging around in 100 B, a room at the Tropicana, would show up in the song too.

Moon Davis clarified for me that 100 B was no room to hang out in for long. "It was directly above the prep room for Duke's restaurant, where they cut the onions," Moon said. "The minute you walked in, your eyes started watering. The Tropicana desk had given us 100 B, me and Arty." Johnny, the shot-caller for the band's finances, insisted on the guys in the road crew sharing rooms. "So there's this onion smell, and I'm like, 'I'm not staying in here. It's disgusting.' They wouldn't give us another room, so I slept in the truck, in the Ryder, and Arty stayed in Joey's room." Moon and Arturo Vega responded to Room 100 B's repulsiveness by making it worse, decorating it like the yellow Ryder truck with the disco footstep decals but with trash. "Little Matt was always using Crazy Glue to fix Johnny's guitar. We took it and started gluing cans and ashtrays full of butts on the ceiling. The cleaning ladies freaked out. We had to give them money just to make them happy. 'Sorry, we're being silly again,' we said."

This last day at Mount Carmel, Marky and his drum kit were going to be rolled down the hall on a wheeled platform called a riser. The production's art crew, like graffiti artists, had spraypainted the wall with references to The Who and their songs, like "I know what it means but I can't explain" and "The kids are all right" and a pitch for Joey Ramone to be school president. Also filmed was the symbolic elevation of Riff from teen songwriter to member of the Ramones' extended family with the guys giving her her own leather motorcycle jacket. Not everything was fun that day. Roxy was deep into her cups, which bothered Johnny, Marky attests in *Punk Rock Blitzkrieg*, and he "dragged her into the nearest empty classroom." The sound of fighting redounded through the hallway, the terrible sound of "grunts and smacks and the sound of desks and chairs sliding around a linoleum tile floor, sometimes toppling over."

DOWN AT THE ROCKATORIUM

The Ramones had just three days of shooting before their commitment to *Rock 'n' Roll High School* was up. With all their school-set scenes in the can, now the guys were needed to film the concert sequence at the Rockatorium, the movie's musical centerpiece, along with a scene leading up to the spectacular show, when the band arrives at the club by convertible, and one following, a backstage meeting between Riff and the band, which plays in the finished movie like a parody of Arkush's first conversation with Marky, Dee Dee, Joey, and Johnny at Hurrah.

There wasn't a single rock club in Los Angeles in 1978 that had the layout or look that Arkush wanted in his effort to evoke the Fillmore East, which was his intention, and he and Finnell and Cundey for the scenes based at the Rockatorium wound up using three different sites: the Whisky a Go Go and the Roxy on Sunset Boulevard in West Hollywood for interiors and, downtown, the Mayan, a porno theater, which would serve for the rock hall exterior. These three venues were all scenic, and the use of them, rented one day each, one day at a time, was cheaper than trying to create anything comparable on a leased soundstage.

The first day of shooting the Rockatorium scenes, Tuesday, December 11, took place at the Mayan on South Hill Street, which was going to provide the outdoor space where Riff camps in front of a box office to have first chance to buy tickets for the upcoming concert. The Mayan had been built in 1927 as an homage to Mexico's pre-colonial history, with idealized renderings of life in the Yucatan and abstract designs made from vibrantly hued tiles that ran along the building's walls. The Mayan had a recessed entrance and a wide sidewalk running along the front and an enormous rectangular marquee, which, that day, had "THE ROCKATORIUM PRESENTS THE RAMONES" spelled across it. Promotional stills of the band clung to the Mayan's arabesque walls. Posters promoting *Road to Ruin*, with Holmstrom's cartoon and the band's name written in bright yellow (a design element introduced by Spencer Drate), had been hung up over the spicy posters the theater used to lure in its regular crowd.

The day's first shots had P. J. as Riff setting up a folding chaise lounge outside the Rockatorium's box office. Riff makes the space outside the Rockatorium as much a home as she can. She's brought along a drying rack for clothes, and a cardboard record-store display (contributed by Sire Records' PR department) of the Ramones for company: same lineup again, when Tommy was still in the band, but larger than the black-and-white cutout of the band in her bedroom. Riff briefly obscures the band's first drummer's face with a scarf. She herself wears catsup-red leggings, buttercup-yellow socks, a shiny sateen red-rose jacket with blue stripes on the sleeves, plus oversized high-tops. She's also brought along food—pizza—that she offers to Joey's cardboard likeness. A massive thermos dangles from the armrest of her beach chair. For exercise, she does calisthenics—jumping jacks. She relaxes reading copies of a Ramones fanzine called the *Gabba Gabba Gazette* and *Crawdaddy!*, which Arkush supplied himself. Riff is so comfortable, she's even able to sleep in her chair above the dirty sidewalk, keeping an alarm clock close, while clutching, like a loving parent with a newborn, a well-worn envelope stuffed with the songs she's written for the Ramones in Mr. McGree's music class. At El Centro a month later, when Allan and his editing team were cutting this sequence, they chose to run this footage fast, speeding it up as fast as a punk rock song, but which they set to Chuck Berry's "School Days."

As the morning progressed, extras collected around the Mayan, some of them drawn by the marquee, and lined up on the sidewalk that ran between the theater and the street. P. J. was eventually joined by actress Lynn Farrell. The two were to do a dialogue together, with Riff meeting her second nemesis in the movie, Angel Dust (another drug joke), who fancies herself, like Riff, as the Ramones' number one fan. An argument develops between the two, which grows nasty with name calling ("You're a groupie!" "You're a cheerleader!"). Their fight stops with the band's curbside arrival at the Rockatorium.

The Ramones, who'd been dropped off at the Mayan around 8:00 a.m., spent the first half of the shooting day waiting around, yet again, for something to do. The time was easier to get through than it had been at Mount Carmel, though, because they weren't penned up like restless farm animals. Johnny, for instance, could stroll around the sidewalk on South Hill, Mark Helfrich recalled, playing "his guitar to the extras and fans who happened to be around. He would hold court and play some Ramones' song, and everybody would sing."

In the early afternoon, the call came for the guys to climb into a parked pink Cadillac convertible Finnell had rented, the "Ramonesmobile" as it's referred to in the film's shooting notes. Allan wanted the band to get an entrance scene as jolting as Jerry Lee Lewis's in *High School Confidential*, when the Killer and his band cruise past a high school on a truck, playing the movie's theme song. Upholstered with leopard skin, the Ramonesmobile had a customized license plate bolted to its front fender that read "Gabba Gabba Hey." The song the guys were going to "perform" from the vehicle would be "I Just Want to Have Something to Do," the opening track on *Road to Ruin*.

Under Allan's guidance, the four rockers squeezed into the rear of the car. The top was down and Johnny and Dee Dee flanked the right and left sides, pressing their haunches against the backseat's shoulder rests with Joey planted between them. A box of chicken vindaloo rested on the floor, near Marky, who squatted in the footwell behind the driver's seat, holding a pair of drumsticks (the musical sort). Actor Herbie Braha, the band's manager, was going to ride shotgun, with KROQ radio's Rodney Bingenheimer holding the steering wheel.

A camera car tracked the convertible as it rolled through downtown Los Angeles. Joey clutched a chicken leg like a toy noisemaker as he moved his lips to the lyrics of "I Just Want to Have Something to Do," namechecking the band's favorite dish, chicken vindaloo. As he pretended to sing, the breeze tossing his long, black hair, his pale hand raised the wobbly chicken leg toward his chin, but instead of taking a bite, he tossed it toward the street past Dee Dee's chin.

Arkush and his assistant directors had arranged for the production assistants and the set decorators to set up sawhorses on the sidewalk to divide a line of extras from the street as Bingenheimer pulled the Ramonesmobile up to the curb outside the Mayan. The deejay with the teased strawberry bangs parked close, very close, near a tree, about a half-block from the box office, where P. J. and Lynne remained standing. The Ramones were going to march down the dirty sidewalk, playing their instruments unplugged, much as the real Ramones, not the scripted ones, rehearsed before shows. Allan had them empty out of the convertible and come toward the extras as "I Just Want to Have Something to Do" roared from the production's mobile PA system.

The Ramones' tour manager, Monte A. Melnick, hung behind the boys as they ambled down the sidewalk. "I come right across the frame," Monte told me, "and then I walk behind the band. . . . You can see me talking to the manager. The manager is holding a silver Halliburton briefcase—that's my briefcase, actually." In the finished cut of the movie, the sight of the Ramones promenading past ardent fans evokes the early moments in *A Hard Day's Night* when a gaggle of frenzied admirers chase the Fab Four through London's Marylebone Station. Marky told Robert Nuñez that he felt the "funniest part of the movie . . . was when we approached the front of the movie theater, with Rodney Bingenheimer driving in the Ford or Caddy convertible. Kids in line with red hair, green hair, punks, and all the chains and the belts, and people driving by going, 'What the heck is this?'"

The band's trek along the sidewalk stopped at the box office, and the dialogue between P. J. Soles and Lynn Farrell resumed, with the two continuing their characters' contentious conversation under the Rockatorium's marquee that ends when Herb Braha's manager character invites the junkie-thin Angel rather than the wholesome high schooler into the concert hall with them. Angel may get the victory here, but her departure also restores Riff to the front of the ticket line.

That night, after Monte delivered the Ramones back to the Tropicana Motel, Dee Dee got into trouble. Vera told me that she and Linda Danielle had gone to Los Tacos to buy dinner, and while they were out, Dee Dee found his way to the Dead Boys' Stiv Bators's room at the Tropicana, where the singer and his bandmates had also been staying. After Vera and Linda returned from the taco stand, "We didn't know where the guys were. When we heard they were in Stiv Bators's motel room, we went over there. Dee Dee was pretty fucked up. He took Quaaludes, and he was barely coherent." In her memoir *Poisoned Heart*, Vera explained, "Tish and Snookie from the Sick Fucks, the Dictators and the Dead Boys were having a party, and the place was overflowing with punks. . . . [S]omeone had given Dee Dee a handful of Quaaludes, Tuinals and some methadone. . . . He was drinking hard liquor and doing lines when I found him. . . . [H]e was completely incoherent, running around like a lunatic."

Marky had been drinking with Phil Spector that night in his own suite. "[P]unk partiers had spilled out" from Bators's room, he recalled. "There was a lot of yelling and banging." The LAPD soon arrived and handcuffed Dee Dee and led him to one of their cars with the intent of taking the beleaguered bass player to jail on a disorderly conduct charge. But in the back of the patrol car, a black-and-white Plymouth Fury, Dee Dee turned blue. "He completely overdosed by the time they got him to jail," Vera recalled, "so they put him into the hospital."

"I woke up in Cedar-Sinai," he lamented "with a $3,000 bill."

Wednesday, December 12, the production moved to the Whisky a Go Go to shoot several interior action scenes and a dialogue sequence between Riff and the Ramones, but nothing musical. The rent Lou Adler and David Geffen were charging was quite dear, though, and to counterbalance the hit to the production budget, they were going to have less to pay the extras they still needed to make the rest of the film.

The Whisky a Go Go had opened in 1964 as a West Hollywood nightspot with female dancers in glass boxes, which dropped from the ceiling like the pendant lights in a cathedral. The Ramones had played the Whisky for the first time in 1976 and were scheduled at the club for three nights later that month between the Christmas and New Year's holidays. The Ramones were much loved in LA. Trudie Arguelles-Barrett explained: "I don't know of *anyone* who *didn't* like the Ramones. They were infectious." It was everywhere else in the country where the four rockers were misunderstood and shunned. Monte A. Melnick told me an illustrative story. "In the late 70s, we're driving around Texas in a van, seven hours in a van. We pull up to a gas station, a general store there. Everybody kind of stumbles in, and then we go pay for the gas. The woman says to me, 'Hey, it's sure nice of you taking care of these retarded boys.' This is what she said to me. And I said, 'Yes, ma'am, that's my job.'"

Shooting at the Whisky began that morning with a foot chase, with Tom Roberts turning hero and recovering from the Ramones groupie, Angel Dust, a manila envelope stuffed with music she's stolen from Riff during the Rockatorium concert. The chase had Vince Van Patten and Clint Howard run after Lynn Farrell through the club's backstage area— the mainstage and auditorium were not to be used that day by request of the owners—with the Mitchell BNC filming in a tight hallway, into which the shooting crew had placed three members of the Ramones "family," Rodney Bingenheimer, Monte A. Melnick, and Arturo Vega.

For several shots featuring the band, a backstage dressing room served as the set, with posters of rock stars adorning its grimy walls—one of Cherie Currie, another of Mick Jagger. In this room, Riff meets the band after the concert, during which she offers them, like the drummer boy in the Christmas carol, the gift of her music, including the song

"Rock 'n' Roll High School," as the guys eat pizza for dinner. The influence for the scene, Arkush said, had been the Saturday night dinner at the Steins' apartment in Central Park West when the Ramones balked at the fancy food put out for them and demanded pizza instead.

Dee Dee, still sick from the previous night's excesses, had the hardest time thinking and talking that day. All the woozy bassist had to do was cry, "Hey, pizza!" as he shambled toward a tiny round table in the cluttered dressing room, bearing a stack of cardboard pizza boxes in his shaky hands. But he continuously blew his delivery. Linda Stein explained in *Please Kill Me*: "Dee Dee was supposed to have one line in the movie, something like, 'Is there a pizza?' or 'Can we get pizza?' or 'Order pizza'—something about pizza. He had one line—he couldn't get it. Did about forty takes. And we were all so nervous that Dee Dee wouldn't get it. And he didn't get it! We tried to rehearse Dee Dee and everything, but we knew it was going to be a problem, and it was a problem.'" The bass player concurred: "I just couldn't function. I couldn't do anything. So they just did their best with what they could."

Filming Joey was far easier. The singer had a scene in which the band's manager shoves a wad of alfalfa sprouts and powdered wheat germ into his mouth, after Joey, seeing the pile of pizzas Dee Dee's just brought in, shouts, "I want some!" Joey claimed to John Holmstrom that he had partly scripted the gag himself. He believed in the healing power of vitamins, supplements, and raw foods, that they could ease pain and stave off illness. All his life, he'd had health problems, and understandably he just wanted to feel well. He'd been born May 19, 1951, with a softball-sized teratoma tumor growing from his lower spine—an incompletely formed conjoined twin—and physical and mental ailments followed after him like Pigpen's dust cloud in *Peanuts*: sinus trouble, OCD, alcoholism, and just bad luck—he died of lymphoma, still young at forty-nine, in 2001. The initial idea for gagging Joey with health food also had come to Arkush during the trip to New York in August, when he'd watched the singer guzzle a Hemo-Tonic shake.

There's a moment in the dressing room scene, as well, that was shot when Riff walks up to Joey, Joey recognizes her, and the high school rock 'n' roller coos, "You remembered my name." Through the garlic-scented air the manager's blusterous voice zings: "Hey, girlie, this is the big time. This is rock 'n' roll." He's as protective of Joey as Eugene Landy was of Brian Wilson (and similarly creepy). With a scarlet scarf cinched around his throat, he grants the teenager permission to give her songs to her heroes, which prompts Joey, once his mouth is again empty, to say: "Yeah, we're gonna be in town one more day, and if we like 'em we'll come pay you and Mr. McGloo a visit." But he messed up his own pronunciation, adding a closing consonant to McGloo, which some hear as "b" and others as "p." In return for her song, Riff gets to leave the dressing room with a souvenir—a slice of pizza.

While the Ramones and P. J. worked inside the Whisky, the production assistant Mark Helfrich had his own adventure. In addition to his van, on occasion Mark drove "a Winnebago, a big Winnebago motorhome that was used whenever we were on location. This thing was huge, and I was young. I'm driving this giant motorhome down the street, and I would pick up hitchhikers. I had all this room, so it seemed like the thing to do. When I was on the job, I would give people rides. I also had to park the Winnebago behind the Whisky, which was very, very difficult. In fact, as I was backing it into the parking lot behind the club, there was a telephone pole with those metal protrusions that the men used to climb. Well, I backed into one of those and ripped a hole in the side of the Winnebago."

The last and most demanding day of shooting the Rockatorium sequence—and the final day of the Ramones' contracted obligation—came Thursday, December 13. This would be the toughest day of filming yet, an eighteen-hour stretch for the Ramones and longer for Arkush and the production crew, at the Roxy Theatre. The concert was to be a fantasy, a totally contrived event, with nonmusical material intercutting the band's performance. Needed were hundreds of extras to fill the rock hall. But there was no longer sufficient budget to pay off a huge crowd with so much spent on renting out the Whisky and the Roxy. So, in a manner that revealed the influence of the parsimonious Roger Corman on their thinking, Mike and Allan figured out how they could get extras to stick around the Roxy for several hours without remuneration: They would recruit actual Ramones fans—the more fervent, the better—and exploit their love for the band by promoting the faux concert as a real concert.

Mark Helfrich, *Rock 'n' Roll High School*'s peripatetic PA, in the days leading up to the Roxy shoot, posted promotional flyers to the telephone poles outside punk-friendly clubs in and around Hollywood like the Masque and Cathay de Grande. "BE IN A MOVIE!" screamed the words on the bill. "AND ATTEND AN EXCLUSIVE CONCERT! EXTRAS NEEDED . . . LIMITED SEATING AVAILABLE. TICKET RESERVATIONS REQUIRED." The campaign worked. "We get every fucking crazy punker in the world in there. If you look at those shots in the movie, you can see Darby Crash from the Germs. You could see members of the Alleycats, the Bags, Circle Jerks," Allan recalled for Daniel Griffith. Pat Smear, the Germs' guitar player, came too. The account of the story varies by who tells it, but in some versions, the Ramones played three concerts that day. Others argue two. The Helfrich flyer announced two: one at 8:30 a.m., another at 5:30 p.m. Johnny remembered three, as he recalled in *On the Road with the Ramones*: "The morning audience got in free, the afternoon audience paid two dollars and the night audience was five dollars. So, extras had to pay." Arkush told me: "I remember only two: but it was a very, very long day. Maybe twenty hours."

To the consternation of the "audiences" who filled the Roxy, several nonmusical scenes were to be filmed throughout the day, and when Arkush was busy, shooting the band mostly stopped. The crew early on shot a group scene away from the stage with McGree, Riff, Kate, and a second giant-mouse character (again with Rob Bottin inside), seeking admission into the concert hall. The ticket taker, played by Arkush wearing a T-shirt with "Fillmore East" stamped across the chest, denies admission to the Ramones-loving rodent. "Sorry, you can't come in. We've had too many mice exploding at these concerts." The mouse, in response, gestures to a pair of noise-blocking headphones he's brought along, and the ticket taker waves him in. Arkush had read an article in the *New York Times* about an experiment conducted on mice that gauged the potential for damage caused by loud sounds, which he'd thought would make for a good joke. As Arkush explained to Daniel Griffith: "This reporter had gone to the owner of a nightclub named Steve Paul. They said to Steve Paul, 'This information says that the people who come in your club are exposed to loud music. . . . It seems to be destroying the hearing of white mice.' And Steve Paul says, 'Absolutely, from now on, I will not allow any white mice into my club.' So, when I read that, it made me laugh, and it stayed in my head till I made the movie. That's where the white mouse thing came from and the blowing-up mice."

Other non-music shots included the two Fritzes riding a motorcycle, using a camera and a flash to photograph the kids at the concert, whom they'll report to Miss Togar. Loren Lester rode in the motorcycle's sidecar—the bike had been used in *Deathsport* and still featured the metallic plating it had been fitted with for the earlier picture. "I didn't relate to the whole rock and roll thing at all. I didn't understand it. The first time I heard the Ramones music was at the concert that we filmed, and I was deaf at the end of it. So I was perfect for that part because I couldn't get into it. I was Miss Togar's perfect lieutenant, to be fighting the rock-'n'-roll people. But then after the movie was over, I bought the soundtrack album, and I listened. I went, 'This is great. I wish I could have heard it during the concert.'"

The extras in the Roxy, especially the ones who paid admission, experienced few of the pleasures usually associated with rock 'n' roll concerts. One of Roger Corman's assistants Gale Anne Hurd—who'd go on to have a tremendous career as the producer behind the *Terminator* film series and *The Walking Dead* TV show—had been sent over from New World to the Roxy "to help out however I could." She wound up as an extra, standing on the dance floor in a swell of angry punks who "thought they were going to see a Ramones concert. They weren't being paid. They didn't realize that in order to film a sequence, you had to start a song, and the Ramones would play a few bars. Or there would be playback. And then it'd stop and start over again. They were not particularly happy with what they thought was a . . . concert that turned out to be, as anyone who's spent time on set, a rather tedious experience."

Finnell kept a watchful eye on the crowds throughout the day, monitoring the amount of frustration the extras could take before going nuts. "Just when they were about to riot and kill us, we got rid of them and brought in a whole new batch of extras, paying also. And then they were all fresh and all enthusiastic, excited," he told Jared Cowan.

Outside the Roxy, ensconced in a mobile recording truck like a hermit crab in its shell, Ed Stasium worked all through the day, into the night and the next morning to get clean "live" takes of "Blitzkrieg Bop," "Teenage Lobotomy," "Pinhead," "California Sun," and "She's the One" for the movie's soundtrack. "It was grueling. It was a long, long shoot," Ed said. The long pauses and the frantic, sputtering, abrupt manner in which the songs stopped and started extended the recording process over eighteen hours or so. "But we got certain takes that we could use." Ed later mixed the five-song set at Media Sound in New York, where he and the Ramones and Tommy Erdelyi had recorded *Road to Ruin* and where he had mixed the *It's Alive* concert record only a few months earlier. The five "live" songs recorded that day would appear on the soundtrack album Sire Records was planning to release in the summer of 1979, to line up with the film's theatrical release, which Seymour Stein had been told to expect by Arkush and Finnell.

Some extras grew so incensed over the stoppages that they attacked the actors. During the scene in which Riff and Kate move through the Rockatorium crowd so that Riff can hand a note to Joey asking him to dedicate a song to Tom and Kate, extras grabbed at P. J. and Dey, pawing at them, tugging their clothes, yanking their arms. "I was genuinely threatened when they started to roll the cameras. I had to literally push my way through," Dey remembered. "I was pinched, shoved, kicked, screamed at." The extras didn't understand that the actors had privileged access to different parts of the club, including the stage. "A few times, Allan had to stop, and with a bullhorn, say, 'Look, if you could please let our actors through. They're making their way from the back of the crowd to the front of the crowd.'" Dey added: "The Ramones had to speak on our behalf because we were trying to get through. We were being brutalized, pushed and tugged at. I was in total awe, shocked by it all." Michael Goodwin, keeping a safe distance from the scrum while observing it closely, noted that Dee Dee from the stage beseeched the audience, "The actors are real scared. They don't understand you. So you have to be nice to them."

The angry extras also knocked around Rob Bottin in his mouse costume. He was shooting a gag scene with Paul Bartel as Mr. McGree and an actor who'd been done up to look like an Indian chief: during the concert the trio—mouse, Native American, music teacher—pass a peace pipe back and forth, probably one packed with pot. Two days earlier at the Mayan, the crew had filmed the same Native American character approaching the line of extras, swinging a tomahawk and thrusting con- cert tickets at them; the joke is he's a ticket *scalper*. (Watch the Three Stooges, and you'll soon see caricatures of a similar sort, and these low- brow gags seem to be similarly done for laughs, not out of cruelty. Even so, the scalper character sorta hurts *Rock 'n' Roll High School*.)

Darby Crash, the front man for the Germs, and Lorna Doom, the band's bass player, had been enticed to the Roxy by Rodney Bingen- heimer's announcements on KROQ promoting the concerts and the flyers Mark Helfrich had posted around Hollywood. They were friends with Moon Davis, the Ramones' merch-table guy, who came to him saying, "We're drinking outside in-between shoots. Come out, and have some beer with us." But Moon had to decline. "I really don't have time for that," he told them. His boss, Arturo Vega, a few minutes ear- lier, had "come up to me, and said, 'Hey, Johnny wants you to be "the pinhead."'"

Johnny earlier had thought it would be funny if Rob Bottin made a mask that looked like the microcephalic people in *Freaks*, the inspira- tion for their "Pinhead" song. While Cundey and his camera assistants were filming, Johnny wanted the band to play the song as it always did, with Joey raising the "Gabba Gabba Hey" sign about halfway through. But now Johnny also wanted one of the crew to come out on the stage wearing the mask. Johnny felt that Moon was the right guy to hop up and down on the stage in simian fashion with the oversized mask on and a cotton shift.

"They brought a mask over to me, and I'm like, 'Well, this thing is hideous, and it's kind of big—It's big on me!'. . . . The Ramones were always getting thrown tubes of airplane glue on the stage when they were doing that 'Sniff Some Glue' tune. It was a joke. I mean, kids actually would throw tubes of Testors airplane glue on stage, and I guess Johnny saved some and used like half a tube on the face of the mask, on the mouth, to make it look like it was drooling. And the glue was not dry. I put the mask on just to try it out. I'm like, 'Oh, it's big, and I can't see where I'm going. And the inside of the mask is full of airplane-glue fumes. I didn't want to sniff glue. It's ridiculous. I'm like 'Can you hit it with a blow drier, and dry it off a little?' And they're like, 'Well, no. We need to do this right now.'"

Moon bounced across the stage in the clumsy mask and dress. "They shot it in one take. Johnny didn't want to do takes and takes because they'd been doing that at the high school over there at Mount Carmel. I put that mask on, and I got out there on stage. I'm not even in the movie for fifteen seconds, but I couldn't wait to get it off because I was just getting completely stoned."

The mask would become a constant feature at Ramones live shows. Monte A. Melnick in his memoir recalled: "After we included the pinhead character in *Rock 'n' Roll High School*, it became tradition for the drum roadie to put on the pinhead mask and run out during the song to dance onstage with the Gabba Gabba Hey sign." The original mask made by Rob Bottin disappeared not long after its creation, lost or stolen for a fan's reliquary, probably when the Ramones were touring the western states in the spring of 1979. "Over the years close friends of the band would ask to do the pinhead, such as Eddie Vedder, Rob Zombie and Lars Frederiksen. I even did the pinhead once when the drum roadie cut his hand on a stage fan right at the end of the show, so I went out in the mask. Damn that mask smelled!"

A camera problem affected the condition of the footage shot that day. "At the Roxy, Roger's big old Mitchell BNC, which was actually my age, kept losing synch and going off speed," Arkush explained to me, and as a result several shots appeared to be sped up when they played on a projector at regular speed. The editors at El Centro who assembled the film in January would allow some of this compromised content into the film, including a shot of Riff and Kate on the dance floor at the Rockatorium bouncing with accelerated intensity.

When the shooting for the day at the Roxy at last was done, Johnny had the band play a short show, with songs uninterrupted, as a gift of atonement to the crowd. "I felt bad because these kids had paid five bucks, and we had played the same five songs over and over again. So, when it was all over, I said I wanted to play more songs, and we played a few more songs. Then they pulled the plug on us."

It was almost 3:00 a.m., and the Ramones' commitment to the movie was finished. Allan thanked the guys and said goodbye. His body felt profoundly run down, but the white Ford Falcon carried him home safely along Sunset Boulevard, and he got in a couple hours of heavy, dreamless sleep, despite the ringing sound that lingered in his weary ears.

CHAPTER THIRTEEN

GIRLS' GYM

Some days were easier than others during production, and for the next one, Friday, December 15, Allan, working with a lighter crew, shot outdoors around the city, harvesting the dependable and always free daytime-LA sunlight for another car scene: this time, with Riff and Kate driving in a red Mustang to meet Tom and Eaglebauer to "get drunk," as Tom worded the invitation on his phone call to Riff from inside the Warlock: paltry recompense for missing the world's greatest punk band. Using cameras mounted to car doors and a camera car that tracked the Mustang as it was towed, this time around Van Nuys, Arkush and Cundey shot P. J. and Dey talking in the front seat and listening at the same time to Screamin' Steve's radio show. "I've got two free tickets to tonight's Ramones concert for the person who can call and tell me what album this song is on," the hyped-up radio jock hollers. "You know what to dial."

The song that Screamin' Steve plays is "Questioningly," the melancholy track from *Road to Ruin* that Arkush had confessed to disliking to

Ed Stasium months earlier. Riff after a second's consideration cries out the song's title. She not only has a vinyl copy of *Road to Ruin* at home in her bedroom but also a cassette copy in her car, which she and Kate quickly consult, confirming that the song playing on the radio indeed appears on the album. The two pull over at the next telephone booth they spy along the road. The crew would finish the scene the following week, with Riff and Kate rushing out of the Mustang into a payphone to call in to Screamin' Steve's station with their answer.

That evening the crew shot another street scene, this time with the two Fritzes—wearing leather airplane pilot caps and long scarves—riding their armored motorcycle madly through West Los Angeles. "We were towed," Loren Lester pointed out, who occupied the motorcycle's side-car. "We weren't actually driving the motorcycle. That would have been scary."

Fifteen shooting days out of twenty now on *Rock 'n' Roll High School* were done, and the weekend was here, but Allan couldn't really slow down. His hair had always been thick; over the course of the shoot it had grown shaggy, piled up on his head like Dylan's on the front of *Blood on the Tracks*. He still felt rough, yet he was happy with the film's progress. In a week, principal photography would wrap, after which he was going to have a day or two off before returning to his editing bench at El Centro to cut the picture.

At Nosseck's that Saturday, Allan met with Roger Corman and Mike Finnell to review the most recent batch of dailies. Corman said again that he liked what he was seeing, but, as he had before, he cautioned against overusing the Ramones, whose looks and mannerisms, while fascinating, carried, he warned, a potential to confound the teen demographic for which the picture, Allan and Mike had to remember, was being made. The Ramones that same day also swung by the screening room, but after Corman had left. They weren't happy with what they saw of the Ramones, either. "We were watching dailies of the scene where they drive up to the high school, and Dee Dee turns to me and goes, 'We look like we're from another planet.' I laughed. 'Exactly.' That was the theme of the movie. You identify with music that moves you, and you become part of a different society than the one you're in. You become part of a peer group of people who like that music and dress and act like those people," Arkush told Monte A. Melnick.

Johnny admitted to *Trouser Press*: "I didn't like going to see myself in the rushes. . . . I don't mind seeing films of ourselves in concert, but you see yourself in the movies, and you just know you could have been better, but you don't know how you could've done it. You get there early in the morning and spend most of the day sittin' there waitin' for your scene to come up. Then you have a two-minute scene, and you're all sleepy and wilted by that time." Joey in the same article sighed, "I came out depressed."

The fourth week of shooting had arrived with the production now at Van Nuys High School, the production's final location. Arkush and Finnell had been first attracted to the site because it "felt suburban" and because, unlike Mount Carmel, the campus had a spacious outdoor seating area and a central quad for shooting outdoor scenes. Most of the work Monday was done inside, however, in a classroom the set decorators had turned into a crude animal laboratory. Miss Togar is not merely a crypto-Nazi; she's a vivisectionist too, and joining her in the lab to witness one of her cruel experiments are faculty members Mr. McGree and Coach Steroid and Togar's bootlicking cronies, the two Fritzes.

Woronov for the scene drew hard on her Play-house of the Ridiculous days—leading her guests' attention to a white lab mouse she's stashed in an otherwise empty aquarium, grasping and swinging the animal by the base of its tail for what seems like an interminable period. "You're probably wondering why I asked you here," the harridan caws. "Since assuming office this morning, I've noticed a number of peculiar incidents among the members of the student body—all having to do with rock 'n' roll music. . . . Recently, I've been doing a study of mice subjected to rock 'n' roll music." Hard and sharp like the needle-leg of a compass, Togar pivots toward an easel that props up a large cartoon drawing of a mouse. "Here we have a picture of this mouse, a typical member of the genus *Rattus Rodentus* as he appeared before the start of my investigation," she intones, her words sodden with malice. "Clean, good natured, content to scamper playfully about his cage. This is a picture of the same mouse, one week after the introduction of rock 'n' roll music—oh, the results were dramatic." Miss Togar lifts the mouse drawing to reveal a second image of the same creature now wearing a leather motorcycle jacket, like a rodent Ramone. "He lost all interest in keeping his cage tidy. He played his electric guitar far into the night, keeping the other test animals awake. And he met this female mouse, and they have been sharing a cage together out of wedlock."

The principal's elucidation prompts a sycophantic Coach Steroid, played by Alix Elias, to declare, "That's fascinating, Miss Togar." Elias had been offered the Coach Steroid role after principal photography started, after Mamie Van Doren, the platinum-blonde veteran of numerous exploitation pictures, including Roger Corman's *Voyage to the Planet of Prehistoric Women*, and a face, too, in *High School Confidential*, who'd been considered for the part first, ultimately passed. Van Doren wanted her name given enhanced recognition in the movie's promotional materials and sought for more in terms of salary than Corman had been willing to give. Alix Elias was an acquaintance of Joe Dante's and Paul Bartel's and had appeared in a bawdy underground comedy Bartel directed a decade earlier called "Naughty Nurse." "My agent didn't want me to do *Rock 'n' Roll High School*. Roger Corman films were not the artistic treasures that they're considered today. They were considered pretty low rent, but I didn't care, I just wanted to work."

As the scene in the animal room progresses, Togar recounts: "I investigated reports of hearing loss by individuals due to the large number of decibels involved in the playing of rock 'n' roll music." She places the mouse-quarium near some speakers. "I will now play a song by the Ramones at a decibel level consistent with that found in the average rock 'n' roll concert hall." A device called the Rock-o-meter sits among the other pieces of equipment Miss Togar has arranged for her sonic experiment. On the machine appear the names of popular musical acts ranging from the milquetoast pop of Debby Boone and Donny & Marie to the hard rock of bands like Led Zeppelin and The Who, and the machine's highest level—its 11—the Ramones. Togar after returning the mouse to its glass box, switches the Rockometer to Ramones-level and "Suzy Is a Headbanger" (a track from *Leave Home*) thunders out from nearby speakers, causing the mouse's box to shake and rattle and the little creature inside to explode (a special effect, thank goodness).

Much of the shooting scheduled the next day would take place outside, starting with a second unit led by Joe Dante getting shots of the school in the morning light and around the patio area that extended from the school cafeteria. It's in this outdoor eating area filled with tables and sunlight where Tom Roberts, in the film's opening minutes, can be seen sitting in his varsity sweater reading a copy of Anne McCaffery's fantasy novel *Dragonsinger*—a nerdy book for a nerdy guy. Tom's teammates, wearing green-and-gold Green Bay Packers knockoff uniforms, barrel over the patio, bearing the bewildered freshman, played by Russ Dvonch, like a battering ram.

Nearby on the Van Nuys quad, Cundey and Arkush filmed the scene in which Riff and Miss Togar meet for the first time. The principal has stormed across the quad to find Riff and Kate at a jerry-rigged radio station, which they've concocted using spliced wires, a turntable filched from Mr. McGree's music class, headphones, and a mic. It's everybody's first day back at Vince Lombardi since winter break, the start of a buoyant new year. Although set at the start of the school day in the film, the scene was actually shot in the mid-afternoon, with long shadows spreading over the pavement in the school quad as the sun dropped ten miles away into the Pacific.

Riff has chosen this day to unleash the power of rock 'n' roll at boring, suburban, lily-white Vince Lombardi, calling out "This is rock 'n' roll high school!" and lowering the tone arm. The shot of Riff appears at the start of the picture, initiating the credits sequence behind which the students bop to the rolling thunder of "Sheena is a Punk Rocker." Rattled by the sound ripping through Vince Lombardi's PA system, the principal just moments into her appointed term storms across the schoolyard to the table where Riff stands wearing headphones, demanding her name. With sanguine smile and extended hand, the film's protagonist declares: "I'm Riff Randell, rock 'n' roller."

The next morning, Allan woke up feeling sick, but he headed out to Van Nuys High School in the Ford Falcon. Hurting though he was, the work had to be finished. Yet after he parked, his condition went down, down, down. He arrived at the school around 6:30 a.m., according to the *Penthouse* writer Michael Godwin, and entered the gymnasium, where he was going to direct the girls'-gym scene. "I was deeply green and deeply nauseous. I recall lying down and feeling it would be easier to direct the picture from the floor." He told Chris Nashawaty, "I *thought* I was having a heart attack. They called an ambulance, and I had to go to hospital. What I had was arrhythmia. My heart was beating too fast. . . . mostly from exhaustion." He was suffering, the doctors determined, from "dehydration, flu . . . and food poisoning," the consequence of "eighteen-hour days, lousy catering and excessive proximity to the high-decibel Ramones."

It was Alix Elias's second day on the production. "I arrived as an ambulance pulled out with Allan in it. He'd had some kind of a collapse. It turned out to be nothing, but they were concerned enough that they wanted him to go to the hospital and get an EKG and make sure that he wasn't having a heart attack." The production needed another director who could take over immediately. Mike Finnell reached out to Joe Dante, and he agreed to fill in as replacement director.

Ron Howard showed up at the high school that day too but not to assist with directing; he'd been scheduled to be an extra in a scene in which Eaglebauer orchestrates the creation of a human pyramid for Tom Roberts to climb atop and peer from into the women's shower room at Vince Lombardi. None of this content, however, found its way into the completed film. Dante said, "It wasn't a particularly interesting scene, but that's not why [the editors] decided to cut it out—and it was not because they didn't want Ron in the movie. . . . This was not going to be an R-rated movie. It had to be a PG movie that could play a lot of places." Keeping the footage with Tom leering at his semi-naked friends would have sullied the audience's perception of the character anyway. Part of the film's thematic concerns is Tom's maturation as a person—the perplexed geek, albeit an all-American square-jawed one, who ultimately conducts himself chivalrously when he recovers Riff's music from Angel Dust, the result of which is his epiphany that the ideal romantic cohort for him is not the anarchic songwriter but her comparatively staid best friend.

Dante and Cundey also filmed in the school's cafeteria Clint Howard and a pack of extras hurling scoops of Tuesday Surprise and, for dessert, Brown Betty, at their torturers—their betrayers—the school lunch ladies. "We were only following the recipes!" one of the cooks cries, echoing the "We were only following orders" defense used by the Nazis at Nuremberg. A cannibalism gag with Russ Dvonch, looking out bewilderedly from a vat, was also filmed—the featured hot lunch meal that day at Vince Lombardi is Freshman Helper.

With Allan still stuck in the hospital on Thursday, the production's penultimate shooting day, Joe Dante and Dean Cundey were left to figure out how to film the musical number in which Riff Randell sings "Rock 'n' Roll High School" during P.E. as gymnasts in pastel leotards flounce about her. The mood in the Van Nuys gymnasium as the day started was not good. "All of us were concerned about Allan," Soles said. "We were all blaming Roger Corman for his poor health. He'd been feeling all the pressure to prove that he could bring this movie in on budget and on time and deliver a great product."

Joe Dante had never shot a dance sequence before, and he hadn't read the Whitley-Dvonch script, either. So Joe asked Dean, "Did Allan have a plan?"

"Yeah," the DP answered, handing him a notebook with an inscrutable sequence of Xs and Os sprawled over its pages, prompting the replacement director to ask, "What the fuck is this?"

"I had never choreographed anything, so I figured the only way to make it work was to shoot it in little pieces, like a Beatles movie and just . . . not worry about staging it or choreographing it, but just doing it shot by shot," Joe said. "So Dean and I really couldn't figure it out at all. We basically decided to do it in a sort of Richard Lester style, where it's just pieces. We shot all the pieces separately, and then cut them together in a sort of music-video kind of a way. And for a salvage job, it was pretty good," he told Robert Nuñez.

For the nonmusical moments in the girls'-gym scene, Dante adhered to the shooting script closely, starting with a shot of Kate grasping the top of a climbing rope, up near the gym's ceiling—her face knitted with anxiety. Then Kate's grip slips, and she plummets and fortunately—inexplicably—isn't hurt. Loren Lester's hall monitor subsequently swings into the gymnasium using the same rope from which Kate just fell—and passes a note (another one!) on to Coach Steroid: Togar wants her in the animal room.

To keep the students occupied, the coach presses the play button on a tape deck and the fangless piano pop tune "The Alleycat" starts. The students form a line and get to it with calisthenics, but once the unpleasantly stern coach departs, Riff springs at the tape player and drops in her recording of "Rock 'n' Roll High School," the song she's written for the Ramones.

After Riff cries, "Gym called on account of boredom!" she bounds along, holding a microphone, jumping rope and singing as her classmates shimmy and dip around the auditorium, while the gymnasts caper on balance beams, flip around parallel bars, and arc through the air. Riff's and Kate's schoolmate chums, Cheryl and Shawn, in their tight tops bop; Riff takes up the jump rope and like a boxer hops; Kate at first seems a little lost, but soon she's swaying to the beat too. When the song ends, so does the dancing, and as Coach Steroid returns from her visit to the animal lab accompanied by Miss Togar, Mr. McGree, and the swinish hall monitors, she finds the students exercising, doing jumping jacks, as she's instructed them, with "The Alleycat" again tinkling from the tape deck's speakers.

P. J. was in especially good physical condition during the shoot: She'd been taking kickboxing lessons at an academy in Hollywood. "Jumping rope was part of our routine: hit the bag, jump rope, run up the stairs. 'Well, I'm not going to compete with the gymnasts,' I realized, 'but I can jump rope.' So I brought my jump rope to the high school. Riff's character, more than gymnastics or dancing, is athletic." Altogether, the actress was pleased with the day's work. "It was really fun. It was beautifully choreographed. It was just movement," she admitted to

Robert Nuñez, "and the energy was all there, and it was great, with the exception that Allan wasn't there with us."

The work on the climbing rope for the actors was tough too. "They kept bringing me up and down," Dey told film scholar James M. Tate, which left her with rope burns on her hands. "[T]hat was a really wicked rope and getting me up there was always a challenge, because I had to shimmy." Yet Dey was again playing her character in a manner much different from her actual self. "You know, the interesting thing is I'm really athletic. So not playing athletic was . . . I mean, I was a real tomboy growing up. I was on all the athletic teams, and everything like that. So that really wasn't that challenging for me, but I had to make it look like 'Oh, my God, I'm about to. . . .' You know, and I'm afraid of heights and all of that, and I'm stuck. But to tell you the truth, it wasn't a painful thing for me, except for I had to act like it was."

Loren Lester remembered, "The way the scene was originally written was that I was supposed to be at the top of the rope and sliding down. They had this huge ladder, and they put me up at the top of the rope with my feet on the knot. 'Okay. Camera's rolling. Slide down!' I had never slid down a rope in my life. I didn't know what was going on. I was, like, *terrified*. And they're like, 'Cut, cut. Can you slide down?' I said, 'I don't know how to slide down a rope. I've never done this before.' I was at least twenty feet off the ground, probably more, because it had to be out of the sight line of the camera. I said, 'I know it's in the script, but I don't know how to do this.' So they changed it to my swinging in on the rope."

On the twentieth and final day of shooting, Friday, December 22, Dante and the crew started with a scene filmed outdoors on Sepulveda Boulevard, a few blocks from Van Nuys High School. Riff and Kate, having recognized the song "Questioningly" on Screamin' Steve's radio show, have pulled over Riff's Mustang at a telephone booth to call in with their answer to win a pair of tickets to the Ramones concert that night at the Rockatorium. Arkush had overseen the shooting of the two friends driving in Riff's Mustang with the radio the previous week, but now Dante had to finish the scene. What he needed was for Riff and Kate to spring from the watermelon-red car toward a telephone booth and force out a guy who's inside it at that moment proposing marriage to someone. As the high schoolers force the flustered bridegroom-to-be from the glass telephone booth, he drops the engagement ring he's brought and starts to search for it, crawling along the pavement. Riff wins the contest, and she leaps out of the booth, stomping up and down gleefully, smashing the engagement ring and the poor man's hand under her tennis shoes. The male actor in the scene, George Wagner, was an editor at El Centro.

Everyone sped over to Van Nuys High after this wild scene that plays like a bit from a Three Stooges short to shoot footage of Riff and her classmates in a shower room, washing away the sweat they've worked up dancing to "Rock 'n' Roll High School" in Coach Steroid's gym class. An accompanying take of Tom leering at the girls through a window and one of P. J. with her top off were also shot but never used. Dante and Cundey got a long-take shot of Riff, Kate, and their classmates in white towels drying themselves, studying their reflections in a wide mirror as Riff implores them to join her at the Rockatorium to buy tickets for the upcoming Ramones show. But no one wants to or can. This is Riff's *High Noon*, and like Sheriff Will Kane she retains her resolve, and as her friends make rationalizations for not joining her, she scrawls "TOGAR SUCKS" with a tube of lipstick across the washroom's mirror and then, like the Little Red Hen, announces that she will get the tickets herself: "I guess it's up to me . . . I'm taking a three-day leave from Camp Lombardi and be first in line."

One final scene, of Vince and Dey and several extras in the shower room, was shot that night, during which, unfortunately, Dey got hurt. "We were in a jacuzzi with bubbles, I'm not sure it even made the final edit," she said. "That's when Vince Van Patten and I actually slipped and cracked each other's heads. I really hurt the cartilage in my nose." Dey would notify New World about the injury, but as she'd signed a liability waiver the company had no obligation to cover her medical costs. "I was so green, I have no idea what I signed back then."

And then that was it: shooting on *Rock 'n' Roll High School* was a wrap. Joe Dante had come in, like a good relief pitcher, and carried

Make the music go bang: Riff and the Ramones blow things up at Vince Lombardi High.
Photo by Carin Abramson / © New World Pictures

Dee Dee Ramone, Joey Ramone, P.J. Soles, Johnny Ramone and Marky Ramone star in
ROCK 'N ROLL HIGH SCHOOL, a New World picture. The original soundtrack featuring
The Ramones is available on Sire Records and Tapes.

Riff and her idols, the Ramones.
Photo by Carin Abramson / © New World Pictures

Roger George's early-morning detonations woke up Watts.
Photo by Carin Abramson / © New World Pictures

On a roll with the Ramones.
Photo by Carin Abramson / © New World Pictures

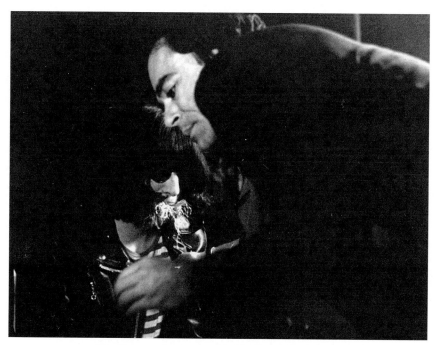

The Ramones' manager (Herbie Braha) feeds Joey.
Photo by Carin Abramson / © New World Pictures

Hey, pizza!
Photo by Carin Abramson / © New World Pictures

Mark Helfrich: the peripatetic PA.
Courtesy Richard Whitley

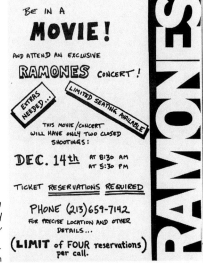

The flyer Mark Helfrich posted around Hollywood to promote the Ramones' concerts at the Roxy.
Courtesy Mark Helfrich

BE IN A
MOVIE!
AND ATTEND AN EXCLUSIVE
RAMONES CONCERT!

EXTRAS NEEDED...   LIMITED SEATING AVAILABLE

THIS MOVIE/CONCERT
WILL HAVE ONLY TWO CLOSED
SHOOTINGS:

DEC. 14th AT 8:30 AM
AT 5:30 PM

TICKET RESERVATIONS REQUIRED

PHONE (213) 659-7142
FOR PRECISE LOCATION AND OTHER
DETAILS...

(**LIMIT** of FOUR reservations)
per call.

The Ramones at the Roxy.
Photo by Carin Abramson / © New World Pictures

Riff approaches Joey in the Rockatorium.
Photo by Carin Abramson / © New World Pictures

Rob Bottin in his mouse costume with friends.
Photo by Carin Abramson / © New World Pictures

Moon Davis, the Ramones' first pinhead.
Photo by Carin Abramson / © New World Pictures

Dey Young and P. J. Soles: friends on both sides of the slate.
Credit: Photo by Carin Abramson / © New World Pictures

The girls' gym number Joe Dante would end up directing. (In the foreground, left to right: Marla Rosenfield, P. J. Soles, Chris Somma.)
Photo by Carin Abramson / © New World Pictures

The faculty aghast! (Left to right: Mary Woronov, Paul Bartel, Alix Elias).
Photo by Carin Abramson / © New World Pictures

Kent Beyda & Mark Helfrich

Michael Finnell & Allan Arkush

Gail Werbin

Joe Dante

The post-production team at El Centro.
Photo by Carin Abramson / © New World Pictures

Bill Stout's lobby poster for Rock 'n' Roll High School.
© New World Pictures

the production to completion. He's always been self-effacing about his contributions to the picture. "[It] was a really fun movie to make," he told Chris Nashawaty. "Then Allan got sick, and he couldn't finish the last couple of days. So I came and shot a couple of days. But it's Allan's movie." For his efforts, Dante would receive a note of special thanks in the film's closing credits.

For Christmas, P. J. Soles hosted a dinner at her home, having over members from both the film's crew and cast. The Ramones received an invitation too. "I like them very much. In fact I invited them all over to my house for a big family turkey dinner around Christmas time. When they arrived at my house that afternoon they were all dressed up and looked very nice, like little gentlemen! They were very sweet, and my family enjoyed them very much." Soles elaborated on her memories of spending Christmas with the Ramones to *Shock Cinema*'s Anthony Petkovich: "[I]t was at my home with Dennis in North Hollywood on Huston Street. . . . So the Ramones came over and just took a look at everything—I had yams, mashed potatoes, green beans—and they said . . . 'Ohhhh. We don't eat that kinda food.' I'm like, 'What do you mean?' They go, 'Yeah, we don't like that. We never had that.' I said, 'You never had Christmas dinner or Thanksgiving dinner?' 'Not Really. . . . Is there a good pizza place nearby?' And I literally had to send Dennis out to bring back pizza for them."

POST

It was in the editing rooms at El Centro where Allan could again infuse the creation of *Rock 'n' Roll High School* with his ideas and personality. "After I got out of the hospital, which was about, actually, three days after I got in, I go to the editing room, [and] we start cutting the picture," Arkush disclosed to Daniel Griffith. The pressure was intense to get something semi-coherent for Corman to review. "Usually, Roger *insists* upon seeing a movie a week after shooting. He does this because he knows that it's impossible to have a decent rough cut after only one week. And that allows him to step in and 'save' the film. His usual line is 'There's a good picture here somewhere, all we have to do is make it work.' And that's when the power play starts," Dante told Roger Corman profiler David Chute. Yet when Allan screened the rough cut at Nosseck's the first Saturday after Christmas, which he'd cut with help from Joe Dante and Larry Bock, the same editor he'd worked with so well on *Deathsport*, he didn't experience much in terms of resistance or interference from Corman. "I think Roger felt a little bad for me," Allan reflected. "He didn't give me many notes."

Frank Moreno, handling New World's sales and distribution, had developed a deep distaste for *Rock 'n' Roll High School*—it didn't strike him as a marketable film, and he'd decided that he was going to release it with minimal support and accommodation from his office. The rock 'n' roll movie he was going to use New World money to promote was The Who documentary he had bought at Cannes, *The Kids Are Alright.* Instead of keeping with the original plan to have the Arkush movie delivered to theaters in the summer, to line up with the end of the American school year, he moved the release up to mid-April 1979, set on using New World's follow-the-sun distribution plan, having the film open not in indie movie houses in LA or New York, where the Ramones had piles of fans, but in drive-ins and hard-top movie theaters in warm Texas—the state where the truck stop attendant had referred to the Ramones as "these retarded boys" to Monte A. Melnick.

The decision to move up the release exasperated Allan and Mike. Having to work faster to get the movie out was one thing. But Sire Records had been told to plan the soundtrack album for a midsummer release. Allan lamented, "The whole point was to do what the big people did: have an album and a movie [like] *Saturday Night Fever, Thank God It's Friday.*" The push to get the movie out in April, which Corman endorsed, impelled him to seek a second editor to assist with cutting the film. "Allan was going to cut *Rock 'n' Roll High School* himself, but then he got sick," said Larry Bock. "Then Allan brought on me and Gail Werbin to edit. When Allan recovered, he was just directing us. Allan was the man with all the knowledge. . . . Joe Dante was involved. So was Paul Bartel; he actually cut a scene, too. Everybody was kind of jumping in and working on it." Gail Werbin, who died in a car wreck in 1982, like Bock, had graduated from USC's Cinematic Arts program; she'd also been a fellow in the American Film Institute's Center for Advanced Film Studies. There seems to have been little direct communication between the two lead editors, however, with Werbin working in a cutting room on El Centro's second floor and Larry Bock on the first. Bock had frequent exchanges, on the other hand, with a pair of assistant editors, Mark Helfrich and Kent Beyda, who shared the hallway with him.

"All the doors were open," Beyda said, "and people were just coming in and out all the time. It was a very free-for-all atmosphere, very collegial: definitely a group of people who had similar interests and similar ideas, who bonded together."

Helfrich recollected. "During production, I'd been the PA who took the film to the lab for development, and I also took the work print from the lab to the editing room, which is how I got to know Kent," Helfrich recollected. "After we wrapped, I didn't want to leave *Rock 'n' Roll High School* behind, so I just hung out in the editing room. There were two editors, and they needed another assistant. So I became the other assistant. I volunteered and worked at El Centro for at least a month every day for free. Everybody was so welcoming and friendly and encouraging, and they liked cool music. We could bring in records and say, 'How about this for this scene?' Everybody would have an opinion, and we felt like we were doing something important. Depending on where you were standing in the hallway, or upstairs, or downstairs, you could hear different songs blasting out of the offices. It was like living in a rock 'n' roll paradise."

"The cutting rooms at 1607 El Centro were small," Larry said. "What else is new? But the great thing was Hollywood Legion Lanes across the street had some classic pinball machines, and the World Theater, which played triple bills of B movies for ninety-nine cents, was only a couple of blocks away."

"The atmosphere at New World was 'If you want to do it, do it.' Everybody was working for the movie, and any wild idea you had got a response like 'Try it. Why not? You have nothing to lose,'" Mark said.

The editors had access to the same archive of previously released feature films and outtakes Arkush and Dante had raided for *Hollywood Boulevard*. In the collection were several movies Roger Corman had directed and produced before 1970, the year he quit directing and founded New World Pictures. "In the cutting room, we could use old Corman movies if we needed a shot of something," said Mark. "They had a rich history of mining and recycling the shots and putting them in different movies."

"That was the New World ethos: just make it work, even if you have to blow it up and make it weird. As long as it works, that's what counts, you know? One of the shots of the school building collapsing comes from Roger's *House of Usher*; it's intercut with the school footage," said Kent.

Handling the editing equipment could be exhausting. *Rock 'n' Roll High School* "was edited on film, 35-millimeter film, on Moviolas," said Mark. "Generally, when you're cutting 35-millimeter films, there were three separate mag reels of sound. One was the dialogue, one was the music, and one was the sound effects. When the film was actually cut, it was just one strip of film and one mag-stripe of sound. When the songs were edited, we would just have the mag-stripe of the transfer of the song. And when the dialogue scenes were edited, you'd just have the dialogue that was recorded on the set. Then, you build a second and maybe a third reel of sound effects. When the paper plane goes in Paul Bartel's ear, for example, we wanted a sound. We just found a sound from the sound library and had it transferred to mag and cut it into that second reel. Now, if there happened to be more sound effects in a specific scene, then of course you could put sound effects in the music reel too."

One sound effect the editors exploited was a recording of birds chirping, which they cut into the establishing shot of Vince Lombardi High School that opens the picture. The birdsong on the soundtrack at once sounds like "cheep-cheep-cheep" and "cheap-cheap-cheap," subtly teasing, as Arkush has claimed in numerous interviews and commentaries, Corman's tightfistedness and the $280,000 film itself.

The editors introduced snatches of numerous songs made available to them through the deal that had been hashed out between Warner Bros. Records and Sire Records. Kent remembered that "Seymour Stein . . . came to the cutting room at least once. And we were in touch with local people at Warner Brothers, who were involved with Sire. We would just go in and get albums. Or they came from our collections. We would go home and say, 'Oh, maybe this will work,' and transfer it to a cassette, and then bring the cassette in and have that transferred to mag." After *Rock 'n' Roll High School*, Beyda went on to edit a pair of rock 'n' roll movies that rank, along with *Rock 'n' Roll High School*, among the most highly regarded examples of the genre—*The Unheard Music*, a documentary about the beloved Los Angeles punk band X, and the heavy-metal mockumentary *This Is Spinal Tap*. He would also edit Arkush's musical comedy follow-up to *Rock 'n' Roll High School*, *Get Crazy*.

The editors had access to songs from other sources, too. "We used some of Brian Eno's *Music for Film* in the chemicals-mixing scene," said Allan—a moment in the movie when Kate creates the explosive compound the students used to blow up Vince Lombardi. "Eno had that album out . . . and all you'd have to do was call up the number they had on the back [and] send him a check for $200," Allan remembered on the DVD commentary he cut with Finnell and Whitley. The editors introduced songs from the Velvet Underground ("Rock & Roll"), Nick Lowe ("So It Goes"), Alice Cooper ("School's Out"), and MC5 ("High School")—thirty-four tracks altogether. They also had an unreleased song from Paul McCartney to work with, "Did We Meet Somewhere Before?" a happy coincidence for Allan and all the others who'd adored *A Hard Day's Night*. McCartney with his band Wings had recorded the song for *Heaven Can Wait*, a Warren Beatty romantic comedy about a professional football player who dies and comes back to life. But the song, a clarinet-soaked lullaby that evokes the Beatles' "When I'm Sixty-Four," hadn't made it onto the Beatty film's soundtrack. For $500, Finnell had secured the rights to use the song, which can be heard during the film's opening sequence as the sweet light of the Southern California morning dapples the trees around the entrance of Vince Lombardi High. It finds use again in the scene when Eaglebauer drives Kate to Lovers' Lane for her sex-ed lesson with her training partner, Tom.

Joey's recovery from his earlier mentioned tea kettle mishap led to the recording of another song that would show up on *Rock 'n' Roll High School*'s soundtrack, a revved-up take on Ritchie Valens' "Come On Let's Go," which the three Ramones in LA recorded with another Sire recording act, the Paley Brothers, at the end of 1977. The western part of the Ramones' tour had been canceled after the accident, but they had gone to LA anyway to "do interviews and anything else their establishment record company told them they should do," according to the *Los Angeles Times*. Seymour Stein in his memoir *Siren Song* explained: "Johnny, Dee Dee and Tommy were getting restless sitting around the Tropicana Motel with nothing to do. There was mutual respect between the Ramones and the Paley Brothers because both bands were into power pop. The Paleys were in the Beach Boys' studio in Santa Monica with Earle Mankey. So one night I brought the Ramones over and, with Joey's blessing, cut a song . . . 'Come On Let's Go'. . . . My wife, Linda, insisted they use the song in the Ramones movie *Rock 'n' Roll High School* in the scene where the school blows up."

Andy Paley, who'd subsequently work for Sire as a producer and make great records with Brian Wilson and Jerry Lee Lewis, explained: "Danny Fields had called. He was managing the Ramones, and he said, 'The Ramones are in LA. They're in Hollywood, and they're staying at the Tropicana Motel. Why don't you guys get together? You're friends anyway.' We knew the Ramones from New York. My brother had been hanging out at CBGBs all the time. I was not. I would just go once in a while, but my brother was there, like, every night. Anyway, we were all friends with the Ramones, and they said they'd like to do something, maybe come over to a studio, the Beach Boys' studio, Brother, and maybe record something. Seymour Stein and Danny talked, throwing ideas around for songs to do. Earlier on the Bang label, the McCoys had recorded a version of Ritchie Valens' 'Come On Let's Go.' We all knew that version. Johnny Ramone was very enthusiastic about it. The Ramones showed up, they came to Brother and set up Marshall amps. And then Jonathan sang lead; I sang the harmony. As I remember it, the recording didn't take very long. It wasn't like we had to rehearse. We just played it. Earle Mankey, the producer, was on the other side of the glass. We were in the room singing and playing. My brother and I were off to the side, and Earle was in the control room, producing the track."

"Brother studio at that time had a very, very mellow vibe—laid-back-California, Beach-Boys-ee," remembered Jonathan. "And they had a fish tank in the control room, a big fish tank with all these tropical fish in it. The Ramones came in, and they began laying down the basic track.

They went through it a few times. They were playing really loud—I mean really, really loud. Even in the control room it was loud. Even with the volume down it was coming through the triple-glass-pane window. I noticed at one point, during playback, that all the fish in the aquarium had burrowed down into the sand at the bottom of the tank. Then Andy and I cut the vocals. I was singing lead, Andy's doing a low harmony, and we added some hand claps."

"I don't think we did that many takes of it," said Andy. "It was a single in the UK, but I don't know why it didn't come out in the US. Maybe the Ramones didn't want it to come out. Maybe Joey didn't want it. I really don't know. The funny thing is Joey told me he really liked it. But it could have been also just a thing where they didn't think it was smart to release it because the Ramones were trying to get a hit on their own. The Ramones were very much in search of a hit record. I don't think they wanted to have it with the Paley Brothers singing lead. I don't blame them. But everybody liked it."

"It's actually the last studio recording with Tommy playing drums with the Ramones," Jonathan noted.

The editors at El Centro used "Come On Let's Go" twice in the finished picture, not, as Seymour Stein remembered, when the school blows up, but rather as the final credits roll, *after* the explosion. It can be heard, as well, when the Ramones shove the hall monitors through the second-floor window of the high school.

Whenever an opportunity to work on promotional content for *Rock 'n' Roll High School* presented itself, the assistant editors, Kent Beyda and Mark Helfrich, would jump. "We asked whether we could cut the trailer. . . . They needed a trailer, so they said, 'Yeah, go for it.' So Kent and I cut the trailer. On your first movie that was crazy. Joe and Allan had started out cutting trailers, so just to get a 'sure' from Allan was a blessing. Kent and I took it very seriously. We spent nights there putting together the trailer because we wanted it to be fun and good, and then to show it to them for their approval. We ordered all the opticals. They were done literally next door, at Jack Rabin's, in the same hallway, the next office over."

Kent said, "I remember working on the trailer on New Year's Day in the cutting room, and Joe Dante was there. There was an earthquake. The whole building started shaking. We all waited outside, stood in front, and when the shaking stopped, Joe said, 'Well, the Hollywood sign's still there, so I guess it's okay to go back in.' So we went back in and went back to work."

One of their contributions almost got the assistant editors into real trouble. "There had been so much footage shot of the concerts because they'd had a lot of cameras. So much of it we hadn't even been able to get through, but we were having a screening," said Kent. "Mark and I came into the cutting room that morning to get everything ready to bring to the screening. We were just running some reels, and we saw this one that had Dey Young and P. J. Soles at the foot of the stage watching and cheering. There was a camera glitch; the camera started slowing down, but for some reason, the exposure didn't change. So the girls start moving faster and faster and faster and faster until they become a blur. We were like, 'Ah, this is great. We have to cut this in.' So we put it in the movie and then raced over to the screening. Mike Finnell was there. He was very upset, yelling at us, saying, 'If Roger knew about this, we could lose our jobs.' We screen the movie, and my memory of it is that it went really well. When that particular part of the concert came up and people saw that shot of the girls, they started cheering and just laughing—because it was totally unexpected."

"I thought we would get fired for going in and recutting a scene without telling anybody and then screening it for the main producer, which was like 'What? Unheard of!'" said Mark. "But because of the atmosphere at the cutting room there, it was fine."

"On a normal movie the assistant editors would not have the wherewithal, the ability, or the permission to do anything like that," said Kent. "But at the Corman School and on *Rock 'n' Roll High School* it was a whole different thing, you know?"

Steering the advance advertising campaign for *Rock 'n' Roll High School* were Jeff and Steve Shank, who, like Jon Davison before them, assembled press kits, planned out trailers and radio and TV spots, and often the visual promotional materials, like lobby posters and lobby cards. It was Corman himself, while the film was still in production, though, who asked commercial artist Bill Stout to design the lobby poster.

Stout recalled in a 2021 interview that Corman's "directions to me . . . were really simple. He said, 'Bill, you can do whatever you want as long as it looks like [the poster for] *Animal House*.' That's why it's drawn in the Rick Meyerowitz style." Meyerowitz had done the cartoon poster for *Animal House*. "And it was a fun gig. To get the photo reference," for a sense of what the actors and settings of a movie look like, "I went to where Allan Arkush and Joe Dante were doing the editing, which was just down the street from my apartment. And I remember entering the editing room, and it was like seeing two kids in the ultimate candy shop. They were having so much fun, and they said, 'Look, wait, let me just cut this scene. You want to see the scene?' It was just fantastic. These guys were so enthusiastic. And because they were shooting the film in town, I was also running into the Ramones at my favorite taco and burrito place, Los Tacos. It seemed like almost every time I went in there, there was at least two of the guys from the band there. I had a reputation for being fast, and I developed that reputation because my favorite artist, Jack Davis, made over a million a year doing posters. So I thought that's a good goal. I developed styles in which I could work very quickly. I think the *Rock 'n' Roll High School* poster probably took a week or two at the most."

Allan and the editors began the process of getting the film rated for release, a task overseen by the Motion Picture Association of America. Joe Dante told me, "We submitted the rough cut, often in black & white to save money, and if there was an issue they'd ask to see it in color. That went for the features, trailers and TV spots. If they assigned a rating we didn't want we would have to make cuts and resubmit. At no point would they tell us what offended them or what to cut. 'That would be *censorship*.' This hypocrisy made everything three times as difficult, and sometimes we'd have to go back several times with different cuts. And since they had no editing equipment at their office they could never tell exactly what we had changed—sometimes it was nothing!" They submitted until they got the coveted PG rating, with a final running time between ninety-three and ninety-four minutes.

As *Rock 'n' Roll High School* moved closer to completion through post, New World found itself on the receiving end of a complaint Joseph McBride had filed with the Writers Guild of America West over his credit for his contributions to the film as a screenwriter in 1977. McBride felt that he deserved a first-position writing credit, for his name, that is, to appear above Whitley's and Dvonch's on the screen—a first-position credit carries more recognition, more professional prestige, in Hollywood. The WGA ultimately sided with New World's recommendations regarding the credit, but while investigating the paper trail left by everyone who'd worked on the script—not just McBride, Dvonch, and Whitley, but also Griffith, Dante, and Arkush—the WGA arbitrators found that Corman had been too stingy with payments for services rendered by the writers. Corman's efforts to get around WGA rules, at least this time, kicked back at him like a gray mule, and he eventually pulled away from the WGA, no longer acting as a signatory.

In March, *Rock 'n' Roll High School* had a private preview screening at the main offices of Pacific Theatres, a company located on North Robertson Avenue, near the office Finnell and Arkush had used during preproduction, which managed a powerful transnational movie theater chain. The screening went well for the majority of those who attended—various exhibitors, distributors, and marketing people—but one evaluator attached to "Pacific Theatres did not like this movie, saying there was a problem with blowing up the school." This lone expression of worry carried great weight for Frank Moreno, validating what Arkush referred to as his "suspicions about the movie." New World audiences came to their exploitation-grade releases to look at pretty actresses taking showers, not Ramones. And blowing up a school, thematically, was reprehensible.

Toward the end of March, *Rock 'n' Roll High School* had its first public screening at the World Theatre on Hollywood Boulevard, just blocks from Jack Rabin & Associates, where it was triple-billed with the Who documentary, *The Kids Are Alright*, and an original New World

Pictures country-music drama from 1976 called *Nashville Girl*. The admission tickets that night were discounted, with the expectation that attendees would complete questionnaires about what they perceived as the featured movies' defects and attributes. The World Theatre—owned by the Pacific Theatres chain!—catered to audiences that liked violent action-adventures, heavy on T & A, stunts, and car chases, not much of which a PG-rated *Rock 'n' Roll High School* could offer. Kent Beyda said. "I remember wondering why the hell we were screening it at a Hollywood Boulevard grindhouse. That was obviously not the audience for that movie."

But some local punk rockers showed up at the World Theatre that night, around thirty or so, a coincidental happening. Yet when Corman and Moreno watched as the kids with mohawks, piercings, fishnet stockings, and combat boots streamed into the theater, they presumed they were ringers coached by Allan to say nice things about the movie on the response cards in the lobby. Yet, as the director explained it, the punks lived in "this abandoned apartment building . . . right next to the Masque, which was *the* club at the time. So, they're coming there because there's music-movies playing. They have no idea *Rock 'n' Roll High School*'s going to play there. The tickets are just $1.50 this one night. So, Frank asks, 'What's going on here?' I say, 'Frank, this is their local theater. I got no control over them coming in.'" He elaborated for Griffith. "It didn't help that one of the stars of the film showed up at that night at the World Theatre, too. Roger keeps saying, 'I hope none of your friends are showing up here,' and who comes walking up in sunglasses and a beret, trying to look, with a newspaper over his face, like he wasn't there—Paul Bartel."

A favorable response from the audience left Allan feeling confident for the film's future, especially if Moreno and Corman got smart and marketed it properly to audiences like the punks who'd showed up tonight, and in big cities like New York, Chicago, San Francisco, and Los Angeles, where people who'd heard of and loved the Ramones lived. Moreno was unmoved. "Everything in the movie plays like gangbusters. Everything about the Ramones gets a huge reaction. We come out of there. I feel great. But Frank is beside himself. He hates the movie. 'This is not our audience!' He's absolutely convinced that I have cooked the books, so to speak."

Corman, on the sidewalk outside the World Theater, informed Allan that he wanted him to gouge away the middle sections of the musical sequences: The Ramones slowed the movie down, and they were unappealing. Allan had created a New World movie that people who liked New World movies and associated them with a certain predictable balance of sex, violence, comedy, and left-wing social statement—the company's house style—would reject. But the director, who'd been working for Corman for five years by then, would not hear it, telling him that recutting and remixing the movie would be too costly to justify the effort, and Corman backed off. Unfortunately, Corman's retreat made Moreno angrier at Allan, and the possibility of having the picture held until summer, when the soundtrack album from Sire would be ready, was scotched.

What should have been a great night for Arkush was anything but. For Richard Whitley and Russ Dvonch, however, the opportunity to attend the first public screening of the picture they'd worked on so thoroughly was only positive. Rich said, "We went to Western Costume. We went and had dinner at Musso and Frank's. We'd rented top hats, tails and walking sticks, and with jeans and Converse, of course, to honor the Ramones. Then we strolled down Hollywood Boulevard dressed like that to the theater." The two writers would go on to work together again, contributing a script ("The Guns of October") to the *Delta House* TV show, a series adapted from the John Landis comedy *Animal House*, which ran on ABC in the winter and spring of 1979. Whitley would subsequently write for programs like *Roseanne*, *TV Nation*, and *The Daily Show* and is now a faculty member in USC's School of Cinematic Arts, where he teaches screenwriting technique. Dvonch continued writing for several years, as well, working, in fact, on an independent film titled *Rock 'n' Roll Hotel* (1983), which had no direct connection to *Rock 'n' Roll High School*, before pursuing a successful career in insurance.

LOOK OUT BELOW

Working with a $12 million advertising budget, New World's sales office under Frank Moreno's stewardship had a heavy load of films to release in 1979, a mixture of original New World productions (*Saint Jack*, *Up from the Depths*, *Starcrash*, *The Lady in Red*, *Rock 'n' Roll High School*) and several pictures the company had secured North American rights to distribute, including a Don Knotts/Tim Conway comedy *The Prize Fighter*, David Cronenberg's *The Brood*, two films by Francois Truffaut, *The Green Room* and *Love on the Run*, Ingmar Bergman's *Autumn Sonata*, and the rock documentary *The Kids Are Alright*.

Per Moreno's insistence, *Rock 'n' Roll High School* opened on April 18, 1979, a Tuesday night, with no soundtrack album tie-in, with screenings all over Texas—Austin, El Paso, San Antonio, Fort Worth, Houston, Plano, Dallas, and Corpus Christi. That same week a bad case of April showers beset the Lone Star State, with storms strong enough to knock over church steeples, headstones, and drive-in movie screens, dampening ticket sales. Another problem: Texans had little if any basis for appreciating the Ramones and their music. "To open a punk rock movie in Texas . . . showed so little understanding of what the film was about," Allan complained to *Starlog*. If the Ramones looked like aliens to themselves and like special-needs adults to truck stop clerks, how else would they seem to the teenagers of Texas but strange? Diego Cortez, a stringer for *Punk Magazine*, who saw *Rock 'n' Roll High School* at the Thunderbird Drive-in in Houston, where it was double-billed with *Avalanche*, observed that "The drive-in wasn't too full. . . . It was weird 'cause the audience was not Ramones fans. They were middle-class teens. I think the picture confused them."

The early reviews for *Rock 'n' Roll High School* tended toward praise or censure, sometimes both. Michael Spies in the *Corpus Christi Times* wrote: "Even to admit seeing a movie called *Rock 'n' Roll High School* may be enough to lose a reviewer his credentials, but to admit enjoying it may be enough to risk expulsion from society. . . . It's a silly film with many old jokes, but it has an energetic rock spirit. At its best, it is down-right rude in an innocently anarchic way. . . . The humor sometimes rises to the Monty Python level, as in a running joke about white mice that explode when exposed to high levels of rock music. . . . *Rock 'n' Roll High School* is really cheap. It should be arrested for contributing to the delinquency of minors. But, hey, it's legal, and the kids have got to do something at night, right?"

The *Austin American-Statesman*'s Joe Nick Patoski enjoyed the movie, but at the same time thumped it as lowbrow: "There's a line from a song the Ramones frequently sing that repeats over and over: 'D-U-M-B, everyone's accusing me.' That pretty much sums up the artistic value of *Rock 'n' Roll High School*, a dumb ode to the dumb kind of B-movies executive producer Roger Corman has specialized in for several decades. No doubt many people will accuse Corman of cranking out just another piece of junk for teenagers to make out to at the drive-in. But then there will be those, most of them either *Beach Party* enthusiasts or Ramones fans, who will not only find it socially redeeming but dumbly funny as well. . . . As the first punk-rock exploitation movie, *Rock 'n' Roll High School* should not be missed, it's so D-U-M . . . uh, so stupid."

After the film's release, Corman reviewed the receipts and considered pulling the picture from circulation and having it reworked with the Ramones and their songs pared down. He floated a new title, too: *Rock 'n' Roll High* (another bit of drug humor). But the cost of recalling and remixing the film was still, as Allan wanted to tell him, prohibitive, and *Rock 'n' Roll High School* stayed out there, playing drive-ins and movie theaters for two-week runs around the country, region by region, often double-billed with New World's *Starcrash*, *The Kids Are Alright*, *Eat My Dust*, and *Grand Theft Auto*.

In May, Sire at last had the soundtrack album for *Rock 'n' Roll High School* pressed and ready for release and started shipping out copies for critics' review. Side A led in with the version of "Rock 'n' Roll High School" that Ed Stasium had produced (and which later Spector remixed in an effort, presumably, to get the songs to sound more "commercial," though the producer himself had been slumping since George Harrison's quixotic and beautiful *All Things Must Pass*, which had yielded the 1970 hit "My Sweet Lord"). The five-song set from the concert also showed up, as did P. J. Soles's take on the title song—the lead-off track on Side B.

Ken Paulson, writing in the *El Paso Times*, characterized the album as "a smorgasbord of power pop, punk and AM radio classics. . . . The Ramones' repertoire of rapid-fire-bam-bam tunes is infectious, and their catchy lead cut, 'Rock 'n' Roll High School,' which is given a Jan & Dean treatment, has all the elements of a hit record. Their rendition of 'Come On Let's Go' moves with the energy and drive of the 1958 Ritchie Valens original—not an easy accomplishment."

The *Austin American-Statesman* gave the record an ambiguous endorsement, just as it had the movie: "The soundtrack to Roger Corman's latest grade-B flick celebrates youthful energy. Not youthful creativity or intelligence, mind you, youthful energy." The hoped-for synergy between the movie and the soundtrack tie-in never really materialized, however, and the album failed to yield a hit.

In May, in the fifth week of the film's release, *Rock 'n' Roll High School* was booked at three independent movie houses in San Francisco simultaneously—the Egyptian, the Balboa, and the Serramonte—where it was paired at each on a bill with George Romero's independent cult hit *Dawn of the Dead*. "Frank Moreno did not like the Ramones but we had a commitment to Sire and the Ramones were playing in San Francisco. I talked to Roger about it and went up to San Francisco to do a radio promo with the band, especially Joey." A review in the *San Francisco Chronicle* noted: "*Rock 'n' Roll High School*, which opened Wednesday at the Egyptian Theater, is bound to become a classic of sorts. Produced by Roger Corman, who brought us all those . . . teensploitation movies of the sixties, this new film is an affectionate send-up of such old-time, lightweight summer fun and rock and roll flicks. Novelty alone is on the side of *Rock 'n' Roll High School* since nobody has made movies like this in years."

Moreno's responded to the bookings in San Francisco with little interest and saw that *Rock 'n' Roll High School* moved upward and outward from the southern states through the spring of 1979. Early signs of the film's becoming a cult sensation were starting to surface, with a small but fervent following of fans watching the film multiple times, drawn, rather than repelled, by the awkward splendor of its featured musical act and its story about students who blow up their own school. A magnet for these cultists was the Addison on West Lake Street in downtown Chicago, which in May, had booked the movie on a late-night triple bill with an AIP low-budget horror film called *The Evictors* and the Cheech and Chong drug comedy *Up in Smoke*.

The *Chicago Tribune*'s movie critic Gene Siskel noted the strange fascination the movie was generating and in his review of the film, published May 22, less than five weeks after the first rollout in Texas, he predicted: "*Rock 'n' Roll High School* is a standard summertime teen-age movie, a *Grease* imitation featuring liberated students battling a haughty school principal. The story is very funny in an appropriately sophomoric manner and features the punk rock sounds of the Ramones, who also appear as themselves. I wouldn't be surprised if this film achieved the cult midnight show sing-a-long status of *The Rocky Horror Picture Show*."

With Roger Ebert, his counterpart at the *Tribune*'s crosstown rival, the *Chicago Sun-Times*, Siskel hosted *Sneak Previews*, a nationally syndicated TV show in which the two tastemakers, whose opinions often clashed, would screen excerpts from new releases and offer their appraisals. That summer, Siskel and Ebert gave the movie national exposure for the first time. On the June episode of the program, Siskel reiterated what he'd stated in his print review—that *Rock 'n' Roll High School*, low-budget campy musical that it was, had potential to find a following and yield new fans long after its initial release. "In the movie business," the professorial Siskel intoned, "there's a peculiar creature known as the 'cult film,' films that aren't necessarily hits when they're first released but eventually they find an audience, and it's typically young people these cult films end up playing for, for years and years at midnight shows and at revival film houses. Now I think an innocent little high school comedy called *Rock 'n' Roll High School* has a chance of becoming a cult film." Ebert, in contrast, withheld his applause, presuming obscurity lay ahead for the movie, not cult immortality. The low-budget comedy's appeal was too limited, too dumb, and in his icy, imperious manner, he gave the movie the thumbs down. "I found this movie kind of a close call. Now, I can't really recommend it, but I did enjoy it. It's got a lot of energy. I enjoyed the Ramones. I like the girl who played Riff Randell—P. J. Soles. I like the situation: kind of *Our Miss Brooks* with pop rock thrown in into it . . . I can't quite recommend it. But yet I wouldn't quite tell you not to go. How's that for sitting right on the fence?"

By August, *Rock 'n' Roll High School* had played most of the country—but not yet New York. The film was going to have a two-week run starting August 3rd at the Eighth Street Playhouse in Greenwich Village, just a few blocks from NYU and CBGBs. Arkush flew back for the first screening, on a Friday, a week and a half shy of one year since he'd met the Ramones at Hurrah. While he was in New York, he and Joey gave an interview to WFMU, an independent radio station, which, like LA's KROQ, had been playing the Ramones when other stations wouldn't. The Ramones could not attend the Friday showing, though—they had a gig in West Hartford, Connecticut, but even without them, "the

audience reaction was sensational, unbelievable. When Miss Togar
burned the Ramones records, people got up and screamed! I mean, it
was one of the greatest nights of my life. This was the audience it was
meant for, it was the audience that I really wanted to like the movie."

The reviews in many of the New York papers were surprisingly
withering, though. J. Hoberman at the *Village Voice* condemned the
PG-movie for being what it was, a PG-movie. "At one point the film's
dauntless heroine goes home, lights a joint, plops a Ramones record
on her stereo and imagines that the band has come to pay a house call.
With Joey Ramone hulking over her bed, Marky the drummer outside
on the lawn and another Ramone lurking in the shower, it's a funny,
but telling scene—a masturbation fantasy as friction-free and sweatless
as the rest of the film." The *New York Times'* John Rockwell found that
while the movie "has its charms," calling it "zanily unpretentious," he
concluded, "[I]t's a real movie, as opposed to a vehicle for a rock act.
This is partly by design; it has a plot and actors and everything. But
it's also partly by omission. The Ramones are so blank and nebulous
on screen that they never emerge as individuals, in the manner of the
Beatles in their films."

The *New York Daily News* ran a mid-week pocket review of the
film, comparing *Rock 'n' Roll High School* to fluffy teen pix like *Hey,
Let's Twist* and *How to Stuff a Wild Bikini*, condemning it on the same
grounds for being "a pleasantly silly production for the young at heart,
but the very young." Yet the same paper's pop-culture columnist,
Martha Hume, penned a supportive piece that appeared in the *Daily
News's* Sunday edition: "Nearly three months ago, I saw a screening
of a movie that I thought was a lead-pipe cinch to be the 'teenage hit of
the summer'—even though it came straight from left field. The film was
Rock 'n' Roll High School, starring Forest Hills' very own Fab Four, the
Ramones: a B movie for sure, yet one of the funniest flicks I've seen since
Duck Soup." Hume attributed the movie's poor box office performance
to Frank Moreno's distribution plan: "New World officials . . . decided
to release the picture on a staggered basis, beginning in the South and
hoping it would build up enough momentum there to carry it into

bigger, northern cities," which, she felt, had hindered the movie's commercial performance. And not only had the follow-the-sun rollout hurt the film, mourned Hume, but if it "had been properly promoted and distributed, *Rock 'n' Roll High School* might have turned [the Ramones] into a major, nationwide draw."

During the film's two-week run at the Eighth Street Playhouse, Joey, Johnny, Dee Dee, and Marky each dropped in to watch it. Marky noted in *Punk Rock Blitzkrieg* that the New York audiences really understood and appreciated the Ramones onscreen: "When the four of us came strutting up the street to the Rockatorium to the beat of 'I Just Wanna Have Something to Do,' the crowd at the Eight Street Playhouse clapped along. I looked even sillier than I thought I would, walking along clicking my drumsticks, but that worked, too. I heard feet stomping in the theater. . . . The movie had cult classic written all over it." A piece that ran in the Canadian paper the *Nanaimo Daily News* reported that "Avid *R and RHS* fans have been returning to the theater five or six times to see the film, and theater owners report that audiences are singing along during the film's sing-a-long scenes." Nick Marden, guitar player for the pioneering New York hardcore punk band, the Stimulators, had a chance to see the movie too, and testified to the interactiveness the film could beget: "We definitely danced in the aisle during the end credits."

Rock 'n' Roll High School returned to *Sneak Previews* for further consideration in a special themed episode titled "Take 2: Midnight Movies." That week, Siskel and Ebert gave the show over to discussing a panoply of previously released established cult films—*Harold and Maude, Pink Flamingos, Dawn of the Dead*, etc. They attempted to explain the appeal such movies had for a limited but intense sect, who "see these films as a form of rebellion against mainstream society and culture." *Rock 'n' Roll High School*, though only a few months in release, seemingly already belonged to the same cult set as *Pink Flamingos* and *Dawn of the Dead* because, like them, it was shot through with "anti-establishment ideas popular with young people."

The two appearances of *Rock 'n' Roll High School* on the most popular movie-review show on TV helped with bringing the picture closer and closer to realizing a profit. "It got the attention of the revival theaters," Russ Dvonch said. "It's what blew the doors off. That thing played for years and years and years at midnight showings, and all kicked off by Siskel and Ebert."

Rock 'n' Roll High School found sympathetic and supportive reviewers as it moved through the conservative Midwest in the fall of 1979 as well, most notably Michael Clark at the *Detroit Free Press*: "[S]chlockmeister Roger Corman's *Rock 'n' Roll High School* is hands down the best movie of 1979. But then, it is both misleading and insulting to restrict comparison of this instant classic to the films of any one year. This picture is for all time." The *Kansas City Star*'s Robert C. Trussell, in contrast, responded to the picture with less-than-muted disgust: "Devoid of anything resembling social consciousness or artistic integrity, the film culminates in a student rebellion in which the high school explodes into flames as the Ramones wail away on the front steps of the building. The act of destruction is meaningless, nothing more than the result of the school administration's anti-rock 'n' roll stance."

When, in October, *Rock 'n' Roll High School* at last swung through Los Angeles, it was booked at standard screening times at hard-top theaters in North Hollywood, Hollywood, Torrance, Huntington Park, and Glendora, playing on double bills with *The Kids Are Alright* and *More American Graffiti*. The advertisements worked up by New World featured Bill Stout's cartoon rendering of the principals with lettering across the stop announcing, "AT LAST . . . THE RAMONES."

The *Los Angeles Times*' Kevin Thomas, frequently an advocate for New World, having heaped praise on the anti-totalitarian themes that undergirded the comedy in pictures like Bartel's *Death Race 2000* and Dante's *Piranha*, surprisingly dinged the Arkush picture. "*Rock 'n' Roll High School* is a rambunctious drive-in movie designed to show off East Coast new wave rockers, the Ramones. . . . It's the same old formula of rock-crazy kids in collision with a kill-joy principal. Of course, the film is a fantasy not to be taken seriously, but because it is precisely that, it is all the more disturbing for suggesting that it's perfectly OK to burn down their school when they don't get their way."

On May 1, one day shy of two weeks since *Rock 'n' Roll High School*'s opening in Texas, the Ramones had commenced with recording their fifth studio album, *End of the Century*. Among the eleven songs that appeared on the final record, two had connections to the movie, a new version of the theme song and "Danny Says," Joey's elicitation of his time at the Tropicana Motel the previous December with Linda Danielle watching *Get Smart* and hanging out in Room 100 B. The experience of recording with Phil Spector was troubled—and bizarre. The recording facilities themselves unsettled the band. At Gold Star Studios, as Monte A. Melnick noted, they were "immediately freaked out by the presence of large oxygen tanks (designed by Brian Wilson) and an underground swimming pool that double[d] as an echo chamber." Spector, too, was strange. Sober, he had an affable and witty nature. But he'd drink, which made him psychotic, and as he carried handguns, the Ramones kept their heads down around him, but only to a point.

Spector had thought he heard a hit in "Rock 'n' Roll High School," which he'd remixed for the movie's soundtrack. The song had been a staple on the band's setlist since January. Spector wanted the Ramones to cut another, more ornate version of the anti-school anthem. His fixation on technical perfection, however, led to a rupture with Johnny, who recalled that the 5'5" producer "had me play the opening chord to 'Rock n' Roll High School' over and over. This went on for three or four hours. He'd listen back to it, then ask me to play the same chord again. Stomping his feet and screaming, 'Shit, piss, fuck! Shit, piss, fuck!' over and over. I couldn't take it anymore. So I just said, 'I'm leaving,' and Phil said, 'You're not going anywhere.' I said, 'What are you gonna do, Phil, shoot me?'"

The Ramones moved out of the Tropicana Motel in June after they finished up with Spector and returned to the road, touring through the summer of 1979 and into the fall, occasionally playing theaters in support of the movie. In July, for example, they performed for a crowd of a thousand at the Ontario Theatre in Washington, DC. "It was not exactly a quiet evening at the movies," wrote Joe Sasfy, a reporter for the *Washington Post*. "But then it's not often that a film is the headliner for a rock 'n' roll show. . . . The band mingled with the crowd, shook hands and signed autographs. . . . The crowd treated *Rock 'n' Roll High School* not as a film to be viewed but as a participatory event. With the opening credits, the Ramones' surf classic, 'Sheena Is a Punk Rocker,' blared out and the crowd responded—some dancing, some cheering and some clapping." Eighteen-year-old Henry Rollins, the future voice of Black Flag and the Rollins Band, was there: "I always thought the Ramones were larger than life and seeing them on film the first time I saw *Rock 'n' Roll High School* was a thrill. It was at the Ontario Theatre. . . . The band made an appearance and hung out in the lobby for a little while." The movie impressed him. "I liked that there was a push against the school, and rock 'n' roll was the tool. I didn't like my school and survived with music. The Ramones were a huge part of that for me. The way almost the entire student body rebels against Ms. Togar and her authoritarianism is so cool." He added, "Music still has this meaning to me, and this film still embodies it perfectly." In October, the guys played additional shows in support of the movie, first at the Walnut Theatre in Philadelphia, then at the Oakland Auditorium Arena.

The band would see their highest charting album with *End of the Century* when Sire released it in February 1980, reaching the #44 spot on *Billboard*: the effort to link Spector's lush wall-of-sound aesthetic with the noisy squalor of Lower East Side street-rock yielded a pop music tiramisu—the Ramones mixed with heavy cream—very sweet, very dense, intriguing critics, if not winning them over entirely. "*End of the Century* could be explained in terms of an inevitable connection," *New Music Express*'s Max Bell offered. "America's leading exponents of artless popular punk face off against the establishment's first rebel, now an establishment superstar, the gun-toting paranoid tycoon of teen."

Sire Records hired director Mark Robinson to shoot a pair of music videos for two singles the label wanted to release from *End of the Century*: "This Is Rock 'n' Roll Radio" and "Rock 'n' Roll High School."

The Ramones had fired Danny Fields and Linda Stein, wanting to see if new management might lead them toward greater popular exposure and acceptance, and they'd moved on in the summer of 1979 to a music promoter named Gary Kirfust to manage them. Robinson recalled that "Gary or Seymour Stein called and said, 'I want you to do the Ramones, but they don't have any time. You're going to have to meet them on the road.' We had a very short period of time. They had two days off or a day and a half off in San Francisco. So I had to go up to San Francisco, from LA, to do it. A lot of the stuff came up on the fly with them, with Joey mainly. Johnny was the grumpy businessman, the disciplinarian. Joey was the dreamer and the brain stormer. We wrote on the fly. We had to do another video for 'This Is Rock 'n' Roll Radio' during the same twenty-four-hour-or-so period. It was very crazy, and they were really, really tired by the end."

Filmed entirely indoors, the music video for "Rock 'n' Roll High School" features Joey, Dee Dee, Johnny, and Marky seated in a school's detention room with a teacher monitoring them, played also by Marky, in drag, resembling at once Mary Woronov's Miss Togar and Dr. Frank-N-Furter, the "sweet transvestite from Transsexual, Transylvania" played by Tim Curry in *The Rocky Horror Picture Show*. Robinson, in fact, had been Curry's understudy in the original theatrical production of the musical *The Rocky Horror Show*, which had premiered at the Roxy Theatre in 1974. When the detention teacher steps away, the four leather-jacketed detainees, as unsupervised as Riff and her pals in *Rock 'n' Roll High School*'s girls'-gym scene, begin breaking rules. Johnny jumps on a desk and plays his banged-up Mosrite guitar. Joey stands at a chalkboard, beside a cartoonish drawing of a chubby, bald, bearded Emil-Jannings-faced teacher (a visual echo, of sorts, too, of Paul Bartel's Mr. McGree). As Marky hoists a boombox on his shoulder and bangs his head to the beat, grinning moronically, Dee Dee noodles around with a chemistry set, at a desk. A trio of female students approach the classroom, their hair bleached blonde, eyelids heavy with mascara, peering at the bad boys. Robinson recalled: "The girls outside the glass door of the detention hall who are pointing in were their girlfriends [Vera, Linda, Roxy] at the time."

A kid with a repulsive, pruney face sits on a stool in the corner of the detention hall, wearing a dunce hat. As Dee Dee toys with some test tubes, doing a troglodytic take on Kate Rambeau with her beakers in Vince Lombardi High, the dunce's hat lifts off, like a nuclear thermal rocket, revealing the strange creature's conical head underneath. The kid with the pruney face is the same pinhead guy the Ramones first brought out at the Rockatorium. The video ends with a jump cut to a mushrooming atomic cloud. Dee Dee has blown up the school and maybe the world.

The idea to include the pinhead character had come from the band. "Throughout the shoot, the Ramones kept referring to their mascot. I said, 'Who's the mascot?' 'Well, you don't want to know.' 'Really, who's your mascot?' I remember Joey kept laughing," Robinson the video director remembered. "He said 'No, no.' I said, 'Well, why?' 'He's just too ugly to put in.' He was laughing and laughing. Then they brought out the pinhead mask. Their mascot came from *Freaks*. *Freaks* was a motivator for them: 'Gabba Gabba Hey.' Had I known about it earlier, I would have stuck the mask in more because when I saw what it was, I said, 'We've got to put this in.' So we stuck it at the end. The opening shot—that's Venice High in Los Angeles.

"The Ramones were between gigs. They had to be out of town the next day. Joey was into it, but Johnny wasn't into anything. He was permanently grumpy. He was quite a right winger. The *Rocket to Russia* thing, he wasn't kidding about that. A real law-and-order guy. Johnny would say, 'Don't let any drugs come on the set.' He was worried about Dee Dee."

A shot of a guitar smashing through a TV came out of the shoot with Robinson, as well, and was used in the video for "This Is Rock 'n' Roll Radio." "We put a Stratocaster guitar through a television screen. . . . That particular guitar going through the television became MTV's logo for several years after that." Launched in August 1981, MTV had, early on, given the Ramones bits of precious airtime. "When MTV was first coming up in New York, they would beg us to do stuff," Monte A. Melnick groused in his memoir. "But as soon as they got big, they ignored the Ramones and banned their videos. We did a lot of stuff early on in New York, and they never returned the favor. We helped them build a reputation, and then they got huge and never played our videos. That sucked."

The music channel spurned punk rock, generally, and if a video by any band perceived as transgressive got past the channel's censors, at best it would be featured on late-night programs like *120 Minutes* and *The Cutting Edge*. Mark Robinson, fortunately, experienced sustained success during the '80s music-video boom and was responsible for several "heavy rotation" hits, most notably, perhaps, the extraordinary Tina Turner's "What's Love Got to Do with It?" which dominated the channel for a time.

MTV eventually gave the Ramones valuable exposure, though, when it started screening iconoclastic and subversive feature films on Sunday nights, many of them culled from the midnight-movie circuit—*Reefer Madness*, *Phantom of the Paradise*, and *Rock 'n' Roll High School*. Although the New World picture carried a PG rating, the censors at MTV ordered the removal of much of the drug humor that seeps through the movie. Joe Dante recalled how *Rock 'n' Roll High School* played in "heavy rotation on MTV for a long time, except they cut out the best scene, which is the scene in Riff's bedroom where she's smoking and sees the guys in her bedroom. It's a terrific scene. And it was always gone from MTV because they had a no-drugs policy."

The broader recognition *Rock 'n' Roll High School* obtained in the wake of the MTV broadcasts wasn't entirely positive, however. In May 1985 on a CBS broadcast of a tournament at the tony West Side Tennis Club in Forest Hills, Queens—the Ramones' homeland—one of the standouts was Vince Van Patten. "Vince was a really good tennis player," said Allan. "He went pro and played in a lot of big tournaments, including Forest Hills. I got a phone call from someone to tell me that Vince's match at Forest Hills was on CBS 'Right now!' And he was doing well. So I tuned in, and it was really exciting. There were two announcers. One, Chris Schenkel, knew tennis inside and out, and the other supplied color: his name was Pat Summerall. In New Jersey, I grew up a New York Giants fan. Pat was a hero to me. I saw him kick many field goals and extra points. Wow! He's color casting the match and talking about Vince. 'You know, folks, Vince Van Patten is quite an actor, and he comes from a Hollywood family of actors. It's ups and downs in that business. They tell me that Vince was in the worst movie ever made, *Rock 'n' Roll High School.*' Chris Schenckel says, 'Never heard of it.' Pat replies, 'I bet Vince wishes that was true of everybody. All right, 40-love.'"

The Ramones had taken up their instruments and become a band back in 1974 with the goal of saving rock 'n' roll from blandness. They never kowtowed to the fads that might have helped them find a larger listening audience as even bands like Blondie and KISS had with disco. Their attempts to recruit radio programmers with the power pop of *Road to Ruin*, the glitz of *End of the Century*, and their appearance in *Rock 'n' Roll High School* didn't work, didn't punch them through to the Top 40, even as the '80s saw the release of strong records like *Subterranean Jungle*, *Pleasant Dreams*, and *Too Tough to Die* and several pop singles that flourished briefly on college radio, "My Brain Is Hanging Upside Down (Bonzo Goes to Bitburg)," "Pet Sematary," and "Merry Christmas (I Don't Want to Fight Tonight)." Mainstream FM stations would ignore them to the end, sadly, and the band stayed forever cult, adored during its time from the fringes, never the center. So, what must Johnny, Marky, Joey, and Dee Dee have thought, in 1991, when the music video for Nirvana's "Smells Like Teen Spirit," an homage of sorts to *Rock 'n' Roll High School*, became, like the grunge trio's song, a huge hit? The video's director Samuel Bayer told *Interview* that he and Kurt Cobain, a Ramones devotee, had worked out the video's stylistic and thematic elements together. "At the time, Kurt had an idea to do a rebellion at a high school. He wanted it to look like *Rock 'n' Roll High School* by the Ramones, mixed with a movie that Matt Dillon did called *Over the Edge*, I heard him say that and came up with something very dark and gritty." Jonathan Kaplan's *Over the Edge* was the movie Joe McBride had used in his efforts to persuade Allan Arkush to blow up Vince Lombardi High School.

The video for "Smells Like Teen Spirit" has Cobain and his bandmates, Dave Grohl and Krist Novoselic, accompanied by tattooed cheerleaders, performing before a crowd of charged-up teenagers in a school gymnasium—actually, a soundstage in Culver City. As the trio rocks the crowd, kids mosh and crowd surf, swirling up and around the band as intimately as the students do when Johnny, Dee Dee, and Joey take their rockin' stroll down one of the Vince Lombardi corridors with Marky rolling behind them banging on his drums. The Nirvana video also ends with a shot of a dunce on a stool, a reference seemingly to the pinhead sitting in the corner in Mark Robinson's video for "Rock 'n' Roll High School."

Thanks to steady home video sales (starting in 1983 with Warner Home Video releasing the movie on Betamax) and numerous TV broadcast deals dating back to the fall of 1979, *Rock 'n' Roll High School* moved into the black, the preeminent measure for Corman of a film's success; "It made a very substantial profit," he told *Billboard* in 1991. And with the film's profitability came Corman's increased support for the picture and his eventual recognition of *Rock 'n' Roll High School*, with *Grand Theft Auto* and *Piranha*, as one of his favorite New World releases, validating Charlie Chaplin's axiom that "Numbers sanctify." "Roger will now say that 'Oh, yes, I produced *Rock 'n' Roll High School*,' or whatever, yet he had no idea what that movie was. It was really Allan, just pushing and pushing, to make it as good as it could be, given the constraints he was under. Roger had no clue, no clue at all. *Rock 'n' Roll High School* is like the number one moneymaker of all time for New World Pictures. I don't know if that's true or not, but that's what I've heard. So now Roger of course is very proprietary and very proud of his involvement, but at the time it was just like he just didn't get it," Kent Beyda told me.

In 1983, Corman sold off New World Pictures to an investment group, though he retained the rights to the movies produced by the company during his thirteen-year tenure. He had no intention of retiring, and immediately after New World's sale, he founded another independent film production-distribution company, Concorde-New Horizons, which made movies in the same fast, cheap manner as New World, and for similar audiences. Lana Clarkson, the woman Phil Spector shot to death in his castle in Alhambra in 2003, starred in a 1985 Concorde film titled *Barbarian Queen*.

Toward the end of the '80s, Concorde-New Horizons financed a profitable run of sequels based on such New World releases as *Big Bad Mama* and *Slumber Party Massacre*. Deborah Brock, who directed *Slumber Party Massacre II* for Concorde, had an idea to do a sequel to *Rock 'n' Roll High School*. "Roger had been redeveloping older properties—*Hollywood Boulevard II* and *Bucket of Blood*—in the 80s and 90s. He made *Rock 'n' Roll High School Forever* because I proposed it to him. It was my idea. I gave him a story synopsis, and he read it over the weekend and gave me the greenlight on Monday. I think the fact that I had made him a film, *Slumber Party II*, that grossed over $6,000,000 on a budget of less than $400,000 probably greased the tracks on that one."

Brock's *Slumber Party Massacre II* featured a demon with a rock-star complex who uses an electric guitar equipped with a giant drill to prey on his victims. She brought a similar gust of extravagance and camp to *Rock 'n' Roll High School Forever*. The story Deborah developed focuses on a student named Jesse Davis, the leader of a teen alternative-rock band called the Eradicators, who run afoul of the administration at Ronald Reagan High School, the name that Joseph McBride had used early on in his *Girls' Gym* and *California Girls* scripts. Corey Feldman was approached to play the film's lead. Feldman in the early-90s had a wide fan base thanks in part to his friendship with actor pal Corey Haim. "The 'two Coreys'" as the popular press referred to them, "were 'hot' then," Brock said, "and we agreed to use some of Corey's songs in the picture, which thrilled him, and so he said, 'Yes.' With Corey as a star, this enabled us to get a bigger budget than usual from Roger.

"I wrote the screenplay with Jed Horovitz, the producer, and it was informed by my taste and sensibility. The only thing it had in common with *Rock 'n' Roll High School* was conflict between the students and school administration, musical scenes, a crazy out-there style and some references to 'Rock 'n' Roll High School Day'—the day the students celebrate the school being burned down twelve years before in *Rock 'n' Roll High School* by 'going crazy': flushing toilets, dancing in the halls, etc. Jed and I used various student hijinks we remembered from high school or had heard about.

"The character of Doctor Vadar, the assistant principal played wonderfully by Mary Woronov, was based on the mythic character in Kubrick's *Dr. Strangelove*—the advisor played by Peter Sellers in a wheelchair who didn't seem to be able to control his body movements. His arm had a life of its own and kept trying to snap up into what I believe was a Nazi salute. . . . I came up with the idea that she was missing a hand and had a metal claw instead, which would go crazy on occasion with a life of its own. I firmly believe Doctor Vadar was the first non-binary character to appear in an American movie. As one of the students says during the movie's prom scene: 'Doctor Vadar's a woman?' We had a wonderful young production designer, Virginia Lee, who put Doctor Vadar into a uniform reminiscent of a Nazi great coat. The special effects guys loved creating her metal claw and after the shoot mounted it on a wooden base like a trophy, had it inscribed and gave it to me. I've still got it on the mantle of my living room fireplace."

For the movie's soundtrack, Brock found herself negotiating with a record company much as Arkush and Finnell had in 1978. "Roger actually had a music guy on staff when we were in pre-production in *Rock 'n' Roll High School Forever*. He knew an executive over at EMI Records—a big company!—and told her about *Rock 'n' Roll High School Forever*. EMI bought the soundtrack rights to the movie, which gave us use of EMI artists and publishing rights. She suggested we have Mojo Nixon write a song for the film and appear in it. Mojo came up with "High School Is a Prison," and we put his performance into a crazy dream scene. Working with Mojo was lots of fun. Virginia Lee, the production designer, created a wonderful set for Corey's bedroom and gave it a crazy German-Expressionist hallway. Dee Dee Ramone and Jean Beauvoir did a song that EMI provided for the movie, but, frankly, my memories are of Mojo Nixon, the Pursuit of Happiness and Mark Governor and his band's fun performance of 'Love at the Laundromat.'

"Corey Feldman had a drug habit, which we didn't know when we hired him. He would occasionally give me trouble on the set. I had to come up with various director 'tricks' to control him. One night when we were shooting at a school, he decided to start directing the other actors. I was sitting on the camera dolly and by that time had had enough. I threw my coffee cup across the set and yelled at Corey to 'quit being a mother-fucker' and to 'go back to position A,' and we were going to walk through the scene like I wanted it, and he was going to do his part as an actor. You could have heard a tiny pin drop when I threw that coffee cup—it was paper—across the set and let him have it.

"I think the film came out quite good for a high school comedy musical. It's bloody amazing considering its budget—just over a million dollars. Unfortunately, Corey getting arrested for drugs while we were finishing up the post-production put a kibosh on the theatrical release. Live Entertainment, which also financed Tarantino's *Reservoir Dogs*, had bought the video and theatrical rights from Roger before the film was even finished, got cold feet from Corey's bad publicity and didn't want to put money into the theatrical release. Roger, I want to say, released it in a drive-in chain in the South he owned [in 1991], but then Comedy Central bought the cable rights and played that sucker every afternoon after the kids got out of school for two years, creating a bigger audience than it probably would have had with a bigger theatrical release."

In 2002, twenty-three years after *Rock 'n' Roll High School*'s release in Texas, American-radio superstar Howard Stern confirmed the film's ongoing potential for commercial exploitation when he announced that he and independent producer Dan Gross would remake the movie, having optioned the rights from Concorde-New Horizons. Roger Corman fully supported the venture, even agreeing to reprise "his role as exec producer." Stern and Gross felt confident that having the shock jock's name attached to the remake would resonate with his listeners: "It means something to them. It means that it's going to be crazy. It means that it's going to be different, and they know I'm not going to be giving them any schlock." But the project never progressed, and a second attempt fizzled similarly in 2008, when, now partnered with TV producer Larry

Levinson, Stern retained Alex Winter (Bill in the *Bill and Ted* movies) to write a script.

Twelve years later, during the COVID-19 crisis, comedy writer Jake Fogelnest had an opportunity to redevelop *Rock 'n' Roll High School* as a television series, after Stern let the project lapse. In 2018, Corman had sold off a huge chunk of his cinematic oeuvre to Shout! Factory, a home video-streaming service company, which included ownership of *Rock 'n' Roll High School*. In 2020, a contact from Shout! Factory sent an email to Fogelnest, asking him, "'Hey, are you interested in turning *Rock 'n' Roll High School* into a TV show?'" "I said, 'Yes.' I went and met with Shout! Factory, and they didn't meet with any other writers. My friend, Natasha Lyonne, had just started a company with Maya Rudolph called Animal Pictures. They were calling me every week: 'Hey, did you get the rights to *Rock 'n' Roll High School*? Did you get the rights?'

"Finally I did. I'd called up Shout! Factory and said, 'How would you like it if Natasha Lyonne and Maya Rudolph came on board as producers? Somebody's going to do this in Hollywood, and it's going to stink. And if anybody's going to do it and get paid for it, it should be me.' I wrote a pilot, and I sold it to FX. That was my COVID project: turning *Rock 'n' Roll High School* into a TV show, making sure that it was 'period,' making sure that it paid homage to the Ramones. There was no press announcement. There's nothing on the internet about it, but it's something I worked on for about a year."

As Fogelnest crafted the pilot script he asked himself: "How do you do a show where the high school blows up in these times?" He "thought about everything the show can't be. I said, 'There's no replacing the Ramones, and I can't have another band come in.' The pilot takes place, basically, the day John Lennon is shot"—December 8, 1980, eleven months after the kids in the film overtake Vince Lombardi—"and Riff Randell has her own band. I made it about the kids, a more-grounded-reality-version of *Rock 'n' Roll High School*. I would've loved a *Rock 'n' Roll High School* TV show that was just jokes and songs, but that's not going to be a TV show, and nor should it be because the original is sacred material. There're some things that are universal truths about *Rock 'n'*

Roll High School. Authority is always clashing against rebellious youth. Adults are scared of the music that their kids listen to. Adults are usually doing most of the bad things in this world. And when we look back, teenagers are usually the smart ones who are on the right side of history.

"We had a bunch of pitch meetings set up. The one that went the best was at FX. They bought it, and we canceled our other pitch meetings. We didn't try to start a bidding war. Then I did an outline, and I started writing the script March 15, 2020, the day that we went into COVID lockdown. It was December 2020 I handed it in. If we got a pilot or we got picked up straight to series, whatever happened, then the next call was going to be to Allan Arkush to say, 'Oh, boy, they're going to make a TV show out of your classic movie. Here's what I've done. What do you think? And can you come aboard?' Allan is an incredible TV director. But it didn't get to that point. The executive who was in charge at Shout! Factory is no longer there. So, the script's been taken out and run its course. It's done. I didn't want to proceed further with the script and development. I wanted to move on to other things. Though if any network is willing to do a fun, silly Ramones cartoon series, I would be first to hop on to do that."

The dream may always persist for a return to *Rock 'n' Roll High School.* Back at least as far as 1999, Joseph McBride noted in his recollection of the film's making that appears in his *Book of Movie Lists*, that "Arkush, P. J. Soles and Dey Young are still hoping to do their own sequel, although if they wait much longer it might have to be called *Rock 'n' Roll Retirement Home.*" P. J. Soles in her filmed conversation with Dey Young and Vince Van Patten back in 2009 expressed her hopes about reuniting the characters from *Rock 'n' Roll High School* for a sequel she'd call *Rock 'n' Roll Nursing Home*, but "with just Marky, since he's the only one left." Johnny Ramone died in 2004 of prostate cancer. P. J. imagines in this exchange with her old castmates that Riff, being Riff, has the task of convincing her old chemistry-loving best pal, Kate Rambeau, to help her lead an assault on the prison-like facility where they find themselves trapped: "'Come on . . . Kate, let's blow up the nursing home. Don't you hate these nurses? . . . We don't want this mush. We want pizza!'"

After the January 6 insurrection at the US Capitol, unfortunately, finding financing for a remake of a movie in which raging youth assail a public institution seems more remote than ever. Yet there's evidence all over the popular-culture landscape that the appeal of *Rock 'n' Roll High School*, like the pale blue eyes in the Velvet Underground song, lingers on. In April 2021, for example, *Rolling Stone* ranked the Arkush-Ramones collaboration fifth on its list of the "25 Greatest Punk Rock Movies of All Time": "To see the beautifully sloppy, brilliantly simplistic band at its best . . . head straight to this Roger Corman-produced teensploitation gem, in which Joey, Johnny, Dee Dee and Marky help P. J. Soles and the student body of Vince Lombardi High stand up to authority, three chords at a time."

The frequency with which the film is still booked at movie theaters around the world validates claims to its incontrovertible charm further. Consider: On June 4, 2021, the Circle Drive-In in Dickson City, Pennsylvania (a two-and-a-half-hour drive from Lancaster), hosted a drive-in screening of *Rock 'n' Roll High School* for fans to watch from their cars, much like the movie's first audiences in the spring and summer of 1979. The arrangement of the automobiles in the drive-in's parking spaces enabled patrons to social distance at a point when the coronavirus was still killing people regularly. Clint Howard flew across country to introduce the film, to a sold-out audience. And six months later, after the acute gnashing horror of the pandemic had lifted and after Kino Lorber released a Blu-ray edition of Arkush's second wonderful rock 'n' roll musical comedy, *Get Crazy*, the New Beverly Cinema in Beverly Hills, a sit-down theater, marked the occasion booking it on a double-bill with *Rock 'n' Roll High School*. And then, in 2022, Turner Classic Movies, the basic cable channel for cineastes in America, added *Rock 'n' Roll High School* to its programming, featuring it twice that year on its overnight showcase program, *TCM Underground*.

What is it about this cheap-cheap-cheap exploitation teen comedy that ends with kids blowing up their own school that continues to draws new viewers—and fans—year after year, decade after decade? Joseph McBride, now a distinguished professor in the cinema department at San Francisco State University, and the author of an excellent book on screenwriting titled *Writing in Pictures*, thinks the movie that he contributed to so importantly holds on because for all its dumb and dated jokes it is an example of a "well-made" picture, a film of quality, despite its low-budget and its absurdity. *"Rock 'n' Roll High School* is one of the best musicals of the 1970s. It's much better than *Grease*, in my opinion. It may not be as good as *Cabaret*, but it's a good musical, a real musical written for the screen. It's the real deal."

For Roger Corman, the source of *Rock 'n' Roll High School*'s longevity, he explained to Leonard Maltin, is its "anarchy" and "The fact that it is so wild. And the fact that the students act out every teenager's ultimate dream: they take over the high school and finally they blow it up." P. J. Soles, in contrast, credits the film's durability to her character, Riff Randell, who has emerged over the past forty years as a Joan-of-Arc figure for many. A regular at film fan conventions, she has "had forty-five-year-old women crying at my table, seventeen-year-old girls crying at my table, having tattoos of Riff Randell or Joey, and they want my signature on their leg. They love and identify with Riff or wish they could be Riff. . . . [S]he was a very empowered woman, who took her own direction."

Arkush agrees with P. J. The Ramones make the movie, but Riff's the one with the rock 'n' roll heart who "seems to inspire kids to take control of their lives and see through the hypocrisy around them," and that, and no more, Conrad might have said, is everything.

Arkush stayed on at New World Pictures until 1979. His next picture after *Rock 'n' Roll High School* was *Heartbeeps*, for Universal Pictures, a multimillion-dollar picture that failed commercially and critically, with extreme disloyalty displayed by its leading man, Andy Kaufman, who maligned the picture, undeservedly, on talk shows. Allan's next picture, his excellent musical comedy follow-up to *Rock 'n' Roll High School*, *Get Crazy*, came and went with minimal attention. His ability to blend narrative, cinema, and rock 'n' roll did lead him forward professionally, despite these disappointments. Like Mark Robinson, he became a director of music videos, with several that played extensively on MTV in the first half of the early '80s, among them "Breaking the Chains" for the American heavy-metal band Dokken, Bette Midler's cover of the Rolling Stones "Beast of Burden" (which featured Mick Jagger), Elvis Costello's "The Only Flame in Town" (with Daryl Hall), and Christine McVie's "Love Will Show Us How," for which Arkush cast Paul Bartel again in a music-themed role, this time as a blundering music-video director.

He gradually moved onto network television, gaining a reputation for being dependable and innovative, directing for *Fame*, *Moonlighting*, *Ally McBeal*, *Snoops*, *Crossing Jordan*, *Heroes*, and *Parenthood*. He never left features behind entirely, shooting several TV movies, including a remake for Showtime of *Shake, Rattle and Rock!*, in which he was able to cast Mary Woronov, Dey Young, and P. J. Soles as fearful parents who take action against the nefarious influence rock 'n' roll may have on their kids; X's John Doe also appeared in the production. In 1999, he won an Emmy for directing *The Temptations*, a four-hour music-soaked biopic miniseries about the fabulous Motown singing group. Allan now teaches for the American Film Institute's graduate student program, which the *Hollywood Reporter* regularly ranks as the nation's best film school. What must the ghosts of Mr. Kelly and Mr. Raimondo think?

Mike Finnell, who would go on after *Rock 'n' Roll High School* to make several exceptional movies as a producer with Joe Dante, among them *The Howling*, *Gremlins*, and *The 'burbs*, told me that he thinks *Rock 'n' Roll High School* abides "for two main reasons: number one, The Ramones, of course. Inducted into the Rock and Roll Hall of Fame in 2002, I'm amazed at how often I hear them on the radio, including the title track, and, even more telling, how often I see someone decades younger than me wearing a Ramones T-shirt. They have only become more iconic as the years have passed. Number two: wish fulfillment. What teenager deep down, whether they would admit it or not (and in this era of school violence, they shouldn't) wouldn't like to see their school, well, if not actually blown up, at least damaged enough to cancel classes for a week or two? Even though I haven't been a teenager in fifty years and grew up in a particularly anarchic time, I can't believe that at least a little bit of anti-authority sentiment still beats in the heart of every teen."

When I asked Henry Rollins why he thinks *Rock 'n' Roll High School* holds on, he gave me this answer: "History has been kind to the Ramones, and people still want to see them. They make great movie stars. I think the film perfectly balances cult appeal and gets to the root of why people like rebellious music. P. J. Soles's performance as Riff Randell is so great. She's the rock 'n' roll girlfriend you wish you had in high school. I think one of the main appeals of the film is that it's not trying to be taken seriously but it gets at things you might take seriously, which makes you attach to it more. I don't think one can have a casual relationship with rock or punk music. You're either all in or not at all. *Rock 'n' Roll High School* gets to that unerringly."

PLOT SUMMARY FOR
ROCK 'N' ROLL HIGH SCHOOL

It is the first school day of the new year, 1980, and best friends Kate Rambeau, a nerd, and Riff Randell, a rock 'n' roller, have seized the PA system at Vince Lombardi High School, through which they plan to transmit the music of the Ramones rather than the morning announcements to everybody on campus. It is also Miss Evelyn Togar's first day on her new job as VLHS's principal. As the new administrator's supervisors on the local school board host a welcoming ceremony for Togar, Riff lowers the tone arm on a vinyl copy of *Rocket to Russia*, letting loose the loping licks that lead into the Ramones' "Sheena Is a Punk Rocker," which, in turn, prompt students to bolt from their desks and rock 'n' roll. Exasperated by this show of teenage malfeasance, Miss Togar marches toward the source of the dangerous music, where she meets the do-it-yourself disc jockeys, Kate and Riff, and threatens to place damaging marks on their permanent records.

The mighty, the fierce, the unkillable Ramones are coming to town to play a show at an arena called the Rockatorium, and Riff wants to cut class to wait in line outside the rock hall's box office to buy a ticket for herself and ninety-nine friends, including Kate, who doesn't share her buddy's infatuation with the band. Riff's love for the Ramones is such that she's written a song for them titled "Rock 'n' Roll High School," which she performs for her friends during phys-ed class when their teacher, Coach Steroid, answers a request from Miss Togar to attend a meeting in the school's animal room, a laboratory, where the principal has been running tests to determine the extent to which rock 'n' roll music can endanger the creatures who hear it, including mice.

Riff may love to rock, but Kate loves Tom Roberts, their school's starting quarterback, who's as awkward as he is dumb. Tom doesn't notice Kate, though, because he's hot for Riff—an attraction that begins when the Ramones' number one fan passes him in a hallway as she's listening to "I Wanna Be Sedated," off the Ramones' latest album, *Road to Ruin*. Sensing his limitations as a suitor, Tom retains the services of a seamy entrepreneur named Eaglebauer, who conducts his business out of a bathroom stall in the restroom, to help him win Riff's heart. Kate hires Eaglebauer for help too, dreaming of a time when she and Tom will go steady.

For three days, Riff camps out at the Rockatorium. On the day the box office is due to open, she wakes up from a doze. Standing in front of her is Angel Dust, a tough cuss, who claims, like Riff, to be the Ramones' biggest fan. The two bicker and then stop as the Ramones show up at the Rockatorium in a magnificent pink Cadillac convertible. The band's manager knows Angel and permits her to join him and the band inside, leaving Riff and a long queue of fans to buy their tickets to the concert.

When Riff returns to Vince Lombardi High she gives out all but two, one for herself, one for Kate. Miss Togar punishes her for having hooked school for three days, giving her detention and forcing her to surrender the last two tickets to the Ramones show. Kate receives the same punishment, having provided fraudulent excuse notes for her friend while Riff has been away.

After school that afternoon, Riff goes home and smokes a joint in her bedroom, which precipitates an intense daydream in which the Ramones come over and serenade her with a song called "I Want You

Around." Kate shows up soon after, and sits with her pal and they talk about boys, Tom Roberts and Joey Ramone in particular. While Riff was at the Rockatorium, Kate and Tom took an interactive sex-ed class together, which Eaglebauer facilitated. Thus Kate's heart breaks a little when Tom calls Riff on the telephone and asks her, now that she can't go to the Ramones concert anymore, if she wants to hang out with him to get drunk, to which Riff, having fun with Kate's heart, answers that she will, as long as Tom can find a date for Kate. He can: Eaglebauer.

Riff and Kate head out in Riff's convertible—the movie is filled with hot cars—and win a pair of tickets to the Ramones concert through a radio contest promoted by disc jockey Screamin' Steve Stevens. The two friends change their plans. They dress up for the concert in "punk" outfits, to Tom's chagrin. Inside the rock hall, Angel Dust spots Riff and steals an envelope filled with songs she's brought along, which she plans to pass on to the Ramones. A foot chase follows with Tom and Eaglebauer recovering the tunes from Angel, during which the klutzy quarterback knocks himself out, hitting his head into a door. Kate aids him, and the kindness arouses in the athlete a desire to start dating the science nerd. The two have much in common—they can both disco dance.

The concert that night at the Rockatorium is monitored by Miss Togar from her office through a radio simulcast. When Screamin' Steve announces to the crowd that Riff and Kate are the winners of the radio contest he hosted earlier in the day, Miss Togar responds by sending her two henchmen, a pair of hall monitors, both named Fritz, to the Rockatorium to bring back proof of Riff and Kate's presence at the show. The louts rip through the Rockatorium on a motorcycle that has a sidecar, taking photographs, which they bring back to their boss. Riff isn't worried, though. After the concert, the Ramones not only agree to meet her backstage, they also agree to take a look at her song "Rock 'n' Roll High School." If they like it, they'll visit Riff at her school to talk about recording the tune in the studio.

The following day, however, Miss Togar sets fire to a pile of rock 'n' roll records she's seized from students, thanks to the aid of their complicit parents. The bonfire is such an outrage that the students, led by

Riff, seize the school, rushing inside, where they break all sorts of rules, like dancing and riding motorcycles in the hallways. The Ramones it turns out have enjoyed Riff's song immensely, and they drop by Vince Lombardi High to tell Riff and her music teacher, Mr. McGree, a sympathizer with the kids' cause. Before the boys can get inside the school building, Miss Togar stops them, grilling them about who they are and what they want. Like McGree, the Ramones support the student uprising, and after pasting a kick-me sign to the principal's back, they enter the school building, where they soon begin to play the song "Do You Wanna Dance?" further riling up the running-wild teens.

Outside, Togar meets with a local constable, Chief Klein, who agrees with her that the insurrection and the Ramones have to be stopped. An attempt at a negotiation between the police and the students flounders. Simultaneously, Kate uses her skills as a chemistry ace to create an explosive, which is eventually packed inside a detonation box that winds up in front of the Vince Lombardi High. The Ramones have set up their gear under a flagpole, ready to play a song. Joining them is Riff, who now wears a leather jacket they've given her—she's one of them, the gesture conveys. The rock 'n' roller presses on the detonator as the band lets loose with their version of "Rock 'n' Roll High School," and a huge blast follows, wrecking the building. The school's undoing marks the total failure of Miss Togar's regime, prompting her to sink into a catatonic stupor. The film closes with a shot of a campus map visible through a layer of fire as the Ramones play on.

CAST LIST

Riff Randell	P. J. SOLES
Tom Roberts	VINCENT VAN PATTEN
Eaglebauer	CLINT HOWARD
Kate Rambeau	DEY YOUNG
Miss Evelyn Togar	MARY WORONOV
Police Chief Klein	DICK MILLER
Mr. McGree	PAUL BARTEL
Coach Steroid	ALIX ELIAS
Screamin' Steve Stevens	DON STEELE
Fritz Hansel	LOREN LESTER
Fritz Gretel	DANIEL DAVIES
Angel Dust	LYNN FARRELL
Manager	HERBIE BRAHA
School Board President	GRADY SUTTON
Shawn	CHRIS SOMMA
Cheryl	MARLA ROSENFIELD
Norma	TERRY SODA

Cop   JOE VAN SICKLE
Stunt Players   ANN CHATTERTON
                             DEBBIE EVANS
                             JACK GILL
                             JOHN HATELY
                             KAY KIMLER

And THE RAMONES
   JOEY RAMONE
   JOHNNY RAMONE
   DEE DEE RAMONE
   MARKY RAMONE

TECHNICAL CREW

Directed by	ALLAN ARKUSH
Produced by	MICHEAL FINNELL
Screenplay by	RICHARD WHITLEY
	RUSS DVONCH
	JOSEPH MCBRIDE
Story by	ALLAN ARKUSH
	JOE DANTE
Executive Producer	ROGER CORMAN
Director of Photography	DEAN CUNDEY
Editors	LARRY BOCK
	GAIL WERBIN
Art Director	MARIE KORDUS
Assistant Art Director	MARK TOEPFER
Production Manager	MARK RADCLIFFE
1st Assistant Director	GERALD T. OLSON
2nd Assistant Director	CAREN SINGER

Wardrobe Designer	JACK BUEHLER
Assistant Wardrobe	LINDA BASS
Makeup/Hairdresser	GIGI WILLIAMS
Assistant Makeup	PAMELA PEITZMAN
Set Decorator	LINDA PEARL
Production Sound Mixer	MICHAEL MOORE
Boom Operator	RHONDA BAER
Camera Assistants	KRISHNA RAO
	PAUL ELLIOT
	THOMAS VANGHELE
Gaffer	MARK DAVIS
Best Boy	STEVE MATHIS
Electricians	SCOTT BUTTFIELD
	STEVE FIERBERG
Key Grip	FRED ROSCOLENE
Grips	TIM DOUGHTEN
	STEVE CALDWELL
Grip/Driver	CHRIS BRIGHTMAN
Assistant Editors	KENT BEYDA
	MARK HELFRICH
Script Supervisor	JEANNE ROSENBERG
Production Coordinator	TERRY HUTNER
Choreographer	SIANA LEE HALE
Special Effects	ROGER GEORGE
	FRANK DeMARCO
Extras Coordinators	ERNIE GUDERJAHN
	SUSAN ARNOLD
Still Photographer	CARIN ABRAMSON
Production Auditor	DIANA ABRAMSON
Production Assistants	BRUCE FRANKEL
	RICHARD GRADDIS
	JENNIFER RADCLIFFE
	MICHAEL SILVERS

2nd Unit Directors	JON DAVISON
	JERRY ZUCKER
2nd Unit Director of Photography	CLYDE BRYAN
2nd Unit Production Managers	BRUCE FRITZBERG
	CRAIG STORPER
"Rock 'n' Roll Rodent" created and performed by	ROB BOTTIN
Special Consultant	JANE ALSOBROOK
Concert Sound	J. A. MARKOVITCH
Special Thanks to	JOE DANTE
	SEYMOUR STEIN
	JONATHAN BRETT
Post-Production Sound	RYDER SOUND SERVICES
Laboratory	MGM

SONGS FROM ROCK 'N' ROLL HIGH SCHOOL (IN ORDER OF APPEARANCE)

Paul McCartney & Wings, "Did We Meet Somewhere Before?"
The Ramones, "Sheena Is a Punk Rocker"
Brian Eno, "Alternative 3"
Eddie and the Hot Rods, "Teenage Depression"
The Ramones, "I Wanna Be Sedated"
Brownsville Station, "Smokin' in the Boys Room"
The Velvet Underground, "Rock & Roll"
Fleetwood Mac, "Jigsaw Puzzle Blues"
Bent Fabric, "The Alleycat"
The Ramones, "Suzy Is a Headbanger"
P. J. Soles and the Ramones, "Rock 'n' Roll High School"
The Ramones, "Teenage Lobotomy"
Chuck Berry, "School Days"
The Paley Brothers, "Come On Let's Go"
The Ramones, "I Just Want to Have Something to Do"
The Paley Brothers, "You're the Best"
The Ramones, "I Want You Around"

The Ramones, "I Wanna Be Your Boyfriend"
The Ramones, "Questioningly"
Fleetwood Mac, "Albatross"
Nick Lowe, "So It Goes"
Brian Eno, "Spirits Drifting"
Brian Eno, "Energy Fools the Magician"
Devo, "Come Back Jonee"
Todd Rundgren, "A Dream Lives on Forever"
The Ramones, "Blitzkrieg Bop" (live)
The Ramones, "Teenage Lobotomy" (live)
The Ramones, "California Sun" (live)
The Ramones, "Pinhead" (live)
The Ramones, "She's the One" (live)
Alice Cooper, "School's Out"
MC5, "High School"
The Ramones, "Do You Wanna Dance?"
The Ramones, "Rock 'n' Roll High School"
The Paley Brothers, "Come On Let's Go"

BIBLIOGRAPHY

BOOKS

Bessman, Jim. *Ramones: An American Band*. New York: St. Martin's Press, 1993.

Blake, Mark. *Punk: The Whole Story*. New York: DK Publishing, 2008.

Bockris, Victor. *Beat Punks*. New York: Da Capo Press, 2000.

Bowe, Brian J. *The Ramones: American Punk Rock Band*. Berkeley Heights, NJ: Enslow, 2011.

Brown, Mick. *Tearing Down the Wall of Sound: The Rise and Fall of Phil Spector*. New York: Alfred A. Knopf, 2007.

Carlson, Zack, and Bryan Connolly. *Destroy All Movies!!! The Complete Guide to Punks on Film*. Seattle: Fantagraphics Books, 2010.

Carradine, David. *Endless Highway*. Boston: Journey Editions, 1995.

Corman, Roger, with Jim Jerome. *How I Made a Hundred Movies in Hollywood and Never Lost a Dime*. New York: Da Capo, 1998.

di Franco, J. Phillip, ed. *The Movie World of Roger Corman*. New York: Chelsea House, 1979.

Fields, Danny. *My Ramones*. London: Reel Art Press, 2018.

Frank, Alan. *The Films of Roger Corman*. London: Batsford, 1998.

Frantz, Chris. *Remain in Love: Talking Heads, Tom Tom Club, Tina*. New York: St. Martin's Press, 2020.

Gray, Beverly. *Roger Corman: Blood Sucking Vampires, Flesh-Eating Cockroaches and Driller Killers*. Santa Monica, CA: Ferris, 2014.

Hell, Richard. *I Dreamed I Was a Very Clean Tramp: An Autobiography*. New York: Ecco, 2013.

Heyling, Clinton. *From the Velvets to the Voidoids*. New York: Penguin, 1993.

Hillier, Jim, and Aaron Lipstadt. *Roger Corman's New World*. London: BFI, 1981.

Holmstrom, John, and Bridget Hurd. *Punk: The Best of Punk Magazine*. New York: HarperCollins, 2012.

Howard, Ron, and Clint Howard. *The Boys: A Memoir of Hollywood and Family*. New York: William Morrow, 2021.

Koetting, Christopher T. *Mindwarp! The Fantastic True Story of Roger Corman's New World Pictures*. Baltimore: Midnight Marquee, 2009.

King, Vera Ramone. *Poisoned Heart*. Beverly Hills, CA: Phoenix Books, 2009.

Leigh, Mickey, with Legs McNeil. *I Slept with Joey Ramone: A Punk Rock Family Memoir*. New York: Touchstone, 2010.

McBride, Joseph. *The Book of Movie Lists*. Chicago: Contemporary Books, 1998.

——— *The Broken Places: A Memoir*. Berkeley, CA: Hightower Press, 2015.

McGee, Mark Thomas. *Roger Corman: Best of the Cheap Acts*. Jefferson, NC: McFarland, 1987.

McLeod, Kembrew. *The Downtown Pop Underground Revolutionized Culture*. New York: Abrams Press, 2018.

Melnick, Monte A., with Frank Meyer. *On the Road with the Ramones*: Bonus Edition. Independently published, 2019.

Naha, Ed. *The Films of Roger Corman: Brilliance on Budget*. New York: Arco Pub., 1989.

Nashawaty, Chris. *Crab Monsters, Teenage Cavemen, and Candy Stripe Nurses*. New York: Harry N. Abrams, 2013.

McNeil, Legs, and Gillian McCain. *Please Kill Me* (20th Anniversary Edition). New York: Grove Press, 2016.

Peary, Danny. *Cult Movies: The Classics, the Sleepers, the Weird and the Wonderful*. New York: Dell, 1981.

Popoff, Martin. *Ramones at 40*. New York: Sterling, 2016.

Ramone, Dee Dee, with Veronica Kofman. *Lobotomy: Surviving the Ramones*. New York: Thunder's Mouth Press, 2000.

Ramone, Johnny. *Commando: The Autobiography of Johnny Ramone.* New York: Abrams Image, 2012.

Ramone, Marky, with Rich Herschlag. *Punk Rock Blitzkrieg: My Life as a Ramone.* New York: Touchstone, 2015

Sarris, Andrew. *The American Cinema: Directors and Directions 1929–1968.* New York: Dutton, 1968.

Stein, Seymour, with Gareth Murphy. *Siren Song: My Life in Music.* New York: St. Martin's Press, 2018.

Tannenbaum, Rob, and Craig Marks. *I Want My MTV: The Uncensored Story of the Music Video Revolution.* New York: Plume, 2012.

Telotte, J. P. *The Cult Film Experience: Beyond All Reason.* Austin: University of Texas Press, 1991.

Thompson, Dave. *Phil Spector: Wall of Pain.* London: Omnibus, 2009.

True, Everett. *Hey Ho Let's Go: The Story of the Ramones.* London: Omnibus, 2005.

Valentine, Gary. *New York Rocker.* London: Sidgwick & Jackson, 2002.

Vanilla, Cherry. *Lick Me: How I Became Cherry Vanilla.* Chicago: Chicago Review Press, 2010.

ARTICLES

"$12 Mil Ad Budget for New World's 1979 Film Releases." *Hollywood Reporter*, December 11, 1978.

Arkush, Allan. "Allan Arkush's Top 10." *The Criterion Collection* (https://www.criterion.com/current/top-10-lists/24-allan-arkushs-top-10).

———"I Remember Film School." *Film Comment*, November 1983.

Armstrong, Stephen B. "Return to *Rock 'n' Roll High School*." *FilmFax*, Spring 2010.

Armstrong, Stephen B., ed. *Roger Corman's New World Pictures (1970–1983): An Oral History, Vols. 1 & 2*. Orlando: BearManor, 2020.

"Behind the Camera on *Heartbeeps*." *Starlog*, February 1982.

Bartel, Paul. "Guilty Pleasures." *Film Comment*, September-October 1982.

"*Bill & Ted* Star Will Write Howard Stern's High School." *Zap2it*, July 31, 2008.

Blowen, Michael. "A Raucous Film and Lots of Fun." *Boston Globe*, October 8, 1978.

Cioe, Crispin McCormick. "*Rock and Roll High School*: The Ramones in Hollywood." *Grooves*, June 1979

Clark, Michael. "*Rock 'n' Roll High*: Not to Forget." *Detroit Free Press*, September 19, 1979.

Cowan, Jared. "40 Years Ago, the Ramones Roamed L.A. in *Rock 'n' Roll High School*." *Los Angeles Magazine*, August 2, 2019 (https://www.lamag.com/culturefiles/rock-n-roll-high-school-40-the-ramones/).

Cromelin, Richard. "The Ramones, the Runaways: Civic Auditorium, Santa Monica CA." *Los Angeles Times*, January 30, 1978.

———"The Group That Sowed the Seeds of Punk." *Los Angeles Times*, January 15, 1978.

Davidson, Bill. "King of Schlock." *New York Times Magazine*, December 28, 1975.

"*Deathsport*." *Los Angeles Times*, April 21, 1978.

Dunkin, Zachary. "Ramones Enroll in *Rock 'n' Roll High*." *Indianapolis News*, June 23, 1979.

Fear, David. "*Rock 'n' Roll High School*" in "25 Greatest Punk Rock Movies of All Time." *Rolling Stone*, April 20, 2021 (https://www.rollingstone.com/tv-movies/tv-movie-lists/25-greatest-punk-rock-movies-of-all-time-103577/).

Garnier, Philippe. "Hollywood High's Cool." *New Musical Express*, January 20, 1979.

Gelmis, Joseph. "Drama, Fun and Disaster." *Newsday*, August 3, 1979.

Godwin, Michael. "Roger Corman's *Rock 'n' Roll High School*: The Last of the Red-Hot Cheapies." *Penthouse*, October 1979.

Goldberg, Michael. "Ramones Look Like They're Hoods, But They're Not." *San Francisco Examiner*, December 24, 1978.

Green, Jim. "The Ramones Finish High School." Trouser Press, July 1979.

Harris, Dana. "Stern Has Gross Idea for Remakes." *Variety*, November 1, 2002.

Hermanns, Grant. "Director Allan Arkush on Cult Musical *Rock 'n' Roll High School*." Comingsoon.net, November 20, 2019.

Hoberman J. "Blitzkrieg Bop Bingo." *Village Voice*, August 13, 1979.

——— "School Is Out Village." *Village Voice*, July 1, 1986.

Hume, Martha. "Ramones Come Home." *New York Daily News*, August 5, 1979.

"Joe Dante." *Shock Cinema*, no. 61.

Konow, David. "*Rock 'n' Roll High School* 40th Reunion: Allan Arkush Interview." *Consequence*, August 24, 2019 (https://consequence.net/2019/08/rock-n-roll-high-school-interviews/).

Kubernik, Harvey. "Ramones *Rock 'n' Roll High School*." *Music Connection*, May 5, 2020. https://www.musicconnection.com/kubernik-interview-with-director-producer-allan-arkush/.

Leogrand, Ernest. "Rock High Is Silly." *New York Daily News*, August 3, 1979.

Lyons, Donald. "Mary Woronov." *Interview*, May 1973.

Marsh, Dave. "*Rock 'N' Roll High School*." *Rolling Stone*, July 12, 1979.

McNeil, Legs. "Punk." *Spin*, January 1986.

Niciphor, Nic. "*Deathsport*." *Psychotronic Video*, Spring 1991.

Needs, Kris. "The Ramones: Ramonin' in the Moonlight." *ZigZag*, March 1980.

Patoski, Joe Nick. "*Rock 'n Roll High School*: Stupid Fun for Ramones Fans." *Austin American-Statesman*, April 25, 1979.

Paulson, Ken. "Sheer Energy Carries High School." *El Paso Times*, June 24, 1979.

Peterson, Gary. "Screenwriter McBride's Film at Cinema." *Capital Times*, May 26, 1979.

Petkovich, Anthony. "P. J. Soles." *Shock Cinema*, no. 58.

"Punk Rocker with a Social Conscience." *Irish Times*, May 5, 2001.

Rausch, Andrew J. "Allan Arkush." *Shock Cinema*, no. 58.

Riegel, Richard. "Dead Boys Tell No Tales (Under an Hour, That Is)." *Creem*, February 1979.

Robbins, Ira. "Joey Finally Gets the Girl." *New Musical Express*, May 12, 1979.

Robinson, Lisa. "Rock Talk." *Ottawa Citizen*, May 4, 1979.

"*Rock 'N Roll High School*." *Daily Variety*, April 23, 1979.

"Rock 'n' Roll Movie Gets Rave Reviews." *Nanaimo* (Canada) *Daily News*, October 7, 1979.

"Rock Remains Soft Movie Plot Line." *Billboard*, June 29, 1991.

Rockwell, John. "*Rock 'n' Roll High School* with the Ramones 'Punk' Band." *New York Times*, August 4, 1979.

Rose, Frank. "Dee Dee Ramone Didn't Wanna Be A Pinhead No More." *Esquire*, April 1, 1980.

Sasfy, Joe. "Rock 'n' Ramones." *Washington Post*, July 26, 1979.

Selvin, Joel. "On the Town." *San Francisco Chronicle*, May 11, 1979.

Shreger, Charles. "Screenplay Credits Involve Egos, Money." *Los Angeles Times*, April 22, 1979.

Siskel, Gene. "*Rock 'n' Roll High School*." *Chicago Tribune*, May 22, 1979.

Spies, Michael. "*Rock 'n' Roll High School.*" *Corpus Christi Times*, April 25, 1979.

Sullivan, Mike. "Dey Young." *Shock Cinema*, no. 58.

Tate, James M. "Dey Young Returns to Rock 'n' Roll High School." Cultfilm-freaks,com, November 26, 2010 (http://www.cultfilmfreaks.com/2010/03/dey-young-rock-n-roll-high-school.html).

Teitelbaum, Sheldon. ". . . And I Can't Get Up: Directors Who've Fallen Down on the Job." *Premiere*, December 1991.

Thomas, Kevin. "Ramones Featured in *High School.*" *Los Angeles Times*, October 12, 1979.

Trussell, Robert C. "Teen Film Has Little Going for It." *Kansas City Star*, October 9, 1979.

Trzcinski, Matthew. "How the Ramones Inspired Nirvana's 'Smells Like Teen Spirit.'" *Cheat Sheet*, May 2, 2021.

Wolcott, James. "A Conservative Impulse in the New Rock Underground." *Village Voice*, August 18, 1975.

Young, Charles M. "*Road to Ruin.*" *Rolling Stone*, October 19, 1978.

Zelazny, Jon. "Do You Wanna Dance? Allan Arkush Remembers *Rock 'n' Roll High School.*" *FilmFax*, Spring 2010.

RADIO, PODCASTS, DOCUMENTARIES

"78: Allan Arkush." *The Fogelnest Files*, February 20, 2014.

"Allan Arkush: Interview," from *Rock 'N' Roll High School* [40th Anniversary Edition Steelbook] (Shout!Factory, 2020).

"An Interview with Allan Arkush, Director of *Rock N Roll High School*," *No Dogs in Space*, July 20, 2020.

"Back to School: A Retrospective," directed by Robert Nuñez (Buena Vista Home Entertainment, 2005).

"Class of '79: 40 Years of *Rock 'N' Roll High School*," directed by Daniel Griffith, from *Rock 'N' Roll High School* [40th Anniversary Edition Steelbook] (Shout!Factory, 2020).

"Commentary" for *Rock 'n' Roll High School*, with Allan Arkush, Richard Whitley and Michael Finnell (Buena Vista Home Entertainment, 2005).

"The Corman/Maltin Interview," directed by Steve Gainer, from *Rock 'N' Roll High School* [40th Anniversary Edition Steelbook] (Shout!Factory, 2020).

"Episode 222: Rock 'N' Roll High School (1979)." The Projection Booth, June 9, 2015.

"Film Director *Moonlighting* on Television." *Fresh Air*, June 2, 1987.

"Former Warhol Protegee Mary Woronov." *Fresh Air*, December 7, 1995.

"Staying After Class," directed by Anthony Masi, from *Rock 'N' Roll High School* [40th Anniversary Edition Steelbook] (Shout!Factory, 2020).

INDEX

ABOUT THE AUTHOR

Stephen B. Armstrong's books include *Picture About Extremes: The Films of John Frankenheimer* and *Paul Bartel: The Life and Films*. He teaches creative writing at Utah Tech University in St. George, Utah.